Rand McNally
Pictorial Encyclopedia of
Horses and Riding

Rand McNally
Pictorial Encyclopedia of
Horses and Riding
Betty Skelton

Contents

Foreword	7
Horses Around the World	8
A History of the Horse	8
Horses of the US	12
Horses of South America	16
Horses of Austria	18
Horses of Belgium	19
Horses of the Netherlands	19
Horses of France	20
Horses of Germany	22
Horses of the British Isles	24
Horses of Hungary	32
Horses of Italy	32
Horses of Russia	32
Horses of Spain	34
Horses of Scandinavia	35
Colored Horses	38
Horses of Asia	39
The Working Horse	42
Riding – Yesterday and Today	46
A History of Riding	46
Riding – the First Steps	52
Choosing a Riding School	54
What to Wear	55
Mounting and Dismounting	56
Position in the Saddle	58
Holding the Reins	59
The Aids	60
Artificial Aids	61
The Walk	62
The Trot	62
The Canter	64
The Gallop	64
Lunging and Exercising	66
Jumping	70
Care of the Horse	74
Grassland Management	74
Stable Management	76
Feeding	78
Grooming	82
The Health of the Horse	86
Care of the Feet and Shoeing	90
Tack and Equipment	94
Buying a Horse	108
Riding for Pleasure	112
Hacking and Trail-Riding Vacations	112
Pony and Riding Clubs	119
Gymkhanas and Mounted Games	121
Training a Young Horse	128
Early Handling	129
Lessons on the Lunge	130
Bitting	133
Side Reins	134
Backing	136
Long Reins	137
Teaching the Aids	139
Jumping	143
Backing Up	144
The Future	145

First published in the U.S.A. 1978 by Rand McNally & Company
Designed and produced for Rand McNally by
Intercontinental Book Productions
Copyright © 1977 Intercontinental Book Productions

SBN 528-81065-0
Library of Congress catalog card no. 77-82259

Printed and bound in Italy

Breeding 146
Mares and Stallions 146
Stud Procedure 148
The Mare in-foal 149
Foaling 151
Handling and Raising of
Young Stock 153
Showing Mares and Foals 156

More Advanced Riding 158
Riding – the Next Steps 160
Dressage 161
The Gaits 162
Counter Canter and
Flying Change 164
The Half Halt 165
Lateral Aids and Movements 166
More Advanced Paces 170
Haute Ecole 172
Side-Saddle Riding 176

Competitive Riding 180
Showing 180
Show Jumping 186
Racing 192
Eventing 196
International Events and
the Olympic Games 200
Driving 206
Endurance Riding 208

Glossary 210

Index 213

Introduction

Perhaps the most famous symbol of the horse is that of Pegasus, the magnificent winged horse of Greek mythology. But ever-increasing numbers of people like to think of horses and ponies in a more tangible form, something to look at directly – even touch. The interest and passion many of us have for horses and the way in which we are drawn like magnets towards them are generally inexplicable. It is echoed in an old Irish saying, "If wishes were horses then tinkers (gypsies) would ride!" In these days, that wish of long ago has become reality for many people. Once the horse was kept as a work animal and had to earn his keep; now he is, first and foremost, a means of pleasure and relaxation. Riding has become so popular that, through sheer demand, it has come within the grasp of everybody in a way that would have been unbelievable a century ago. This book is intended for those people who want to discover what riding is all about and what possibilities a life with horses might bring, but equally it is for anyone who has the merest interest in horses – yet may not want to ride.

My main interest in life, particularly since moving to my present home in 1940, has been with horses and riders of all types. I was born with horses around me. My father won the International High Jump Competition at Olympia, London, three days after I was born! I have no recollection of learning to ride – my brother and I just rode. Ponies were our normal means of transportation – although in the early days, it was a donkey!

The fraternity of the horse world contains a wonderful bond between people linked together in an inextricable way by a mutual interest in, and compelling love for, horses. One person with a more than average interest in horses is Lucinda Prior-Palmer, whom I have asked to write the foreword in this book. Lucinda and I have known each other since she started to ride at the age of five. Her achievements and success are known internationally, and she is a worthy example to inspire the ambitious young rider.

Betty Skelton

Foreword

To all who have known her and been lucky enough to gain from her lifetime experience with horses, Betty Skelton, known affectionately as "Mrs S," has been inspiring and teaching and helping riders of all ages for about 40 years.

That Mrs S's one-time hobby ever turned into a career could be described as something of an accident. It happened around 1934, when, newly married, she realized she had to find a way to continue the riding that had always been an integral part of her life. Ingenious as ever, she began to ride the horses at a local stable – in return for which she gave free instruction to the pupils. Later, during the war years, the Red Cross was to benefit from Mrs S's love of horses, for she sent them regular donations from the money she earned taking children for rides – on a pony she had bought for $10!

Slowly, but inevitably for a person so full of enthusiasm and vitality, Mrs S's stable grew to number over 60 horses and ponies, many of which she bred herself. Over the years she has produced some top-class show ponies and hacks, which her daughter has shown with great success. Some years later Mrs S was kind enough to give me encouragement by allowing me to show some of the next-generation horses and ponies bred from those early winners. Now it is her granddaughter who rides her show horses and who has posed so gracefully for many of the pictures in this book.

Mrs S has been a major factor in shaping my career. From the age of five until I was nine, I had lessons with her faithfully every Tuesday and Thursday afternoon. With patience and humor – and yet I well remember the slight fear I had of her – Mrs S laid the foundations which were to open the doors to such a wonderful and exciting way of life. And like so many others, I have retained a deep-rooted affection and respect for her.

More recently, Mrs S's inspiration to riders has taken on a different form, straying slightly from the purely practical. When a badly injured knee rendered her bed-ridden for many painful months, she in no way weakened in the face of what was truly a disaster for such an active person. Instead she picked up her pen and committed to paper the message she had hitherto been teaching. In addition, her books and articles are full of her personal anecdotes and experiences, so that reading them is like talking to her.

This book is by no means Mrs S's first, and yet it is probably the most comprehensive of its type she has so far tackled. The compilation of such an awe-inspiring task would only be embarked upon by someone with Betty Skelton's bravery and determination.

Lucinda Prior-Palmer.

Horses Around the World

A History of the Horse

The horse as we know him today has arrived in his present form through millions of years of evolution. The animal that was to become our much loved and prized equine began as a small creature, which we are told was about as big as a medium-sized dog. He had five toes and, from pictures we are given of him, looked, to my mind, rather like an otter! He lived on the herbage that the plains and valleys of his environment had to offer; and since he was not an aggressive carnivorous animal, his defense lay in an ability to run faster than his aggressor or predator. This primeval instinct to run away from danger is still uppermost in a horse's subconscious mind today.

By the time man arrived on earth, the horse was getting closer in form to the present *equus caballus*, although it still had a long way to go. Even so, it was clearly important to prehistoric man, as is indicated by the many cave paintings which feature horses in a variety of roles. From that time on, man tamed the horse and domesti-cated him for his own purposes as a beast of burden, a means of transportation and a companion for pleasurable riding and hunting pursuits; this is well illustrated in every field of art. Drawings on pottery, sculptures – both crude and amazingly refined – paintings and tapestries, all depicting man's involvement with horses through the centuries, exist from every land and culture. As events became documented through writing, the millions of references to horses in literature helped us to trace his development still further, giving us a more or less complete insight into how the many different breeds of horse which are currently in existence in the world evolved.

It is obvious that all horses developed from the many herds of small wild horses and ponies that roamed the continents of the world. Different characteristics developed at an early stage between these herds, depending upon the environmental conditions; and so, in my view, began the emergence of different breeds. Those animals living in areas where food was sparse and of poor quality clearly were not likely to

The famous horses in the Lascaux caves in France. The paintings date from the Stone Age.

grow as big as others where the food was abundant and lush. The existence, or not, of various minerals in the different water supplies would have affected the density of the bone. Nowadays, we can draw definite and interesting comparisons. For example, the shape and conformation of the small wild horse called after the Russian explorer Colonel Przewalski bear a strong resemblance to that of one of Great Britain's native breeds – the Exmoor pony. This would indicate that at some stage they emanated from the same stock, although we have no certain knowledge of how or when. Likewise the similarity in bone structure between Norway's Fjord pony and the Icelandic pony indicates that these ponies too have common ancestry.

In saying that all modern horses developed from the herds of wild horses, some sources go further in stating that there were four different types of wild, primeval horse or pony which existed in different parts of the world. Northwest Europe and northern Eurasia apparently both contained distinct pony types. Central Asia, extending as far north as Spain, and western Asia had two horse types – the bigger of which was found in the central Asian areas.

In all areas, horses were still needed mainly as a means of getting from one place to another, to help in cultivating the land and to carry goods. It was only when the native horses in a given area did not conform to any of these particular needs, that man began to experiment by cross-breeding different types of horses. This is the basis of "selective breeding." Then horse trading started on an international scale, and often one of the aims of the wars of conquest was to

acquire horses suitable for breeding new types.

Many countries began striving to breed what finally became known as the "great horse" of olden times, which would be suitable to carry horsemen when clad in their heavy suits of armor. People living in central Asia were probably in the best position to do this, for their native horse was considerably bigger than those found in other areas. By the middle ages the "great horse" existed more or less throughout Europe. A strongly built animal, it was a much treasured possession with pride of ownership centering on its size, general massiveness and pulling powers. But in existence simultaneously were many thin working horses, which led, I believe, to even more organized and deliberate instances of selective breeding. Very heavy horses were not agile enough to work in hill country, for example, so would be crossed with a lighter type, to produce a compromise in terms of agility and size. By selective breeding in England and on the continent of Europe, two main types appear to have been bred during the middle ages – the great horses which were strong enough to carry knights in their heavy armor

as well as work on the land, and the "palfrey," which was a lighter riding horse than the great horse and was also used to pull carts as opposed to heavy carriages or agricultural implements.

In this century there has been a shift of emphasis regarding the role of the horse. He is no longer required for warfare, or agricultural work or as a major means of transport; consequently there has been a corresponding shift in the types of horse bred. With the tremendous upsurge of interest in the many fields of riding for pleasure, there has been an enormous increase in demand for essentially riding horses. Heavy horses are now bred almost entirely to satisfy an interest in them as breeds, rather than for any practical purpose – even though we are assured that it is cheaper and more reliable to run horses and carts than it is to run motor vehicles!

Planned selective breeding has been practiced in most areas of the world; and now nearly every country has its own national, as opposed to native, breeds of which it is justifiably proud. In each case, these breeds have been developed

Examples of the primitive breed known as Przewalski's horse.

10

to meet the interest, demands and requirements of the individual country. The US, for example, has a great many national breeds nowadays, although at the time of its discovery it had no indigenous horses at all. The first horses were brought over from Spain by the early settlers, who went on to breed horses that would help them in establishing their homesteads and provide a sporting interest as well. These sporting interests took the form of trotting races, which is how the trotting breeds emerged in the US. By continually importing the best horses to meet their specific requirements from abroad, the US now owns some of the finest racehorses and trotters in the world.

Another huge country, the USSR, has as many breeds as the US but these are generally of a different nature. In the USSR horses were used considerably longer as a means of transportation, to pull sleighs over the snowy terrain. As a result, tough, hardy horses, able to withstand the extremely cold weather, were produced. The USSR has about 40 recognized breeds – among them the Karabakh, the Budyonovsky, the Akhal-Teke and the Donsky. One area of interest that it shares with the US is trotting races, and the Orlov Trotter bred in

Russia was at one time among the finest of all the trotting breeds.

A great number of breeds are found in the countries of Europe nowadays. Again, although some horses are still bred for work on the land, particularly in the mountainous areas, most of the attention has been given to producing riding horses for pleasure and sporting pursuits. In these areas they have produced some of the finest and most outstanding breeds of all time. One of the supreme examples of these must surely be the English Thoroughbred – a universally recognized horse which is of comparatively recent origin.

Above: The huge figure of a horse that has been carved out of the chalk hills on Cheshill Down in Wiltshire, England.

Below: Part of an old tapestry which depicts the labors of the months from July to December.

Horses of the US

The American Quarter Horse

This powerful horse gets its name from the races started by the early settlers. Since the tracks were cut out of virgin woodland, they were not usually more than a quarter of a mile long. The horse was bred to suit these "race paths" and was able to move very fast over a short distance. The breed started by crossing Thoroughbred stallions with lighter work mares, probably of Spanish and English descent. The great ancestor of the breed was a small Thoroughbred stallion called Janus. Alive from 1756 to 1780, he possessed very strong quarters and, like Justin Morgan (see below), he stamped his stock very strongly with this characteristic. Nowadays the Quarter Horse is very popular in America, particularly for cow cutting on the ranches and for competitions related to this. Its strength, quiet temperament and docility enable it to start and stop with great speed and precision, without becoming over-excited. It is an ideal breed for Western riding generally. A great many Quarter Horses have been exported to England to western riding establishments and a number have also gone to Australia and New Zealand to work on the vast cattle stations and properties.

The Morgan Horse

This is one of the best known breeds in America today, yet its origins could almost be termed ignominious. It was founded by a tough little stallion, 14.2 hands high, which was foaled in 1789 and given as payment for a bad debt to a school teacher named Justin Morgan. The little stallion proved to be a great worker and extremely versatile, happy to pull a plow or loads of timber, and yet highly successful in races under both saddle and harness. He became known as "Justin Morgan's horse" or just "Justin Morgan" and people began to send mares to him. However ordinary the mares, the foals seemed to be a replica of their sire, with the same useful characteristics. Thus a breed was established. The exact breeding of the original stallion is unknown, although he is said to have been by a Thoroughbred stallion out of a working mare. It is also thought there may have been some Arabian blood in his ancestry. He apparently changed hands several times, but was eventually bought by the US Army, which established the famous Morgan stud in Vermont. Morgans will now be found all over the US in many roles – as family horses, show horses, show jumpers or challengers in pulling matches. The docility, strength, toughness, constitution and endurance of the original

The Morgan Horse.

The American Quarter Horse.

horse are reproduced perpetually from generation to generation, along with the other breed characteristics – long neck, short-coupled body and strong quarters. Usual colors are brown or dark bay.

The Tennessee Walking Horse

Like the American Saddle Horse, the Tennessee Walking Horse was originally produced by planters to carry them around their plantations at a sedate, comfortable pace. They were bred from a stallion, foaled in 1886, which itself was descended from mixed ancestry, mainly featuring Morgan and English Thoroughbred. Similar to the original Morgan stallion, he reproduced his type regularly through a number of successive generations, and the most notable breed characteristic is the "running walk" gait, which was popular with the planters. In addition, the Tennessee Walking Horse is noted for its quiet temperament and intelligence. Physically it is large and solid-looking with a short neck and very powerful quarters. Usual colors of Tennessee Walking Horses are bay, chestnut and black.

The Standard Bred

This is the official name given to the American pacing and trotting horses bred for the popular harness races. The breed dates from the late nineteenth century, when a set of rules based on speed was introduced for admission to the American Trotting Register. Trotting horses found in the various countries of Europe all owe certain characteristics to the Standard Bred, which developed from a stallion known as Hambletonian. He had strains of English Thoroughbred and Darley Arabian in his blood. Standard Bred horses are similar in physique to the Thoroughbred, although generally they tend to be slightly heavier in build with a longer body and shorter legs. They are also credited with greater endurance and stamina than the Thoroughbred – essential characteristics for the gruelling demands which are placed on them during races.

The Tennessee Walking Horse.

Mexico and spread to the plains of the western United States and to a certain extent into South America as well. Appearing as wild horses, they were all given the name Mustang. The Indians caught them as they needed them, while the cowboys roped them to tame and use in their work. As these horses bred naturally out in the wild, they tended to be tough, small and wiry – far from good looking, and, in fact, somewhat scraggy and rough. But they did have to survive extremely harsh conditions. Every now and then, one would appear which indicated a throwback to the original Spanish ancestry. Its beauty would stand out so much, particularly beside its plainer relatives, that it would become a local legend. It is these examples which have so often achieved fame in movies about the Wild West. Nowadays there are really no true Mustangs left, as the range ponies have been improved by the introduction of stallions of various breeds, including Arabs, Thoroughbreds, Quarter Horses and other breeds recognized in the US.

The Pinto

The colored Pinto horses are another breed well known to all followers of Wild West adventures. The name is now applied to those horses or ponies whose coloring is referred to as Piebald or Skewbald, meaning irregular markings of black and white or brown and white, with either the white or the dark markings predominating. Pintos were very popular among

The American Saddle Horse

This breed evolved at a time when the settlers required an energetic horse that could stand hard conditions, but would be bright and comfortable enough to enjoy riding over long distances. In fact, it originated in Kentucky, where the planters were anxious to develop a horse to give them a comfortable ride at a slow pace as they inspected their plantations. As imported horses were used to produce it, it has a mixture of Spanish, French and English blood. The Saddle Horse today is a highly trained animal, and besides the conventional paces of walk, trot and canter, it is taught the artificial gaits of slow gait and rack. Saddle Horses have therefore become known as either three-gaited or five-gaited horses and when moving at the rack they are extremely spectacular to watch. The Saddle Horse has a great following, and its proud carriage makes it well suited to its main role today, which is that of showing. In fact, the high tail carriage is obtained by nicking the muscles of the dock and then setting the tail in position (a practice which was banned in England many years ago). The long neck and proud head carriage, however, are characteristic of the breed.

The Mustang

The name *Mustang* comes from the Spanish word meaning "stray." Originally some of these horses broke away from the settlers in

The American Saddle Horse.

A Pinto mare and foal.

14

The Appaloosa.

the American Indians, since besides being fast and tough, their strange markings camouflaged them. Pinto colorings can be traced from ancient Egyptian, Persian and Chinese origins, and today horses of the same coloration may be found all over North and South America. Western riders show a marked preference for colored (that is, those whose coat is a variety of colors) horses rather than plain ones. It is a fact that, in breeding, certain colors will predominate, and it seems that most colored mares will reproduce their own markings even if mated to a wholly colored stallion. Pinto horses are not recognized as a breed in the strictest sense of the word, and most breed societies around the world ban colored horses. So great is their popularity, however, that a society has been formed in the US called the Pinto Horse Society. The registration rules of the society are very strict, and no horse can be registered unless it has a pure-bred sire (of any breed, except a gaited horse).

The Appaloosa
Another colored horse from the US, the Appaloosa derives its name from the Palouse country of central Idaho and eastern Washing-

ton. It originated from Spanish stock, which was introduced by the Spanish conquistadors and subsequently drifted northward from the early settlements. Some horses were captured by the Nez Perce Indians, who were known to be outstandingly good horse breeders and riders and who prized colored horses above all others. They developed the Appaloosa from these wandering horses, primarily, it seems, for war uses. Today, the Appaloosa's attractive and unusual spotted markings, combined with the refinement and quality that stems from their Arab blood, make them much prized as ceremonial or circus horses. Their markings and colorings can vary considerably, but generally the "blanket" markings will be predominant in any collection of Appaloosas. This means a white area over the rump with dark spots or small patches on it. Alternatively, Appaloosas may have a dark body with white markings, which is known as snowflaking. Yet again, a light body color (not white) with dark markings is known as leopard markings, and a roan background with white markings is referred to as marble coloring. The skin of the lips of the Appaloosa is partly colored and the hooves are often striped.

Horses of South America

The Criollo

These bright little horses with their short, deep backs and broad heads are a native of the Argentine, famous for its cattle ranches and its horses. The Criollo ancestry can be traced to the Spanish landings in 1535, when Don Pedro Mendoza – founder of Buenos Aires – imported 100 Andalusian stallions and mares. After Buenos Aires was ransacked by the Indians, some of the horses escaped to run wild on the Pampas, where the extremely hard conditions led to a natural selective breeding and the survival of the fittest. Hardships the horses had to contend with included great changes of temperature, frost, droughts, floods and dust storms. As a result, many physical weaknesses were gradually eliminated, for weak horses seldom lived long enough to reproduce. Small wonder that one of the most notable characteristics of the breed is its hardiness and stamina, although at one stage the breed was nearly ruined through being "improved" by imported European stallions. Seeing this happen, a number of breeders got together and in 1918 formed a society to protect and perpetuate the breed by using only the most perfect examples of the breed as stallions and brood mares. The society now has backing by the Argentinian government. Criollos nowadays usually average 14 to 14.2 hands high, which is generally smaller than their ancestors – a fact attributable to the harsh conditions under which they live. These conditions have probably also contributed to the evolution of the characteristic dun coloring, which fits into the sandy wastes and burnt-up pastures of the native surroundings. Two Criollo ponies carried the Swiss teacher, Professor Tschiffely, from Buenos Aires to New York, a journey of approximately 13,350 miles (21,500 km.).

Argentine Polo Ponies

Argentine Polo Ponies first made an appearance when the local inhabitants began to select the most agile of their cow ponies to compete in this sport. As it became more important, the ponies were crossed with Thoroughbred stallions, chosen more for their compact conformation

Cowboys in the Andes riding native South American ponies.

16

than their racing ability. English breeders of Polo Ponies adopted the same principle before the First World War. The Argentine Polo Ponies, however, showed remarkable talent, and when the winning teams from both North and South America were mounted on them, it became fashionable all over the world to play polo on Argentine Polo Ponies. They were bred on the vast cattle estates of Argentina, and there were any number to choose from. In more recent times, the breeding has been controlled along stricter lines and now some stud farms will use only mares which have previously proved themselves on the polo field. As a result, they are now recognized as a breed, and every year many trained ponies leave Argentina to supply the polo-playing countries of the world. As such the Argentine Polo Ponies are in constant demand.

The Peruvian Pasa Fino

Like the Criollo from Argentina, the Peruvian Pasa Fino originally descended from the Andalusian Horses brought to South America by the Spaniards during their early conquests. Its most outstanding characteristic is its gait, which is similar in action to today's pacing horses. The pacing gait or "amble" is a movement of the laterals, which means that the hind leg and foreleg on one side move in unison, followed by the hind leg and foreleg on the other side. Most riding horses around the world today perform a trot using diagonally opposite legs. The pacing gait, however, reduces the jarring effect of the trot considerably, thus making a very comfortable ride. The comfort aspect was particularly important in the Peruvian Pasa Fino, as it was originally bred specifically to travel over the vast plains, rocky trails and mountain passes of the country. With this aim in mind, it was also essential to produce a horse of great endurance and willingness. The breed was first developed some 300 years ago and great care was taken in the selection of the breeding stock. Horses were chosen for their conformation, noble carriage and docile temperament, which doubtless accounts for the excellent specimens of the breed in existence today. The Peruvian Pasa Fino may be gray, chestnut, bay or black, of which bay and chestnut are the most common colors. They frequently have white markings, such as a blaze, on their heads. They stand between 14 and 15.2 hands high and, in spite of their fine conformation and appearance of being light of bone, they are extremely hardy and reliable, and are able to cover great distances.

Polo ponies in action during a game.

Horses of Austria

The Lippizana

The beautiful and famous Lippizanas have marked Andalusian ancestry (see page 34), but they are also descended from a specialized type of horse developed in Bohemia, called the Kladruber. They have similar characteristics to the Andalusian, with a small head, powerful neck, short back and short quarters. They are generally 14.2 to 15 hands high. Although small, their magnificent carriage makes them look bigger than they actually are. The name Lippizana comes from that of a stud farm founded by the Archduke of Austria at Lippiza. Since then the breed has become closely associated with the famous Riding School in Vienna and with its style of classical riding and *haute école*. The school dates back to 1572, at which stage it was no more than a wooden building, known as "The Spanish Riding Hall." Here the Spanish horses of the Archduke were trained and gave exhibitions, which is why the establishment is known today as the Spanish Riding School. Lippizanas are ideally suited for exhibition purposes and many of them have been imported into other countries such as Poland, Hungary, Yugoslavia, Czechoslovakia, England and the US.

I first came across this breed in 1947 when I met a Czech refugee named Mr. Keil who had imported two stallions from the Spanish School in Vienna into England. One was a trained horse which taught me a lot and the other was a young stallion I taught to jump. I learned from

Lippizana mares and foals.

Haflingers at stud.

these horses that the breed is both comfortable to ride and easy to train, although their action is quite different from that we have come to know and accept.

The strains of the most famous stallions imported into the stud between 1767 and 1819 – called Maestroso, Conversano, Neopolitano, Pluto, Favory and Siglavy – are still retained in the pedigree and the names are still used as prefixes for the foals bred today. Their traditional white color has been established over the years and they have a peculiarly iridescent skin with occasional black markings. At one time, there were many colors of Lippizana, but the foals bred at the most famous stud farm at Pieba are all born black and then turn to gray as they mature. Other colors are found in Hungary and Czechoslovakia.

The Haflinger

All true Haflingers are descended from a cross-bred Arab stallion called El Bedavi XXII. It is said that the breed evolved from ancient European pony stock which became acclimatized to the mountains and was improved by this oriental blood. Natives of the Austrian mountains, they are hardy little chestnut ponies, usually standing 13 to 14 hands high, with flaxen manes and tails. They are a utility breed with a wonderful temperament and delightful disposition as well as a strong build and a lively way of moving. Their main use is as a work pony on the land and for riding by the small farmers in the Tyrol. The ponies' attractive coloring and hardiness, combined with their docility, have also made them a popular breed in other countries, and many Haflingers are exported.

Horses of Belgium

The Brabant

Along with the Netherlands and northern parts of France, Belgium has long produced heavy horses of great merit, a fine example of which is the Brabant. A cold-blooded horse, its exact origins are a little uncertain, but it would certainly have arrived in its recognized form through the crossing and inter-breeding of many different breeds. A very heavy work horse, it stands between 16 and 17 hands high, and besides being a willing worker, it has a very good temperament. All these attributes have made it extremely popular in other countries as well as its own, and it has been extensively used for crossing with other types in the development of new breeds, the English Shire horse being one. Brabants are also bred in Russia.

Above top: Gelderland mare and foal.

Above: The Brabant.

Horses of the Netherlands

The Gelderland

The name of this breed is derived from the province of Gelderland in Holland, from which it emanates. Strongly made deep horses, they have excellent harness action and as a result are much in demand for driving. Indeed they are much sought after for Federation Equestre Internationale driving events, as they possess both courage and staying power. They are a very old breed descending from native mares which were crossed with Norfolk Trotters, Thoroughbreds and Holsteins many years ago. At the beginning of this century, Hackney stallions were also imported to breed with them, and selective breeding has resulted in a specific type being produced. The most common color is currently chestnut, although there are a few grays, examples of which are rarely seen abroad. Their usual height is 15.2 hands high, although their carriage makes them appear bigger, and some animals do grow larger.

The Dutch Draft Horse

This heavily built horse was bred to meet the need for a heavy horse of good temperament with the agility to work on sandy soils. It has a large head with generous eyes, which denote the breed's characteristic good temperament. The legs are stoutly made with good feet and the animal has an easy walk. Since 1925, no horse of unknown parentage has qualified for entry in the stud book.

Until fairly recently, the Dutch Government controlled the breeding of all horses in Holland. Then control was handed over to the recognized Breed Societies, who were subsequently allowed to license their own stallions. Great encouragement is given to the export of Dutch-bred horses and ponies, to countries all over the world.

The Fresian

Indigenous to the Netherlands, this is one of the oldest breeds in Europe. It has a fine head set on an exceptionally shapely neck, and because of its noble and gay carriage it was frequently depicted as the mount of kings and generals. Its great docility and its ability to subsist on meager rations have always made it popular. At one stage the fineness of the breed was threatened by the introduction of Spanish blood. As a result, the Fresian breed deteriorated, losing much of its substance. A new Fresian Society was started with only three stallions at stud, and with careful patronage the former characteristics were restored. The present-day Fresian is about 15 hands high and, besides being a sound harness horse, is much in demand as a show animal.

Horses of France

The Ardennes

Ardennes horses may be considered a French or Belgian breed, as the mountains of their origin belong to both countries, according to the exact location. It is a hardy breed, which has distinguished itself particularly in times of war – as a cavalry horse in the seventeenth century, during Napoleon's campaigns against Russia in the early nineteenth century and as "artillery wheelers" during the First World War. With influences imposed upon it from other breeds, the Ardennes have been subjected to a variety of changes over the past few centuries, although the small type which exists today, ranging from 14.2 to 15.1 hands high, is probably nearest to the original type. There is also a heavy draft type in existence, but mechanization of transportation and farming is somewhat threatening the need for the continuation of this breed.

The Camargue Pony

The herds of wild horses that are found in the marshes of the Rhone delta, or Camargue region of southern France, are great lovers of freedom. Somewhat resembling the Andalusian or Spanish horse their height is about 15 hands or under. They have robust and powerful limbs, more characteristic of a horse of greater size. The usual coloring of these horses is gray and

Above top: The Ardennes.

Above: Camargue Horses.

Right: The French Trotter.

A Percheron at the Horse du Pin Stud in France.

all foals are born black. Some then remain darker gray than others as they mature. The Camargue region abounds in marshes and salt flats, and as a result these ponies seem to love water, appearing to be immune to troublesome flies and mosquitoes. Breeding of the Camargue ponies is not controlled and is left to nature. However, they are not so abundant as at one time, when several herds of 50 ponies or more could be seen roaming freely across the Camargue. These wild herds of Camargue ponies are a great tourist attraction, while the broken horses have proved quiet and reliable for tourists to ride.

The Percheron

The docile, popular Percheron breed was founded hundreds of years ago by French farmers in the district of France known as La Perche. Now its popularity extends well beyond its native country and it is said to be the most widely dispersed heavy horse throughout the world. The Percheron has a short, compact body and exceptionally short legs. It is surprisingly active for a horse of its build and has always been used primarily for agricultural work, in which it is said to excel.

The French Trotter

It was the Norman coach-horse breeders who were responsible for breeding the French Trotter in the mid-1830s. They used their native Normandy mares, which were an all-purpose breed used for riding and harness work, and crossed them first with English hunters (themselves Thoroughbred crosses) and then later with English Thoroughbreds. This produced a much lighter type of animal than the somewhat heavy Norman horse, and the French Trotter

was actually produced by crossing this stock with Norfolk Trotters. Trotting races began in France in the 1830s. By the late 1850s, only stallions who had proved themselves on the race track were recognized by the authorities and thus allowed to be used for stud purposes. A stud book was opened for the breed in the early 1920s and Anglo-Norman horses able to prove a trotting record of 1 minute 42 seconds to the kilometer ($\frac{5}{8}$ mile) were allowed to be registered. In 1942, it was closed to all horses except for those born of a previously registered sire and dam. The breed has therefore been kept remarkably pure.

The Breton

France is justifiably proud of this strong, hardworking horse. There are three distinct types, bred in various parts of Bretagne, where the rather poor land and rough, winter climate have made them able to stand up to hard conditions. The main difference between the three types of Breton is in size, for they are all essentially work horses rather than riding horses. The largest is the massive draft horse which stands between 15.2 and 16.2 hands high. Next comes the draft post horse which stands between 15 and 16 hands high and is a lighter type of horse. It has the reputation of being a good mover, which made it much in demand for trotting deliveries. It is said to be descended from the early Breton type crossed with Norfolk Trotters. The third type in existence is bred and used in the mountainous area of Bretagne and stands about 14.3 hands high. Representatives of the Breton breeds find a ready market abroad and, when crossed with other local breeds, they produce horses with great power and a tough constitution.

Horses of Germany

Horse breeding in Germany is practiced on a very extensive scale. For some 200 years or so it has been state controlled, and strict policies have been established in the selection of stallions both for performance and conformation. It is true that the theories of selective breeding are both practiced and preached. Many fine Thoroughbred racehorses are found in Germany today, originally descended from English stock, although they are now also imported from the US, France and Italy. The German Trotters are well known too and, in fact, there are now more trotters registered than Thoroughbreds. The first trotting club was formed in 1874 at Hamburg, mostly with Orlov Trotters imported from Russia. Later they began to import trotters with French blood, and, more recently, trotting stallions from America have been imported.

The Germans have also developed many wonderful breeds of horses of their own, producing what are described as "warm-blooded" horses. This, in fact, is an apt description for they are a combination of hot-blooded and cold-blooded horses. The Oriental breeds of horses, such as the Arab and Barb (see pages 39–41) are known as hot-blooded, while the cold-blooded breeds emanated mainly from Northern Europe. The Germans seemed to have a happy talent for combining the two types to reproduce the best of both worlds in one horse, capable of excelling at top-class show jumping as well as dressage. This was

The head of a Hanoverian Horse.

Holstein mares.

admirably demonstrated in the 1976 Olympic Games when German-bred horses took all three medals in the dressage event and a gold in the show jumping.

The Hanoverian Horse

This big, noble-looking horse of 16 hands or over was originally bred for the Royal Stables in Hanoveria to be both a carriage horse and a mount for the cavalry. As a breed, the Hanoverian has seen several changes over the years. In early times, Holstein stallions were used with local mares to produce the new breed. But when George I came to the throne, he sent over many English Thoroughbreds for crossing with the German breeds. The modern Hanoverian developed as a result of this intermixing and can be described as a handsome, heavily built horse which has powerful quarters and shoulders and good legs.

The Holstein

The Holstein is an older breed than the Hanoverian, reputedly dating back to the thirteenth century. It was apparently originally fostered by the monasteries and has Oriental, Spanish (in the form of Andalusian) and Neapolitan blood. In the sixteenth to eighteenth centuries, it became very popular in other countries and many were exported. Then in the nineteenth century, Thoroughbred blood was introduced into the breed, followed by intermixing with Yorkshire Coach horses. The resulting offspring had a more elevated head and neck carriage and were powerful, deep horses. Nowadays, prospective stallions are sent to the Stallion Testing Center at Westercelle at three to four years old. There they are put through various performance tests and those stallions that do not come up to

the required standards are gelded. This procedure safeguards the future standard of the breed.

The Trakehner

This breed can be traced back to the Order of the German knights when there were two notable types of horses – the heavy type used for fully armored knights and the lighter type used for pleasure riding and hunting. King Wilhelm I was most instrumental in founding this extremely successful breed, when in 1732 he founded a stud at Trakenhen. Mares with local blood were put to stallions supplied from the Royal Stud and to imported Arab sires. Later a number of English Thoroughbreds were also used, and by 1913, it is said, 84 per cent of all mares at the Stud had been sired by Thoroughbred stallions. As with so many breeds, the aim was to produce a dual-purpose animal, suitable for agricultural and cavalry use. Again this breed has more than proved its worth as a riding horse, and today the breeding of the Trakehner is still rigorously controlled.

The Oldenburg

The Oldenburg traces its origins to a stud started in the early part of the seventeenth century by Count Gunther, who used a famous gray stallion called Kranich. In the eighteenth century, fresh blood was introduced into the breed from Spanish Neapolitan, Barb and English half-bred horses. Later still, Cleveland Bays, Thoroughbred and Hanoverian stallions were also used, and the resulting progeny was a "coach horse" type – strong and deep with a marked tendency towards early maturity. The Oldenburg is the heaviest of the German "warm-blooded" breeds, and displays many of the characteristics of its "cold-blooded" ancestors. In 1819, the first Oldenburg Horse Breeding Act was passed, and the licensing of stallions and all aspects of breeding were put into the hands of the registered Society. This also uses the Westercelle Stallion Testing Center to conduct performance tests on prospective stallions to preserve the standard.

The Trakehner.

A team of bay and gray Oldenburgs.

Horses of the British Isles

The English Thoroughbred

The Thoroughbred, a name which has come to be associated with the racehorse of today, was first developed as a breed in England and came under control of Messrs. Wetherby's Stud Book in 1793. It is probably the best known breed of any horse in the world and has been exported to almost every country, although its rather delicate constitution means it sometimes has difficulty in getting acclimatized to extremes of temperature. Charles II is often attributed with starting the breed, by establishing racing as a respectable and popular sport. The horses used were the best Britain could find and they were improved by the introduction of Oriental blood with the importation of the famous Darley Arabian in 1705. In fact all modern Thoroughbreds can trace their ancestry to the Darley Arabian, the Godolphin Arabian or the Byerly Turk – three Arab stallions imported into England in the early eighteenth century. Although it is often claimed that these famous sires were bred to English mares, there appears to be evidence to support the theory that the foundation mares of the Thoroughbred stock were also Eastern. Pillars of modern Thoroughbred pedigrees are such famous names as Eclipse (1764) and St. Simon (1883), both direct descendants of the Darley Arabian, while the famous American racehorse stallion Man-O'-War was descended from the Godolphin Arabian. Thus the "English" Thoroughbred actually emanates from foreign blood, but is now attributed with the word "English" because of the length of time it has been bred and developed in that country.

The Hackney.

The Thoroughbred has been one of England's greatest livestock exports over the years. Nowadays, excellent Thoroughbred horses are found in the US and all over Europe. The French, in particular, breed very successful racehorses and the Germans and Italians have some magnificent Thoroughbred stock. In any test of speed the Thoroughbred has no rivals. In addition, as we have seen, they have been used to improve other breeds the world over, although, interestingly enough, they have not produced successful results when crossed with the Lippizana.

A good specimen stands about 16 hands high and should have about 8 in. (20 cm.) of bone below the knee. The whole appearance is one of extreme elegance and refinement – beautifully

The English Thoroughbred.

The Irish Draft Horse.

proportioned and balanced. Any color is acceptable except skewbald or piebald.

The Hackney

Bred as a harness horse, the Hackney is endowed with a characteristic high-stepping trotting action. This unique movement has been bred into the breed, and their origins can be traced as far back as the fourteenth century at least. The most important ancestor of the Hackney was the Norfolk Trotter, which possessed Arab blood and first appeared in the early eighteenth century when it was used as a work horse. Later it became very popular, particularly in East Anglia where it was used to compete in trotting races. But, although it was often in demand as a stud to improve the breeds of carriage horses, its popularity waned. Then the increasing number of horse shows encouraged a demand for a showy class of carriage horse, which in turn encouraged the breeding of "high steppers." In 1883 a society was formed which revived the Norfolk Trotters and took the name of the Hackney Horse Society. A stud book was begun, and most Hackney horses today can trace their origins back to a stallion called Shales who had been sired by a Thoroughbred called Blaze.

The advent of the motor car has meant a demise in any utilitarian demand for the Hackney, so the concentration has been to breed only the very best horses for use in the show ring. Recently a pony section of the Hackney Society has become increasingly popular and, in fact, Hackney horses and ponies have enthusiastic followers all over the world. There are flourishing breed societies in Canada, Holland, South Africa and the US.

The Irish Draft Horse and Irish Hunter

Irish Draft Horses were the original work horses of Ireland before cart horses were imported from England. They are strong, active horses able to work on the land with a good, steady trotting pace. Today, they are found mostly in the hilly or mountainous districts of Ireland, where they are still used for work on small farms. Breeding is now carefully controlled. Only mares and stallions showing no signs of cart horse blood are used to perpetuate the breed. A stud book was started in 1917 and all horses have to be inspected before registration. The breed suffered badly during 1914–1917, when large numbers were commandeered and never returned from the war. Later many were sold abroad for slaughter, although on a recent trip to Ireland I was relieved and delighted to see many excellent examples at a local show in the mountains.

The Irish Hunter is probably even more famous than the Irish Draft Horse, although it was developed by crossing the draft mares with Thoroughbred stallions. The first cross produced a heavy-weight hunter and the next cross with a Thoroughbred produced a middle-weight hunter.

Ireland is justifiably proud of its horse breeding, and many beautiful and successful horses for racing, hunting and show jumping have been produced. The rich pastures on lime soil, and the mild climate which has virtually no frost in winter, make conditions eminently suitable for horse breeding. The Irish Horse Board, which has government backing, encourages all horse breeding in the country. The famous Connemara pony, bred in the west of Ireland, is described on page 28.

Native Breeds of the British Isles

Within the British Isles there are nine indigenous breeds of ponies. Although each breed is quite separate and has its own specific points and characteristics, there are various factors they all have in common. These include overall smallness in size, inherent intelligence, sure-footedness, hardiness and stamina, all of which have helped the ponies to survive the often harsh conditions of their environment.

The Exmoor Pony

Found in southwestern England, Exmoor ponies today are believed to look exactly as they did when the breed first appeared – at least as long ago as the first inhabitant of the land. For centuries they have managed to survive and breed in wild herds in sparsely inhabited, high, bleak moorland country, where conditions, particularly in winter, are harsh and rugged. Growing to a maximum of 12.3 hands high, they are amazingly strong and hardy, quite capable of carrying a fully grown man through a long day's hunting.

Exmoor ponies may be brown, bay or dun in color but have no white markings anywhere. Their most notable characteristic is their mealy-colored muzzle with its black nostrils. The texture of the coat is quite unlike that of any other horse or pony. Springy and harsh, during the winter it is very full. In summer, the shorter hairs are close and hard with a noticeable shine. Exmoor ponies have long been used as children's riding ponies, for which they are ideally suited. They are exceptional jumpers for their size and, when crossed with Thoroughbreds, make excellent teenage mounts, retaining many of the native pony characteristics, yet combining them with the lightness and smooth pace of the Thoroughbred.

The Exmoor Pony.

The Dartmoor Pony.

The Dartmoor Pony

From time immemorial, these good-looking ponies have roamed the rough and rocky moorlands found in the extreme southwest of England. The open high moors of this area, situated between the English channel and the Atlantic seaboard, are bleak and windy and contain many treacherous bogs. Not surprisingly, the Dartmoor ponies display all the hardy characteristics associated with the native breeds. They rarely exceed 12.2 hands in height and are usually bay, black or brown in color. There are some grays, and a few chestnuts (although these are seldom seen nowadays) but in fact no color is barred from the stud book except skewbalds. Some colored ponies will be seen running wild on Dartmoor. They resulted largely from Shetland stallions being turned out on the moors years ago in order to produce a heavier type of small pony, for use as pit ponies in coal mines. This seriously threatened the pure-bred Dartmoor ponies, for the Dartmoor-Shetland cross established a very strong footing on the moors, multiplying faster than the pure-breds. The true Dartmoor pony is essentially a riding-type pony. Its strong, short legs enable it to carry weights that in no way look commensurate with its size. Outstanding physical characteristics of the Dartmoor Pony are a very neat head with exceptionally small ears and a thick mane and tail.

The Dales Ponies

Power is the main characteristic of this pony, which, at a maximum height of 14.2 hands, is among the largest of the native breeds. It is a native of the North of England, emanating from the eastern side of the Pennine Range. From the western side came the Fell Pony, and at one stage the two breeds were almost identical in type. Both originally used to carry lead from the mines in the Dales to the seaports. The Fell has developed more as a riding pony while the Dales pony remains strong and stocky and more suitable as a work horse. The deep body of the Dales pony is set on four well-shaped legs and the pony is usually black or brown in color.

The breed in general was placed in great danger by the modernization of transportation and farm machinery. Renewed interest in riding over the Dales country has brought them back into favor, and their ability to carry the heaviest of riders while being docile enough to entrust with a beginner or child, has made them great favorites for trail rides.

The Shetland Pony

Smallest of all the native breeds, these stocky little ponies rarely exceed 10.2 hands high. They originated in the Shetland Isles off the north coast of the British Isles, where the terrain is rocky and conditions harsh. The islanders used them for pulling carts, carrying peat in baskets and working generally on the farms. Nowadays they are used extensively as children's riding ponies, although their small size often makes it difficult to school them for saddle work. They make fantastic driving ponies and are often seen well up in the list of prize winners in driving competitions. Shetland ponies

may be any color, although black is the most popular for showing. Besides their small size they are characterized by their incredibly thick coats, long thick manes and tails, and small well-shaped heads. The Shetland's short strong back is very deep through the girth.

The New Forest Pony

As their name indicates, these native ponies come from the comparatively small area of moorland and forest known as the New Forest in central, southern England. There were hardy wild ponies running in this district before the

The Dales Pony.

The Shetland Pony.

Roman invasion of Britain. They were used by the local inhabitants to work on the land, and as beasts of burden. These original ponies and those that followed them for centuries were able to sustain themselves entirely on the rough grazing, but the introduction of foreign blood to the breed from time to time, to "improve" them, sometimes led to less hardy specimens being produced. In 1852 Queen Victoria loaned an Arab stallion called Zorah for use in the Forest, and it remained there eight years. Later a Thoroughbred stallion called Field Marshall was used extensively and then Lord Cecil tried crossing the breed with other native-bred stallions such as Highland, Fell, Exmoor and Dartmoor. Not surprisingly with all this mixture of blood, it has been difficult in the past generations to establish a true type, but in 1938, the New Forest Pony Breeding and Cattle Society was formed and since then no foreign blood has been introduced into the roaming herds. There are a number of stud farms in existence – not necessarily in the New Forest Area – where registered New Forest Ponies are being bred. A good export trade exists for the better bred pony.

Bays and browns are the most usual colors and the ponies vary in height from 12 to 14 hands. They are finer looking than many of the other native breeds and are much in demand as children's riding ponies, particularly as their grazing by the roads in the forest makes them unafraid of traffic.

The New Forest Pony.

The Connemara Pony

The pretty Connemara pony is a native of the rocky and boggy west coast region of Galway in Ireland. As with all other native pony breeds, its exact origins are unknown, but there is a theory that its present form emanated from indigenous pony stock crossing with Spanish horses which swam ashore from the wrecked ships of the Spanish Armada in 1588. Certainly a native pony breed existed before this time, and

The Connemara Pony.

The Highland Pony.

certainly Connemara ponies today display physical characteristics of Spanish and Arabian blood.

Compact, strongly built ponies with a well balanced head and neck, and good, easy action, Connemara ponies make excellent riding ponies. They vary in height from 13 hands to 14 or 14.2 hands and may be any color, although piebald or skewbald specimens cannot be registered in the recognized British and Irish Connemara breed societies.

The Highland Ponies

There are two types of Highland pony, both emanating from Scotland. The Western Isle pony comes from the Isle of Rhum and is a light type, active but strongly made, which stands at about 13.2 to 14 hands high. It is said to contain some Arab blood. The mainland pony is known as the Garron and is taller and more strongly made. Garrons were originally used for farm work and as a means of transportation. They were also used in deer hunting, often to bring the dead stag down from the mountain. Today this breed is popular as a family pony and is also used by trail-riding establishments because it makes a reliable mount at slow paces. The lighter type also makes excellent riding ponies. All Highland ponies are noted for their docility and kindness, which has made them popular mounts for the disabled. There is a very active society for the Highland ponies, which imposes no color bar except for piebalds and skewbalds. The most usual color, though, is dun – either blue dun, mouse dun or yellow, usually with a dorsal stripe and zebra markings on the legs. Both types of Highland pony have proud head carriage, small ears, necks which are strong but are not coarse, deep strong bodies and

short powerful quarters. The legs of the Highland pony are strongly built with plenty of feathery hair in the heel.

Children's Ponies

From these native breeds has sprung a type, rather than a breed, of quality small animal used mainly for showing. It has been produced by crossing the native breeds with Thoroughbred and Arab stallions, a practice encouraged by the Ponies of Britain Club, which sponsors classes for these show ponies, as well as the brood mares and the yearlings.

The Cleveland Bay

This is one of the oldest breeds of English horse and is said to be one of those that helped in founding the present day Thoroughbred. It certainly has the same flat bones that are admired in both breeds. Originally bred in Yorkshire, the Cleveland Bay was primarily a coach horse and is powerfully built, active, with a rather large head and strong, clean, muscular legs. It stands between 16 and 16.2 hands high and is usually colored bay with black points. No white is allowed except for a small star on the forehead. They are particularly popular as a foundation stock for breeding hunters and jumpers, as Cleveland Bays show an unrivalled ability to reproduce all their best qualities in generation after generation.

The Cleveland Bay Society was formed in 1884 to protect the breed, since crossing with other breeds and types had seriously reduced the numbers of purebred stock. They are used by reigning monarchs of Britain to pull the state carriages, and teams of Cleveland Bays will often be seen competing in International Driving Competitions.

The Cleveland Bay.

Welsh Ponies

There are four distinct types of Welsh pony recognized by the Welsh Pony and Cob Society. These are:

The Mountain type
The Riding pony
The Riding pony of Cob type
The Welsh Cob

The Mountain type is a beautiful and graceful small pony. Some display distinct Arab characteristics such as a dish-faced head. Excellent riding ponies for children, they usually stand between 11 and 12 hands high and are active and proud with well shaped bodies and attractive flowing manes and tails.

The Welsh pony or Riding pony has very similar characteristics to the Mountain type but is generally larger, standing up to 13.2 hands high. This gives these ponies a little more scope, and besides making excellent children's ponies and hunters, they have proved their worth many times over in almost every field of riding.

Above: The Welsh Mountain type mare and foal.

Left: The Welsh Cob.

Below left: The Welsh Riding Pony.

The Riding pony of the Cob type has to be under 13.2 hands high, but it is heavier in build and stronger in every way than the Welsh Riding pony. Although undoubtedly of cob build, it still retains the pony-type head with the small ears and has the characteristic flowing mane and tail. It is able to carry adults as well as children and may also be driven in harness. These attributes make it an ideal, all-round family pony.

The Welsh Cob is the largest of all the Welsh ponies and may be anything from 14 to 15.1 hands high. It is a strong, active animal with a small head set on to a well shaped neck with good shoulders, and short, but strong quarters. Originally Welsh Cobs were used on the hill farms for every kind of agricultural work, and they were also popular as harness animals, with a reputation for being great trotters. At one time, too, they were extensively used in London for milk deliveries. They have a well earned reputation for being quiet with a good temperament, and they are easily trained.

The Heavy Horses

Until the recent revival of interest in the great Heavy Horses of England, it seemed as if these giant breeds, whose ancestries may be traced back to the eleventh century, would be doomed to die out. With the days of their usefulness as work horses over, it seemed as if they were no longer needed. Then, happily, there was an upsurge in interest shown by the public in the forming of the Plowing and Heavy Horse Associations. Great support was given to "open days" at farms and establishments such as the Shire Center. Many of the English breweries have retained the heavy horses to pull their carts over short distances and in exhibitions. The three main British breeds of Heavy Horse are:

The Suffolk Punch

Renowned for their uniformity of type, these horses are chestnut in color with very slight feathering of the heels. Large muscular animals, standing 16 to 16.2 hands high, they have a deep rounded body and have been bred in East Anglia since 1506, when they were known as the Britannia breed. An infusion of light blood, aimed at improving their working agility, resulted in the present-day Suffolk. All present-day registered Suffolk Punch horses can trace their pedigree to one horse, foaled in 1760 and known as Crisp's Horse of Offord. Careful selective breeding and a thorough ban on selling or exhibiting any horse without a vet's certificate at a breed sale or agricultural show, has kept the breed very pure and sound. Cross breeding with Thoroughbred or Arab stock has not proved very successful.

The Shire Horse

This ancient breed has long been renowned for its size and strength. In Elizabethan times it was known as The Great Horse of England, and as

The Clydesdale.

A Shire mare and foal.

a breed it has always been used for heavy draft and agricultural work. The best types are usually at least 17 hands high. In coloring they are mostly bay, brown, gray or black with a considerable amount of white on their very heavily feathered legs. The Shire Horse is a slow worker but has a very regular walk and is docile and honest. Heavy hunters and good show jumpers have resulted from crosses with Thoroughbreds.

The Clydesdale

This breed evolved from the crossing of local mares with heavier breeds to produce an active horse suitable for draft work. They were much in demand when roads improved and they replaced pack ponies for hauling coal. They became so popular that in 1911 one stallion fetched the unbelievable price of $31,660! Great store is placed on the movement of these animals, and the shoe on each foot should be seen as they walk. The feet must be large and open, and it is from this breed that the adage "No foot, no horse" is supposed to have come. Feathering is on the back of the leg and heel and should not be as heavy as in the Shire. The back of the Clydesdale should be short and well ribbed.

The Clydesdale Society was formed in 1877 and imposes no color bars. White markings are often found on the face and hind legs. Mares of this breed cross well with Thoroughbreds to produce heavy hunters. Sometimes the first cross has a little too much action to make a good riding horse, but the second crosses have proved their worth in the hunting field, time and time again.

Horses of Hungary

Hungary has been responsible for some fine horses through the centuries. At one time the main breeding place of the famous Lippizanas was at the Hungarian State Stud at Babolna, founded in 1789, when Hungary was part of the Austrian Empire. Its most notable breed is probably the *Shagya* which descended from a Syrian Arab stallion, imported in the early eighteenth century. It stands at 14 to 15 hands high and is an excellent mover, besides being extremely hardy. It also stemmed from the indigenous Hungarian horse – a small, hardy, primitive breed. The Hungarian farmers' horse is a descendant of this same horse and is generally recognized as forming the native stock.

The *Gidran* was produced by crossing native mares with Thoroughbreds and half-breds. The big saddle horse that resulted is popular in other countries, Poland in particular.

Horses of Italy

Although Italy has perhaps never had a great reputation as a horse-breeding country, it was undoubtedly one of the first nations to appreciate horses of quality. The Court of Naples fostered a famous breed of horse, known as the *Neapolitan*, during the sixteenth century. They were descended from horses with Spanish blood and were in great demand to improve other breeds. Henry VIII imported some into England. In more recent years the breeding of horses for agricultural and utilitarian purposes

Hungarian Horses.

The Salerno.

has decreased, and more interest has been shown in the breeding of race horses and trotters. A breed known as the *Salerno* was produced from native mares crossed with horses of Thoroughbred and Arabian blood. It proved a serviceable horse that could be used as a carriage horse if necessary. Breeders did not find a ready market for it, though, probably because riding does not enjoy tremendous popularity as a national sport. Those who wanted riding horses tended to import them from Hungary and Yugoslavia. It should not be forgotten, however, that it is Italy's famous cavalry school that is responsible for modern show jumping techniques, and their national riders have had great influence in this sport.

Horses of Russia

Russia has many unique breeds of horses, but possibly the most famous of all is the *Orlov Trotter*, which gets its name from Count Orlov, who started the breed in 1777. Count Orlov was renowned for breeding horses of strength and speed for pulling carriages. He produced his famous trotters by crossing English Thoroughbreds with Arab, Dutch, Danish and German blood. The resulting horse retained the Arab look about the head, took speed prowess from the Thoroughbred and inherited a hard constitution from the Dutch, Danish and German stock. Standing up to 17 hands high, it has a good girth and wide chest, giving plenty of heart room.

From the Orlov Trotters the *Russian Trotters* developed by crossing the best of the Orlov mares with American stallions Only the finest offspring were retained and are now established as a breed with their own State Stud Book. About the same height as the Orlov Trotters, with deep girths, long necks, short legs and powerful shoulders and quarters, they are able to move faster.

In addition to the trotters, Russia has produced some notable heavy draft and saddle horses. The breed known as the *Russian Saddle Horse* came from crossing an Orlov Trotter with the Rostopchin Saddle Horse. This horse was bred by a Count Rostopchin and contained Arabian and English Thoroughbred blood. It is a breed which is noted for its stamina and endurance.

The Mongolian Pony

This ancient breed of horse is believed to be the ancestor of most of our European breeds. It is found both semi-domesticated and wild all over Mongolia. Nomads use the ponies for shepherding and as pack ponies, and in parts of China there is a good market for them for use in racing and playing polo. Mostly, however, they run wild, fending for themselves and being caught when they are needed for a specific purpose or for sale. Usually ranging from 12.2 to 13.3 hands high, they are tough little ponies, with long coats, coarse manes and tails and rather long backs in proportion to their size. Their necks are not well developed, and in fact their conformation shows that they have not had the benefit of care or selective breeding. This, of course, is why they have remained virtually unchanged for centuries. Ponies found in Burma and Northern India stem from the Mongolian Pony and have the same ability to exist on poor and meager rations.

Przewalski's Wild Horse

This strange breed of wild horse can be found roaming in the same area as the Mongolian ponies and is known to interbreed with them.

Although it is of an incredibly primitive nature it only came to light in the late nineteenth century when the Polish explorer Colonel Przewalski obtained the skin and skull of one of these animals. It can be described as being horse-like in appearance although it has such characteristics as a very large head but small ears. It has a stocky, somewhat ungainly body with a thick neck and shoulders. Its coat is coarse and harsh and dun-colored. Living specimens of this wild horse-like creature were collected at the beginning of this century and succeeding generations can be seen displayed in various zoos around the world.

The Mongolian Pony.

Russian Horses.

33

Horses of Spain

The Andalusian

This breed of horses, emanating from the Iberian Peninsula, is regarded by many as one of the most superb breeds of all. It is thought that Arab blood was instrumental in founding the breed, although some sources dispute this theory. It would seem logical to assume that Arab blood would have been introduced into Spain at the time of the Moorish occupation. Although the straight profile of the head does not show Arab characteristics, it is obvious that there is some Oriental blood in their veins.

The magnificent qualities of kind temperament and a general build and make-up that make the Andalusian suited to hard work and pleasure riding have been recognized since the days of Cincinnatus. Grecian friezes depict a horse very similar to the Andalusian, and there

Left: Andalusians preparing for a display.

Above: The Spanish Horse.

is a reference in the *Iliad* to two Spanish stallions driven by Achilles. Spanish horses must therefore have been imported into Greece in ancient times and they are also said to have been used for chariot racing by both the Romans and the Egyptians. Later the Duke of Austria imported Spanish horses when he married Isabella of Spain. In fact, Andalusians have been exported to all parts of the world from the sixteenth century onwards and they have had a tremendous influence on breeds of many other countries.

The Andalusian is particularly well suited to life as a display horse with its proud bearing and prancing action, coupled with its docility and easiness to train. England's great sixteenth century master of equitation, the Duke of Newcastle, called them "the noblest horses in the world." The breed was kept pure with the help of two studs. One was run by the monks of Jerez and the other was known as the Zapstero stud. Usually the breed is gray, but other colors are allowed by the established breed societies.

The Spanish Horse

The Spanish Horse, known also as the Spanish Jennet, is the result of a cross of Andalusians with Barbs and Arabs. The progeny is a beautiful, elegant horse which has proud carriage. It has proved to be an amazing, all-purpose utility horse – used equally for classical riding, in bull fighting and as a carriage horse. Originally they were also used for transportation and light agricultural work, and many were exported to the United States. A vast horse population has descended from the original imported stock, and many new breeds began by crossing Spanish Horses with local mares.

Horses of Scandinavia

The countries of Scandinavia have produced many notable breeds of horses and ponies, and it is from this area that many of the "cold-blooded" types emanate.

Sweden is an important horse-breeding country where the Government has taken a great interest in the breeding of all breeds and has introduced a system of controlling stallion licensing. In addition to the "cultivated" breeds, Sweden has a native type known as the Gotland pony, found on the Island of Gotland in the Baltic sea. It is descended from a very primitive type of horse, which it still resembles in many ways. It may be brown, chestnut, black, dun and gray and is renowned for its stamina and speed.

Denmark's indigenous horse was originally a small thick-set animal, which over the years was crossed with Dutch, Spanish, Turkish and Thoroughbred blood. As a result of these crosses, two main breeds were produced, one primarily for working on the land and the other for riding.

The Swedish Ardenne Horse
Introduced from its native country of Belgium in the 1830s, and subsequently bred in Sweden, the Swedish Ardenne Horse is a small, active heavy draft horse. Its main work is hauling timber out of the forests. A stud book was opened for the breed at the beginning of this century. Pedigrees are kept and foals registered by the Swedish Ardenne Horse Breeding Association.

The North Swedish Horse
The North Swedish Horse was established as a breed at the beginning of this century and evolved through an up-grading of their size by breeding small native mares to bigger stallions. The stallions were imported from Norway. In 1944, there were 400 registered stallions of this breed, producing about 8000 purebred North Swedish horses each year. The hard work they are expected to do in the mountain timber camps takes a tremendous toll on these horses, however, so the Government has also set up an advisory service to help horse owners. This and the licensing of the stallions has undoubtedly maintained the high standard of this very useful national breed.

The Swedish Riding Horse
A very careful selective breeding program rigorously pursued and adhered to since this breed began has helped it in achieving a tre-

The Swedish Riding Horse.

mendous reputation all over the world for ability in dressage, show jumping and cross-country eventing. The breed appears to have been developed as the result of the founding of a Royal Stud in 1621, although the breed as we know it today was produced for the Swedish cavalry when they joined the Royal Stud at Stromshold in 1868. Only the best stallions were imported to cross with local mares and again only the best of the foals produced were retained as breeding stock. Stallions from Oriental, Spanish and Fresian stock were used, and later German blood was introduced by Hanoverian and Trakehner horses. The influence of the German blood is clearly shown in today's Swedish horses. Many Swedish Riding Horses have been imported into England in recent years, and the breed is one which is particularly popular for dressage work.

The Norwegian Fjord Pony

This tough little pony has existed on the west coast of Norway for centuries. It probably had Przewalski's wild horse as one of its ancestors. It is said that the Vikings kept and bred it, and unlike many native ponies from other parts of the world, it had been systematically bred in captivity for many years. Considered as one of the greatest native ponies of all, it stands about 14 hands high and is a dun color with a dorsal stripe running into its short, upright, thick mane. It has a deep body slung on strong, powerful legs with a short thick neck and a well proportioned head. It has good bones and hard feet. Like other animals that originate in mountainous country and are used to roaming over the steep hills, it has developed great power, which makes it invaluable for working the land or as a pack horse. Its good nature and

The Norwegian Dølahest

The Norwegian Fjord Pony.

willingness, coupled with an intelligence that makes it easy to train, also make it a good riding pony and it is popular for trail rides.

The Finnish Horse

There are some 18,000 of this type currently in Finland, according to a state register kept by the Ministry of Agriculture. In fact, only one breed is officially recognized and this is a utility type of horse, heavy enough to work in the forests. All mares and stallions considered for breeding have to pass a weight-pulling test, and their temperament is also taken into account. In addition, their conformation, soundness and action, working at the walk and trot, all have to come up to a required standard. This breed was developed by crossing pony stock with larger stallions and the result is a horse of medium size, lighter than many working horses and leaner in the leg, with strong pony characteristics in the head and neck. They have good bones, strong legs, hard feet and thick, muscular bodies. Standing about 15 hands, or slightly over, their predominant color is chestnut

Finnish Horses.

and their reputation for being surefooted, hard working and immensely tough is well earned.

The Fredericksborg Horse
This Danish horse was bred for riding and takes its name from a stud founded by Frederick II in 1562. The heavy horse previously demanded for armored knights was now virtually no longer required, and instead there was a need for a lighter horse. With the introduction of Andalusian and Neapolitan blood a horse was bred that proved particularly easy to train for classical riding school work. This was the Fredericksborg, and at that time it was considered one of the most elegant horses in Europe. It more or less marked the beginning of the breed of "pleasure" horse. Unfortunately, it was the popularity of the breed which proved to be its undoing, as all the best examples were rapidly sold. In 1839 the stud had to be closed down, because it had no suitable breeding stock left. Only a few private individuals were

Icelandic Ponies.

able to continue breeding and a system of registrations was gradually developed for the breed by 1923. The Fredericksborg is now a weight-carrying riding horse of about 15.3 hands high.

The Jutland Horse
Much heavier than the Fredericksborg, the Jutland breed nevertheless evolved in a similar manner. It is a useful heavy horse originally intended for agricultural work on the plains of Jutland, and it has proved its worth as a draft horse in the town as well. In fact, the breed goes back for centuries, and is mentioned in the Age of Chivalry. Since then, much cross breeding with horses from neighboring countries has taken place, although most present-day pedigrees go back to an English imported stallion called Oppenheim LXII who is thought to have been a Shire. Increased mechanization has led to a marked decrease in the numbers of the breed.

The Icelandic Pony
Icelandic ponies are closely related to the Norwegian Fjord pony and in fact are not a native of Iceland. Reports vary slightly about their history, some sources claiming that they were brought to Iceland by the Vikings, while others say they are of older descent and originate from the time when Iceland was still part of the European continent. There seems fairly convincing evidence to support the theory that they were taken to Iceland by the early settlers who went there towards the end of the ninth century. Since this time, the ponies have changed very little in appearance – except perhaps to become slightly smaller. The extreme cold and harsh conditions have meant that only the toughest have survived to produce a species that can scramble over the rock, ice and snow with amazing agility.

Icelandic ponies are small, sturdy and hard working, possessing great strength and a docile, friendly nature. They are quite able to survive on very sparse rations, but the minerals found in the volcanic soil of their homeland give them excellent bones. Standing from 12 to 13 hands high, they have very short, thick necks with short manes that stick upwards. Good working ponies, able to carry considerable weight, they tend to be classed as riding or pack ponies. Those intended for riding are broken to an ambling gait. Attempts have been made at various times to produce a finer riding horse by crossing with Thoroughbreds but the results have not been successful. Icelandic ponies have also been crossed with Shetlands. A few were imported to England recently for trail riding establishments, but although they were able to carry great weights for their size, they were not very popular and were inclined to get laminitis.

color is shown off to its best in Western classes, when the riders are wearing their colorful traditional Western riding gear.

The color is said to stem from the Spanish horses imported into the United States by Spanish settlers. Queen Isabella of Spain was particularly fond of this coloring, and Palominos were known as "Isabellas" in Spain.

The Spotted Horse

From ancient times there have been spotted horses – a fact borne out by cave pictures found in France dating from about 18,000 B.C. They were also known to have existed in Asia in about 3500 B.C., and horses with spotted markings appear in Egyptian, Greek and Chinese drawings and pottery, dating from about 1400 B.C. The Persians claim that their spotted horses descended from a famous spotted war horse called Rakush, which belonged to their great leader, Rustan, about 400 B.C. And the Chinese imported spotted horses from the West during the T'ang dynasty of 618–907 A.D. The first English pictures showing spotted horses appear in a manuscript dated about 1397. In recent times in England a society has been formed exclusively for these horses, which is known as The Spotted Horses of England Society.

Left: The head of a Knabstrup – a Danish breed of Spotted Horse.

Below: A Palomino pony.

Colored Horses

The Palomino

The Palomino is not a breed of horse: the term refers to the color, which is described as being that of a newly minted gold coin with a white, flowing mane and tail. This lovely coloration is popular in the US and the horse has come to be associated with North America. The Palomino is often known as "the golden horse of the West."

The Palomino Horse Breeders of America and the Palomino Society of Great Britain insist on strict inspections of all horses before they can be registered. Besides the color described above, the best animals will have a dark skin and either dark or blue eyes. A white skin shows a lack of pigmentation and many horses are too light in color. Often two palominos will breed a cream-colored horse known as a "Creamola." If the resulting stock is then crossed with a dark chestnut horse, the best Palomino colorings are obtained.

The Palominos in America are generally divided into three types, known as the Parade horse, the Bridle Path type (a heavier horse than the former) and the Stock Horse. Certainly the

An Arab-Barb mare and her foal.

The Arab.

Horses of Asia

The Arab

From the arid deserts of the Middle East comes the most famous breed of all, and one which has had more influence on the horses of the world than any other – the Arab. This exquisitely beautiful horse has been portrayed in art since the fourteenth century B.C. The purity of its blood has been fanatically guarded through the ages by the nomadic Arabs who have bred it. Living in such close quarters with its masters, the horse has had to develop an even temperament, and its kind nature has undoubtedly attracted many of its followers, just as have its beauty and endurance.

Arab horses have always played a great part in tribal life in war and peace, and they have been taken to all parts of the world by invaders and traders. The result of this has been that nearly all present-day breeds are descended from the Arab, and their hot-blood has done much to improve breeds of colder blood, giving them greater elegance and powers of endurance.

Today there are many different types of Arab, but those with the purest blood still

come from the desert. English Arabs are, for the most part, Egyptian-bred and to a great extent owe their existence to Blunt, the family who started their famous stud at Cralbet. The Russian Arab is also famous and in the first decade of this century a Russian Arab was imported into England. It has had a profound influence on British pedigrees since that time. The Persian Arab is a larger horse with a less pronounced "dish" to his face and, according to racing records, was in use as a racehorse some 2,700 years ago. The American Arab is mostly of English/Egyptian/Polish blood. The Polish Arab emanates from stallions taken to Poland by the Crusaders. In fact, the earliest references to them are in 1570, although it was not until some purebred mares were captured from the Turks that Arabs as such were bred in Poland. Now Polish Arabs are exported to every part of the world, and they have won a great many international awards – such as at the Paris Exhibition in 1869 and 1900 and in Vienna in 1873. The French Anglo-Arab is one of the most famous French-bred riding horses.

As Arabs are bred in nearly every country in the world, the many national Arab Horse Societies are attempting to form a world Arab Horse in deference to this magnificent beast. Undoubtedly, it is the most beautiful of all horses – full of grace and elegance. The broad head, dished face with soft, intelligent eyes, the flowing mane and tail with its high carriage are the proud characteristics of all Arab horses. In fact, they can be divided into two distinct groups – the larger, coarser type preferred by those countries who race them; and the smaller type, which has a more delicate frame, notably smaller ears and is generally more delicate.

Above: An Arab being ridden by a member of the armed forces, during the Maskal ceremony at Addis Ababa.

Right: A part-bred Arab.

Australian Walers.

The Barb

The Barb is a close relative of the Arab and almost certainly came from the same original source. It is generally connected with North Africa, Morocco, Tunisia and Algeria. We hear of "Barbary" horses being imported into England in the time of the Stuarts. Part of Charles II's wife's dowry was the port of Tangiers, which was British for 21 years, and undoubtedly during that time traders brought back horses from there. When one talks of "Oriental" blood in horses, it is a reference to Barb or Arab blood.

In type the Barb has many of the same characteristics as the Arab, but is in no way as elegant. It is generally rather larger and has a straighter profile to its head and more sloping quarters. Barbs are usually gray or brown in color and stand at about 15 hands, although larger ones have been bred at the Royal Stud in Morocco. The Barb is very hardy and a naturally good riding horse, but because it does not hold the same prestige as the Arab it has not been used to the same extent in influencing other breeds.

The Timor Pony

From the far east of Asia comes the tireless, little, sure-footed Timor pony, so called because it came originally from the island of Timor. Some sources say that these ponies were imported to Timor by Chinese traders, centuries ago. But this is not altogether substantiated by the fact that native ponies in all the Indonesian Islands are very similar to the Timor pony in type. On their native island they are used to draw carts and herd cattle, or for riding. Timor ponies are usually ridden bareback in a bitless bridle.

Nowadays the Timor pony is found both in Australia and New Zealand, where it is used as a stock pony for shepherding. Although it is small, it is capable of carrying great weights and possesses all those qualities of endurance and willingness associated with native ponies. Experiments in crossing them with Arab blood have proved quite successful and the resulting progeny are used for racing in Indonesia.

The Australian Waler

Australia has no native horses, so the early settlers, desperately in need of them for transportation, first imported horses in 1795. This stock was mainly of Dutch and Spanish origin and the first horses were small. The settlers crossed them with imported Arab and Thoroughbred stallions to produce a larger, riding type of horse. It became known as the Waler from an abbreviation of the state of New South Wales, where most of the horse breeding took place. At one stage Walers were in great demand in India as army remounts, favored for their hardiness and general ability. They were also used for polo, pig-sticking and hunting with great success, and now all good polo ponies found in Singapore are Walers. In Australia they have proved themselves in racing as well as show-jumping.

The Working Horse

The study of the various types and breeds of horse that have evolved through the ages will have made it clear that the role of the horse in society has shifted dramatically over the last few decades. Clearly, the single invention that has made the most difference to man's relationship with the horse is the internal combustion engine. Where horses were once used as the major, if not only, means of transporting people and goods – as either riding horses, carriage and coach horses or pack horses – and as the major aid in cultivating the land, they have now almost universally been replaced by more modern forms of transportation. They also played a leading role in days gone by in times

Above: Circus horses in the ring.

Left: Breweries in England still retain horses to pull their carts. Here a team is seen at a Horse Show.

Below: Horses in France help to bring in the wine harvest.

of inter-tribal feuds and war, but their usefulness has again been eroded by the sophisticated weapons and methods of modern warfare. And yet it is probably true to say that the horse has never been as popular as it is today, in the latter half of the twentieth century. Its role now, as it nears extinction as a "work" animal, is as a "pleasure" animal – although it is doubtful that the horse distinguishes between the two! It is interesting to note, too, that in spite of this shift to "pleasure," horses are more a big-money business now than they have ever been, even when they formed an essential part of nearly every man's livelihood. The breeding of top-class competition horses in whatever sphere – racing, show-jumping, showing or combined training and eventing – has never been as internationally competitive as it is today, and the sums of money for which horses exchange hands are astronomical.

There are, of course, still many places in the world where horses continue to fulfil a useful function in man's everyday life, and for which no satisfactory replacements have yet been found. In more remote and less accessible places, particularly in mountainous regions, small farmers find that horses are still a greater aid to life on the farm than modern tractors. Not only would tractors be hard-pushed to reach these areas, they are less versatile and markedly less reliable! In such instances, how-ever, it is usually the hardy native ponies of the area that are the greatest help, and the great cart horses of yesteryear – the docile Shires and mighty Clydesdales – that formed a common sight in front of a plow or a hay-wagon on most farms are seldom seen anywhere. As breeds they live on today because of the societies that have been formed to ensure their perpetuation. Many fine examples are owned by the big breweries of England, which use them to deliver beer to restaurants in the big cities, but perhaps more to maintain their public image than anything else.

No replacement has yet been found for the cow horses and ponies used by the stockmen and owners of big ranches in the US, South America and Australia. No modern machinery can fulfil their role of herding cattle, or singling out a steer for branding. Owners of cattle ranches in Australia sometimes use an interest-ing combination of transportation for herding purposes. They first fly over their huge proper-ties in light aircraft, so as to locate the herds of cattle. Then they drive the horses to the spot in trucks, and finally they use the horses to round up the cattle and bring them back to the homestead!

Horses still are used by police forces around the world. Their work in this area is amazingly varied – from traffic and crowd control in London, New York, Tokyo, Stockholm, Stutt-

The Horse Guards in Hyde Park, London.

gart and Sydney to guard and ceremonial duties in all these places and many more. Undoubtedly the most famous mounted police force in the world was, and probably still is, the Royal Canadian Mounted Police, known everywhere as the "Mounties." Originally they were used to patrol a vast area of ungoverned territory, pursuing criminals and trying to keep the peace between the native Indian population and the ever-increasing new settlers. Their practical use continued up to the Second World War. Although the Canadian Mounted Police still breed their own superb horses, their only use now is on ceremonial occasions and as promoters of goodwill between countries. This latter is done mainly by exhibitions of the famous and highly skilled "musical ride," which the Mounties have performed in many countries throughout the world.

When the mounted police force began in Australia in the early nineteenth century, one

Above: Horses being used in New South Wales, Australia, to round up cattle and drive them across the Hunter River.

Left: A horse stands patiently while the hay is stacked in the Belgian Ardennes.

of their more dangerous duties was to protect the early settlers from the outlaws who lived in the bush. For generations, the police force formed the main link between the out-back dwellers and the town communities. The main function now of the Australian mounted police force, besides that of controlling crowds and demonstrations in the big cities, is on ceremonial occasions.

Members of London's Metropolitan mounted police are a familiar sight in all the streets of the City. Each day they are on duty outside

Buckingham Palace at the Changing of the Guard and they can be seen on numerous ceremonial occasions.

Police horses are looked after and trained for their exacting work by members of the police force. A very special kind of temperament is needed for police horses, for they have to be taught to ignore the noise of large, unruly crowds, to move or stand stock-still on command in traffic, unheeding of roaring buses or screeching motor-car tires – in fact, to be unperturbed by the unusual, whenever it may occur. In addition, they are taught to push against a crowd with their quarters, but not to kick or to lean against people who may push against them.

Armies obviously have less use for horses than they did at one stage, but there are still many mounted regiments in existence in almost every country of the world. Once again, ceremonial duties are their primary function, but this in itself is an important part of international life. Probably the best-known mounted regiments in England today are the Life Guards and Household Cavalry, the Blues and Royals, and the King's Troop of the Royal Horse Artillery. The first troops of the Life Guards were formed by Charles II, after he had been so impressed by the French mounted royal bodyguard, the Maison du Roy, which he saw during his exile in France. It is from cavalries the world over that many of the favorite equestrian sports of today have evolved – polo, modern show-jumping, and three-day eventing, for example. In London, mounted soldiers display their "skill-at-arms" annually at the famous Royal Tournament.

Another area where horses have been used as work horses, albeit to give entertainment, is that of the circus. Circuses are international entertainment and, in spite of gloomy reports, are as popular today as they ever were. There are famous circuses thrilling crowds in the US, Russia, Germany, France, Spain and Switzerland; and in all of them, the horses rank as one of the greatest highlights of the circus acts.

Horses in circus acts are used either by the acrobats, who perform their breathtaking acts of balance on the back of a horse as it canters round the ring, or else it is the horses themselves that do the performing. Performances of these "liberty" horses are akin to *haute école* work (see page 172), although some of the movements and exercises they perform extend beyond the purely "natural" airs of the highly trained *haute école* horse. Their training is exacting, for often many work together, performing the movements

in unison, and in a very confined space under artificial lights. Many different types and breeds of horses will be found in circuses, from Lippizanas and Russian- and Polish-bred Arabs to performing Shetland ponies; horses from Hungary to those from Norway and, indeed, almost anywhere else you can think of. Particular favorites among circus troups of the world have always been the Danish Knabstrup and the Appaloosa horses, popular for their attractive and distinctive spotty markings and their fine build and carriage. The Andalusians from Spain are popular for the *haute école* type acts.

Above: A cowboy and his horse. The horse is wearing a bosal nose-band.

Left: The Canadian Mounted Police performing their famous musical ride.

Riding–Yesterday and Today

A History of Riding

The first certain evidence we have of man using the horse as a mount, as opposed to a source of food or a beast of burden, appears to come from an Egyptian figurine that dates back to the fourteenth century B.C. There is some indication from the Chinese holy books that the Chinese may have indulged in a form of equitation, seven centuries earlier. But it is from around the fourteenth century B.C. that we can begin to trace man's riding progress. The wealth of information that helps us comes in the early times from cave paintings, sculpture, pottery and bas relief, and later from literature, tapestries and paintings. That the horse is featured so frequently and consistently in all these fields of art leaves no doubt of the important part he has played in man's life through the ages.

It is clear that, when early man began to ride, he had no thought of saddles and bridles. Instead he rode bareback, astride the horse with his legs stretched down on either side. He stayed in place by balance and appears to have "controlled" the horse, or its direction at least, by using switches. Before long the first bridles came into existence, for man must soon have realized that a link between him and his horse's head would give him considerably more scope in controlling his mount. Archaeological excavations have revealed a number of ancient bits, which amazingly differ little from those which are in use today.

The forerunner of our modern saddles appears to be a kind of saddle cloth used by Assyrian warriors in the seventh and eighth centuries B.C. This was developed into an ornamental saddle cloth to which a type of stirrup was attached.

Like the bit, stirrups were a great invention

Above: An eighteenth century papier maché panel showing a young

Persian prince indulging in the sport of hawking or falconry.

Below: A painting of the start of the Derby in 1844.

that played an important part in developing the use of the horse. They made it possible to ride faster, for a horse can move more quickly if the rider's weight is carried farther forward. The use of stirrups helps a rider to lean forward and to sustain this position for longer periods of time. From the saddle cloths, the modern saddle began to emerge. Initially these were in the form of two cushions, stuffed with hair, which rested on the saddle cloth on either side of the spine, joined by cross straps. Later they were attached to a wooden "saddle-tree" which helped to take the rider's weight off the horse's spine. The idea behind all these innovations was to encourage the rider to sit low behind the withers – as opposed to sitting farther back, virtually on the animal's rump, which had been the earlier practice when riding donkeys or more primitive forms of horse.

There are many famous men and women who have influenced styles of riding and horsemanship over the centuries, but there can be none more famous than the Greek riding master, Xenophon. Born in 430 B.C., he was to write a book on equitation, parts of which are still in existence today.

The riding position he taught in essence remained that used by Europeans until the twentieth century. This was to ride with almost straight legs: in Xenophon's words, "We do not recommend the seat as in a chair, but rather as the rider were standing upright." This position is still the recognized seat used in Western-style riding.

Xenophon trained the Greek warriors and considered cross-country riding an important part of their training. Thus they had to jump over any obstacles in their way – stone walls, banks

A portrayal of the Spanish Riding School's Lippizana horses and their riders, painted in 1755 by Baton Refs d'Eisenburg.

and so on. He trained his horses to jump using their hocks, rather than to "hop" off their forehand. This great horseman also left us with much sound advice on dealing with horses. On riding a spirited horse he said, "You must calm him for longer than an average horse, and in making him advance, use the aids as gently as possible. Sudden actions produce alarm." He advised, "Never lose your temper in dealing with horses. When a horse suspects some object and is unwilling to approach it, you must explain that it is not terrible. Lead him up to it gently. Those who compel the horse with blows make him more frightened than ever." These are words that are as apt now as they were over 2,000 years ago.

After Xenophon, no more books on horsemanship were written for some 2,000 years, and equitation did not appear to develop much as an art over the next few centuries. With the advance into the Christian era, one of the main uses of the horse was in battles and campaigns, so it was aspects of horsemanship that would be useful in these areas that developed. An important invention of this time, however, was the horseshoe, which meant that horses could be ridden all the year around on all types of ground.

Towards the middle ages, methods of warfare became more sophisticated, and horses played a correspondingly less important role in battles. More definite signs began to appear of the horse being used for sporting pursuits and relaxation purposes. Riding became fashionable among the aristocracy and courts of Europe and it became important for noblemen to be able to ride well in the *haute école* style. The famous jousting tournaments between knights of the middle ages demanded precisely trained and obedient horses as well as a high degree of skill in horsemanship.

The courts of Europe developed their own riding schools, each of which had a riding master or masters to train the courtiers and give displays. One of the earliest and most famous of these was the School of Naples, started by Federico Grisone. Pupils went from all over Europe to study under him, although by our standards his methods were cruel and the bits and spurs he used both sharp and extremely severe. Grisone's schools taught the movements of dressage and high school, or *haute école*, as it is called today, putting the emphasis on lightening the forehand and transferring the weight to the hindquarters. He trained horses in circle and serpentine work and simple dressage movements, such as turns on the forehand, as well as teaching the airs off the ground (see page 173). It was about this time, too, that the famous Spanish riding school of Vienna was started.

Grisone practiced during the sixteenth cen-

Above: Part of a Roman sculptured slab dating from A.D. 143, showing a mounted horseman.

Below: Eastern horsemen playing polo — one of the oldest mounted games.

A horse used in classical equitation or *haute école* having weights attached to his feet to make him lift them higher. Weights are still used in the training of Tennessee Walking Horses to make them lift their feet. Note the pillar in the indoor riding school — also much used in classical equitation.

tury, and there was to be a marked difference between his approach and views, and those of later riding masters. In the early seventeenth century, Antoine de Pluvinel ran a young nobleman's finishing school in Paris, with an emphasis on equitation. Pluvinel condemned coarse aids and was altogether more patient and thoughtful towards the horse. As well as advocating greater use of the leg rather than the heel and spur, Pluvinel attempted to study the mentality of a horse and adapted his training methods accordingly. He also introduced the idea of training horses to perform the high-school movements between two pillars.

England's great riding master of this time was William Cavendish, the Duke of Newcastle. Exiled from his own country, he ran riding academies in France and Belgium. He emphasized that a young horse must be trained patiently and not be expected to learn quickly. He says in his famous book on the principles of equitation, "I have not yet seen that force and passion prevail upon a horse . . . I would not hurt his mouth nor anything about him if I could help it."

Undoubtedly one of the protagonists of modern riding and the principles of achieving free forward movement in a horse was a Frenchman – François Robichon de la Guerinère, who was Louis XIV's riding master. He developed many new school aids, aiming all the time at a partnership of horse and rider. He did not concentrate solely on the art of dressage or classical riding, but also did much to further

jumping and riding cross country, so laying the foundations of future eventing.

With Guerinère's influence and the reorganization by the Comte d'Aure of the Cavalry School at Saumur (a guiding light in all French riding for years to come), France became one of Europe's most important centers of educated horsemanship in the late eighteenth and early nineteenth centuries. The British and Irish horsemen preferred their sports of racing and hunting to the Continental-controlled indoor riding. The climatic conditions in England made it possible to ride out-of-doors all year, and so indoor rings were not deemed necessary. Instead, the British boasted that their packs of hounds far outnumbered the indoor rings and riding masters found on the Continent. The penalty for such an attitude can still be seen by comparing British dressage expertise with that of other European countries.

Riding instruction seems to have been universally directed at the military with the aim always to improve the cavalry horse and his rider. The many books published in the eighteenth and nineteenth centuries on equitation mainly deal with the cavalry. Gradually, the different countries and districts developed their own characteristics to suit their own particular needs and requirements. In the US, horses were needed to travel around the vast plantations, and sporting events evolved naturally from everyday riding techniques. In Great Britain, fashion in London during the late nineteenth century depicted fine ladies in smart carriages attended by gentlemen riding beside the carriages. Riding as such did not really enter the lives of many people. The well-to-do rode and drove as a pastime certainly, and the farmer's wife might have driven to market to sell her eggs and butter. But in general people did not travel far, and although coaches ran from place to place they were not widely used.

Perhaps the greatest revolution to take place in riding styles was that instigated by the Italian cavalry officer Federico Caprilli, who was influential at the very beginning of the twentieth century. Caprilli evolved the "Italian seat" or "forward" position, from a belief that a rider should interfere as little as possible with a horse's natural balance. He claimed that any ridden horse was able to adjust its center of gravity to changes of pace or to jumping, without any assistance from the rider, providing the rider adjusted his own center of gravity to conform with that of his horse. In effect, he was saying that the rider's body weight must be equally distributed over the horse's center of balance, and nowhere were his ideas better demonstrated than in jumping. Although most people by this time had realized that leaning back on the approach, take-off and suspension over a fence impeded the horse's action, most people would still lean back instinctively as they landed. Caprilli taught that by leaning forward on landing, a horse was able to stretch out his head, which meant he had no need to rebalance himself as he landed. It took a number of years, and consistent success by the Italians riding in this style at major horse shows, before Caprilli's methods became universally accepted and practiced – as they are today.

Nowadays, modern styles of riding vary slightly from country to country. Many people claim that the differences exist because of the adaptations and modifications that need to be made to suit different breeds. In Germany a very precise style of riding is practiced, and the rider is required to work at his horse all the time. The impression given is that of the rider holding his horse very strictly between legs and hands and almost driving him through his paces. The horses, however, are generally of the heavy Hanoverian or Trakehner breeds. They need fairly hard work from the rider to create the necessary impulsion from the hindquarters, which allows the forehand to be lightened and free forward movement to be achieved. This precision riding, however it may appear to people from other nationalities, is clearly effective, for Germany is considered to be the top country in the dressage world at present. Their riding of figures is exact, and the horses display immaculate and controlled changes of pace with utter obedience.

The French style of riding, particularly in the dressage field, is more supple and elegant,

perhaps reflecting a national characteristic. The horses, however, are generally of lighter breeding, often containing a high proportion of Arab blood, so they do not require the forceful riding of the heavier German-bred horses. Instead, they reflect a lightness of movement which indicates great cooperation between horse and rider.

The Swedish dressage style could be described as a mixture of the German style and the lightness in hand of the French. Thus, their work is exact in execution, yet it appears a less demanding way of riding than that displayed by the Germans. Their horses – often a cross between German breeds and Thoroughbreds – are light in hand and responsive and they make a very pleasing combination with their fine, elegant riders.

The Russians are becoming a force to be reckoned with in equestrian events. They seem to be mounted usually on an elegant type of horse which, when ridden with characteristic

An Italian horseman in 1920 adopting the new forward position. As his horse descends the slope, the rider's body is at a right-angle to the angle of the slope. Previously, a rider would have leaned right back, thus not distributing his weight evenly over the horse's center of gravity.

lightness in hand, shows an ability to execute good dressage movements with excellent paces.

Swiss riders appear to prefer either the French or the German style. One of their most successful dressage riders, Christine Stuckelberger, rides a Hanoverian horse using a very definite German style, whereas Colonel Handler, who won the dressage event in the Olympic Games in 1948, adhered much more to the French style of riding.

In Great Britain, the style of riding taught is undoubtedly that based on Caprilli's teaching. As late starters in the field of dressage, they probably experience some confusion over which style would be most effective, and consequently the British standard of dressage is poor compared with that of other countries. I feel they should take the opportunity to extract all that is best from the various national styles – the German exactness, and the French lightness, which, combined with the British love and respect for the horse, must surely be likely to produce a pleasing and successful end result.

Above: An example of the German style of riding, where the horse is held firmly between the rider's hands and legs. The Germans lead the world in dressage riding.

Right: Swedish dressage rider, J. Jonssan, performing a half pass.

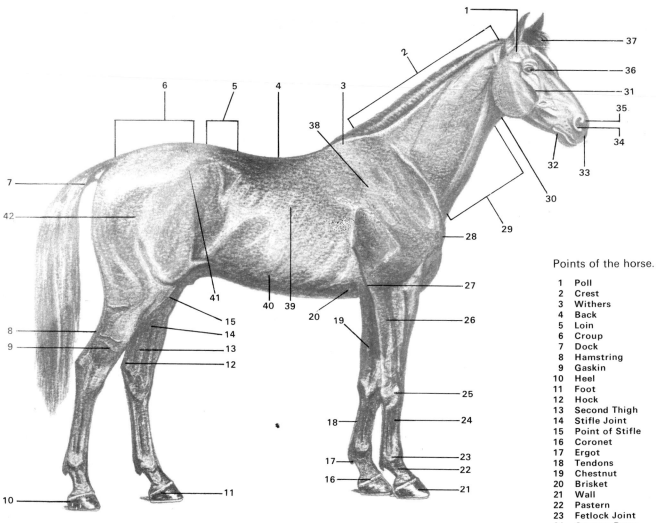

Points of the horse.

1 Poll
2 Crest
3 Withers
4 Back
5 Loin
6 Croup
7 Dock
8 Hamstring
9 Gaskin
10 Heel
11 Foot
12 Hock
13 Second Thigh
14 Stifle Joint
15 Point of Stifle
16 Coronet
17 Ergot
18 Tendons
19 Chestnut
20 Brisket
21 Wall
22 Pastern
23 Fetlock Joint
24 Cannon Bone
25 Knee
26 Forearm
27 Elbow
28 Point of Shoulder
29 Gullet
30 Throat
31 Projecting Cheek Bone
32 Curb Groove
33 Muzzle
34 Nostril
35 Nasal Peak
36 Eye
37 Forelock
38 Shoulder
39 Ribs
40 Flank
41 Point of Hip
42 Hip Joint

Riding – the First Steps

Nobody will ever make a really satisfactory horse owner and rider unless they take the trouble to learn something about the horse's anatomy and physiology. An understanding of these will help to explain why we ride in a certain way, and why a horse requires the care and treatment he does.

As with humans, each part of the horse's body has a name and these are generally known as the Points of a Horse (see above). You should learn these, so that you know what people are talking about when they refer to a specific point. Also a knowledge of them will help to give you a good idea of what to look for in a horse.

A horse's height is measured in "hands" taken from the ground to the point of the withers. A hand equals 4 in. (10 cm.) and if the animal measures over 14.2 hands high (i.e., 14 hands 2 inches – 58 in. or 145 cm.) it is a horse. Under this, it is a pony.

Like all other vertebrates, the horse has a body built around a solid framework of bones, called the skeleton. It is actually composed of nearly 200 bones, but, of course, it is not necessary to know the names or details of these. Suffice it to say that in essence the skeleton comprises the head, the spinal column, the ribs, the forelegs and the hind legs. However, the bones and joints are the source of numerous problems resulting from injury or strain and also comprise an important factor in correct saddling and bridling, so some understanding of them is a help.

From the standpoint of riding, the most important part of the skeleton is the spine, which is divided into two main parts – the back and the loins. The back is supported by the rib cage and is capable of carrying weight, whereas the loins are not. Hence the importance of not sitting too far back in the saddle. The other important point to realize is that out of the bones, or vertebrae, of the spine extend bony projections which run along the ridge of the back. These are covered with only a thin layer of flesh and skin and are not only extremely sensitive but also quite incapable of bearing any actual weight. This demonstrates the importance of using a correctly fitting saddle, which puts no weight along the ridge of the spine, but instead places the weight-receiving surfaces over the ribs.

A notable difference between a horse's skeleton and that of man is that a horse does not have a collar bone. The shoulder blade, therefore, is not attached to the spinal column, but instead is kept in place by various muscles. It is important that the saddle, and thus the rider's weight, is positioned in such a way that it does not interfere with the free movement of the shoulder blades.

Below: The muscles of a horse.

Right: A horse's skeleton is composed of approximately 200 bones.

All the bones and joints of the skeleton are covered with and support a vast number of muscles. These, of course, enable the bones to move. The saddle- and weight-bearing surface of the back are comprised of pads of muscle which act as cushions and give the horse its external rounded shape. As in humans, there are two types of muscles: those that are movable at will, known as the voluntary muscles, and those that control the bodily functions, known as the involuntary muscles. Voluntary muscles are those attached to the bones either by muscular fibers or by tough, inelastic cords known as tendons. It is the tendons that actually affect the horse's movement, for as a muscle is contracted, the tendon pulls the bone. For this reason, tendons are more subject to sprain than the muscles themselves.

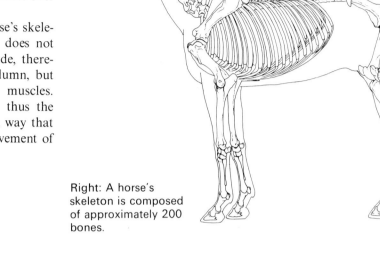

Right: The diagram shows clearly where the saddle should be positioned in relation to the horse's spine. It should not interfere with the shoulder blade or exert pressure on the sensitive loin area, which is not supported by ribs.

Above: The author's stable yard – an example of a typical riding establishment.

Choosing a Riding School

Having made the decision to learn to ride, you will have to find a riding school – that is, unless you are one of those fortunate people who were born into a "horsy" family so that you were put on a horse before you could even walk! Such people, however, form only a small percentage of those who ride, and for others the choice of school is important, since the first lessons will have a marked effect on future confidence and the way you ride.

It may be that there is only one school close enough for you to attend, in which case you do not have to make a choice. In any event, there are certain things you should consider about the running of riding schools to make sure they maintain high standards. Are the horses healthy and well cared for? Is the establishment clean and are the fire precautions adequate? When considering a riding school, it is a good idea to satisfy yourself with regard to at least the first two items.

As a complete beginner, you ideally need the individual attention of an experienced instructor, but for this you must expect to pay top prices. Try to have a few short lessons close together to begin with, rather than joining the "one-hour, once-a-week brigade." You will get a far quicker and better feel for riding if you have, say, half-an-hour's lesson, followed by a rest of an hour or so and then another half-an-hour's lesson, repeated again the following day. By this time you will have consolidated the feel of your position in the saddle and be on the way to feeling the rhythm of the gaits.

Indoor riding schools are common in Europe. This one is at the Park des Expositions de la porte de Versailles, in Paris, France.

What to Wear

The various modes of dress worn for the different aspects of horsemanship all have their basis in practicality. When you are starting to ride, depending slightly on the school you go to, you can probably get away with wearing a strong pair of jeans, leather-soled shoes with heels and no buckles, a jumper and heavy coat (if necessary) and, most essential, a hard hat. More formal and correct establishments may want you to wear all the correct attire – breeches or jodhpurs and boots, shirt and gloves – but these are all expensive items and it is a good idea to make sure you want to carry on with your riding before you invest in them.

These items of clothing are the most commonly worn in many fields of horsemanship, but there are all sorts of additions and variations. People riding in dressage events wear swallow-tailed coats and top hats, which enhance the general impression of elegance. Jockeys traditionally wear silk shirts in the chosen colors of the race-horse's owner. And they wear a more substantial hard hat (usually worn nowadays in cross-country events as well), also topped with the owner's colors.

Riders at internationally famous riding establishments, such as the Spanish Riding School in Vienna, wear what amounts to special uniforms, used only by them.

The riding clothes worn by Western riders doubtless evolved for practical reasons, although we have come to think of them as a traditional "costume." The broad-brimmed hat, checked shirt with bright, knotted handkerchief worn around the neck, "chaps" or leather trousers worn over blue jeans, and high-heeled boots are common to all. So it is easy to forget that the leather trousers, for example, give considerable protection to a person who spends many hours in the saddle at a time, while the hat gives protection to the rider in all kinds of weather.

Below: Riders enjoying an outing near Canberra, Australia, are dressed in a casual and informal manner.

Bottom left: The formal dress worn for a dressage show includes a swallow-tailed coat and top hat.

Bottom right: The traditional "uniform" of the cowboy has its origins in practicality.

Mounting and Dismounting

A horse is most usually mounted on the near (left) side. There are three ways in which to get into the saddle:
1. To be given a "leg up."
2. To use a mounting block.
3. Without the aid of either of the above.

To be given a leg up is certainly the easiest way for a child to mount a pony. The rider faces the side of the pony, with the reins held in his left hand, and the right hand on the pommel of the saddle. He bends his left leg behind him and the instructor holds this to support him as he jumps off the ground. The rider then swings his right leg over the top of the saddle before sitting upright.

Using a mounting block gives the rider additional height so it is easier for him to place his left foot in the stirrup.

To mount without a leg up or a mounting block, a rider has a choice of two methods. The traditional British method is to face the horse's tail, and to place the left hand, which is holding the reins, on the withers. The rider then pulls the back of the stirrup iron towards him with

Girths should be tightened before (above) and (below) after a rider has mounted.

Mounting the English way. Above far left: The rider faces the horse's tail and places her left foot in the stirrup. Above left: She springs up, twisting her body around towards the horse. Far left: She throws her leg over the horse's quarters. Left: She settles into the saddle and takes up the reins.

Mounting the Continental and Western way. Bottom far left: The rider faces towards the horse's side, while standing slightly behind the stirrup leather. Bottom left: She puts her left foot in the stirrup and prepares to spring up into the saddle.

the right hand, places his left foot in it and springs up, turning as he swings his right leg over the top of the saddle. The Western and Continental method is to face the horse's head, instead of his tail, the left hand holding the reins and the right hand on the pommel of the saddle. He then places his left foot in the iron and steps up onto the horse.

Both methods have their advantages and disadvantages. In the former, if the horse moves forward as he is being mounted (often because the rider's foot prods him on the side), the momentum of his movement helps push the rider into the saddle. On the other hand, he has to twist his leg around to get into the saddle, which could take a little longer. In using the Western and Continental method, there is no need to twist the body, foot or leg, nor is there any likelihood of prodding the horse in the side. But should the horse move forward, the rider is often left hopping by his side.

To dismount, the rider should hold both reins in his left hand and take both feet out of the stirrup irons. Placing his right hand on the pommel, he swings his right leg backwards, up over the cantle to land gently by the horse's near side. The Western and Continental practice is to leave the left foot in the stirrup, removing it when the right foot is on the ground.

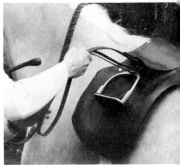

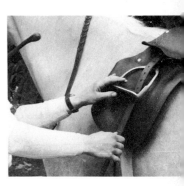

Above: After dismounting the stirrup irons should be run up the leathers against the saddle.

Dismounting the Continental and Western way. Above far left and left: The rider retains her left foot in the stirrup as she swings the right leg over the horse's quarters. The left foot is taken out of the stirrup when the right foot is on the ground.

Dismounting the English way. Above center: Both feet are taken out of the stirrups. With her weight inclined forward, the rider swings her right leg over the horse's quarters and jumps to the ground.

Bottom far left and left: The stirrup irons are run up and the reins taken over the horse's head, so he can be led away.

57

Position in the Saddle

Once on top of the horse, the rider has to learn the correct position to sit in the saddle, while the horse is standing still. It is essential to get this right from the very beginning, for the position in the saddle for all the horse's gaits is based on the position at the halt.

The rider should settle into the center of the saddle, and there should be a hand's width behind the back of his seat and the back of the saddle. The inner part of his thigh and knee should be kept close to the saddle. In fact, at no time when riding a horse should there be any daylight visible between the rider's knee and thigh and the saddle. From the knee down, the leg should hang naturally, and perpendicular to the ground, not pushed forward or back. The feet are placed in the stirrup irons so that the weight is taken on the inside of the foot, which helps to push the knee against the saddle.

For most riding, the length of the leathers can be satisfactorily judged by letting the iron hang down by your leg: the bottom of the iron should be level with the ankle bone. The ball of the foot should rest in the iron, with the heel lower than the toe. You will find that if you ride with your feet too far back it will be almost impossible to keep your heel lower than the

toe. Don't fall into the trap of pushing your legs and feet forward, though, because that puts your weight too far back in the saddle.

The rider's back should be straight, or, to put it another way, he should sit erect and upright in the saddle, with his shoulders square and his head up, looking forward between the horse's ears. This doesn't mean that he should be stiff and uncomfortable – indeed the aim is to be comfortable and sufficiently relaxed to follow and blend in with the horse's movement at all times.

Arms should hang easily down from the shoulder to the elbow, at which point, of course, they are bent, so that the hands can hold the reins in the correct position. The elbows should always be pressed into the rider's side, as this helps to keep the pressure on the reins constant. Arms that flap all over the place will inevitably cause the reins, and thus the horse's mouth, to be jerked unevenly.

The main aim when riding is to keep the body in the middle of the horse to make his work easier. The rider's weight should be evenly distributed over the horse's center of gravity. As a rider becomes more experienced, he will learn to shift his weight at various times, according to what he is asking the horse to do, but essentially this basic position is maintained.

Above: The stirrup leathers are adjusted from the saddle. The rider keeps his foot in the stirrup iron so he can feel the correct and comfortable length.

Below: The correct position in the saddle for western-style riding. The stirrup leathers are longer than in English-style riding, but not so long that the leg is completely straight.

Left: The correct position in the saddle for English and Continental style riding.

Holding the Reins

The reins are the rider's most direct controlling contact with his horse, but as they connect to the most sensitive area of his body – the mouth – they should be handled extremely carefully. When the rider is seated comfortably in the saddle, he must learn how to pick up the reins, which are held one in each hand. They should run through his hands, coming around and through them from underneath to be held between the thumbs and fore-fingers, with the thumbs on top. In effect, this forms a double lock on the reins, but in this position the forward movement of the horse is not impeded in any way. The main work of feeling, controlling and guiding the reins is done by the little finger of each hand. The hands should be held slightly apart, just above the horse's withers.

It is essential that the hands are not held in such a set position that they are unable to "give" with the horse's forward movement. This, of course, does not mean that the horse should be allowed to go at whatever pace he chooses, rather than that of the rider's choice; but at no time should the hands be set against his mouth. Certainly the reins are used to control and guide the horse, but they are not "lifelines" for the rider to hang on to or to maintain his balance. At a walk, a horse's head moves up and down slightly and the hands should move correspondingly with this action. At the trot, a horse's head is held a little higher and should be held in a more constant position, so the rider's hands should be still, but in no way pulling against the mouth.

In the very early stages of learning to ride, it may help a rider to hold on to the pommel with his hands, until he begins to perfect his balance. Some people teach beginners to hold on to a neck strap, but I am less in favor of this as it encourages a forward tilt of the body. How to hold reins – Western style – is explained in the caption below right.

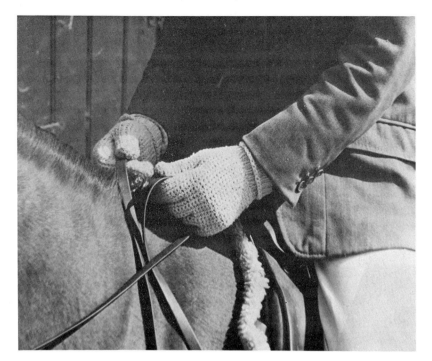

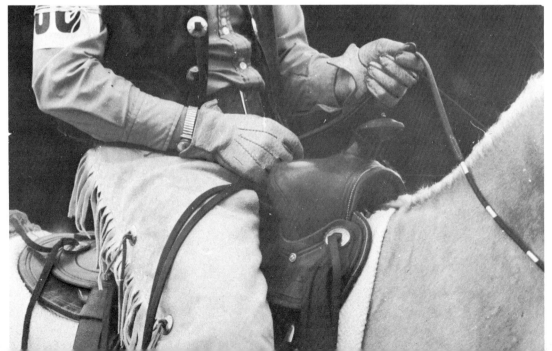

Above top: Reins held in two hands. Note the thumb is on top of the reins pointing forwards.

Above: Reins held in one hand only.

Left: Reins held western style. They are usually held in the left hand, while the right hand rests on the thigh. They are held higher than in English equitation, so as to clear the saddle horn.

The Aids

"Aids" are those means at a rider's disposal for controlling his horse, and the signals by which he lets the horse know what it is he wishes him to do. The simple and natural aids to riding are the rider's hands, legs, body and voice.

Taking each of these in turn – the hands give the direct contact with the horse's most sensitive area, his mouth, and for this reason they must be very sympathetic. In riding terms, they regulate the energy conveyed to the horse by the rider's legs; they directly control the horse's forehand; and they guide, check and allow pace.

The legs control and guide the horse's hind quarters and they are also used to stimulate energy and thus movement.

The body can affect a horse's pace by altering the distribution of its weight. It should always be *very slightly* inclined to the direction of the horse's movement. The importance of the voice as an aid is often overlooked but it is an extremely useful adjunct to the rider. A soothing, sympathetic voice can go far in encouraging an inexperienced horse or calming a nervous one. Used more firmly, it can help in checking

Spurs are one of the artificial aids. They reinforce the action of the leg and should only be used by an experienced rider.

movement, and a sharper tone may warn the horse of impending danger.

Aids should always be given in conjunction with one another. To get the horse to move forward from a halt into a walk, a rider shouldn't flap his legs furiously against his horse's side. Instead, he should press into the saddle with his seat bones, close his legs against the horse's side so that he does no more than give the horse a squeeze behind the girth, and be prepared to give with his hands as the horse moves forward. By the same token, when the

Above: With a young, inexperienced rider on top, an adult leads the pony for safety.

Below: How not to stop! The rider has merely hauled on the reins and is giving no aids with his legs and seat.

How to apply leg pressure. The knees remain in contact with the saddle, with the calf and heel close against the horse's side. The diagram has been exaggerated for clarity. In practice, the angle of the knee does not change when aids are given.

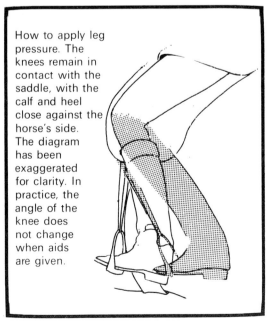

time comes to stop, a rider should not just haul on the reins. Besides resulting all too quickly in a ruined mouth for the horse, it means that he will stop with his head in the air, very likely with his mouth open to try to escape the pressure from the bit, and with his legs and body all askew. The correct aids for slowing the pace or coming to a halt are to cease the movement of the hands, rather than actively pulling on them, while the body weight is placed just behind the seat bones, i.e. on the soft cushion of the seat. The legs are again gently closed against the horse's side, so as to drive him forwards up into the bit. The resistance he meets as he moves forwards will automatically make him slow down.

Before a rider begins to try to put these aids into practice, he should have spent a lot of time being led around by an experienced instructor, while he gets used to the feel of a horse's movements. At the same time the instructor should be explaining the function and implementation of the aids.

Artificial Aids

Besides the natural aids already discussed, there are a number of artificial aids. In my view, these will not concern the rider until he is thoroughly confident and sufficiently good to be doing more advanced work. However, all riders should know a little about the artificial aids, which comprise riding crops, and also martingales and spurs.

Different types of martingales and their uses are discussed more fully on pages 103–104. Riding crops and spurs are a great help to people like me who are blessed with short, weak legs! Those people with long, strong legs should have less use for them. There are endless different types of riding crops on the market – heavy, light, long and short. I prefer a light crop, as the heavy ones are unwieldy to hold and so tend to interfere with the rider's hands on the reins. Crops should only be used to enhance the lower-leg aid and so a rider should only tap his horse with the crop just behind the girth – in the same place he applies pressure with his inside leg. They should be used lightly, and, in fact, their main use is to wake up a lazy horse or to create a bit more concentration.

Spurs also enhance the aid of the leg, but they should be used only by those riders who have a good control of the lower leg. Then they can help a good rider to use a finer and more delicate aid. If spurs are used by an inexperienced rider, they can be very harmful, inflicting unnecessary discomfort to the horse, particularly as a rider may not even realize when he is using them. They are worn on the rider's boot, fitted just above the heel, and their severity is governed by the length of the neck and the shape of the tip.

Right: Pressure being applied evenly on both reins, indicated by the horse's body being in a straight line. Pressure is applied evenly with both legs in the same place.

Below: Pressure applied marginally more strongly on the right rein so the horse's head is flexed to the right. The left hand goes very slightly forward to allow the bend. This is known as direct reining. Pressure is applied on the girth with the right leg and behind it, slightly more strongly with the left.

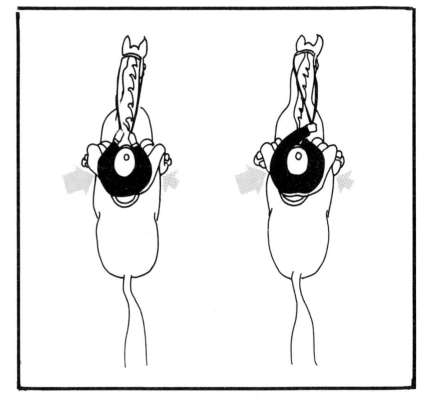

The rowel spur has sharp edges on the wheel fixed inside the end of the neck of the spur, and can really cut a horse's side. Happily, it is not used very much these days. The two patterns in commonest use are the "Prince of Wales" on which the neck slants downwards; and the straight-necked spur, which has a bulbous, blunt end. The latter has a more direct action and is useful when schooling. Not every horse can be ridden in spurs – some horses hate them and will kick as soon as they feel them against their sides.

Above: Aids to turn to the right or left in western-style riding are given by the "indirect" rein, i.e. to turn to the right, the left rein is brought against the left side of the neck. This is known as neck reining. Leg pressure is applied in the same way as in English equitation.

The Walk

Just as it will help a horse owner/rider to understand his horse's needs if he studies something of its anatomy and physiology (see page 52), so it will help a rider to understand his position in the saddle and adjust it accordingly if he knows how a horse moves at its various gaits. There are, in fact, three types of walk, trot and canter – ordinary, extended and collected – but it is the ordinary gait we are concerned with here.

A horse walks in four-time, which means he takes four distinct steps one after another. A well-balanced horse will lead off with a hind foot, followed by the forefoot on the same side, then by the opposite hind foot and, lastly, the opposite forefoot. So it goes, for example, off-

The Trot

The trot is a gait in two-time, in which diagonally opposite hind feet and forefeet (known together as a "diagonal") are moved simultaneously. The sequence of movement is offside hind and nearside fore (the left diagonal) moving together, followed by a moment of suspension when all feet are off the ground, before the nearside hind and offside fore (right diagonal) take a step. The rear feet should hit the ground in, or very slightly behind, the front footprints, and you should hear two distinct hoof beats.

The *sitting trot* is generally adopted for the first few steps after a horse has broken into a trot, when it is being asked to break into a canter, and is used in all advanced school work. Instructors differ in their opinion of whether the posting trot should be taught first, or whether it is better for the beginner to be kept sitting for the first few lessons to improve his balance. I think it should be considered in the light of two factors. First, is the rider learning on a really smooth-trotting animal, which makes it as comfortable to sit as it does to post, and secondly, does he seem happy to sit? If, as the beginner you find yourself wobbling about all over the place, you will probably find it more comfortable to learn the posting trot fairly quickly! Either way it helps to practice the posting movement while the horse is walking, and you can compare it to rising up on your toes and dropping back onto your heels while you are standing on the ground. In fact, the posting motion in the saddle should be no more than this, because if you post too high it not only makes unnecessary work which requires too

The sitting trot. The rider sits upright, but deep into the saddle.

side hind, offside fore, nearside hind, nearside fore. Each step should be of equal length, so that the hind feet tread in the tracks left by the forefeet, and of equal timing, so you hear four evenly spaced hoof beats.

To ask a horse to go from a halt into a walk, the rider sits well down into the saddle and applies leg pressure just behind the girth.

A horse walks with a swinging movement and, although the rider's body remains constantly in the same position, it should gently swing in rhythm with this movement. To bring him back to a halt, the rider again sits well into the saddle and applies gentle leg pressure to drive him forward, but now resists the forward movement by ceasing to give with his hands.

The aids for moving from a walk to a trot are the same as those for going from a halt to a walk. The diagonal movement of this gait means there is no sideways movement of the horse, so the rider's body should remain quite still. Also the horse's head and neck remain

much straighter and more upright, so the hands should remain correspondingly still.

There are two ways of riding at the trot – the sitting trot, which means the seat does not leave the saddle, and the posting trot. These are explained in more detail below.

The posting trot. The rider's body is inclined slightly forwards.

much effort and could throw you off balance, but it also produces extra stiffness in the body from the extra effort.

For the *posting trot*, it helps to begin by holding both reins in one hand and holding onto the front of the saddle with the other. Change over hands frequently. Practice posting to the trot on a hard road first, so you can clearly hear the beat of the horse's hooves, for you rise up and down in time with the "one-two" of the two-time beat. An uphill grade is easier than going along on the flat. The rider is trying to achieve a smooth, non-jerky movement, and the upper part of his body should be inclined very slightly forward with the small of his back supple. Thighs and knees are kept close to the saddle and the legs kept quite still in their usual position. Never trot for too long initially without having a rest, which is best achieved by walking the horse for a while with your feet out of the stirrups and hanging down naturally by the horse's side. When the post is well established, try trotting at a post on soft going and finally over a slightly uneven surface.

63

The Canter

The canter could be said to be a more complicated gait than the walk and trot, for it is a gait of three-time, which means there are three distinct beats to each stride. In addition there is a period of complete suspension in every stride. One or the other pair of diagonals moves together and is always in front of the other, as you will be able to see if you watch a horse cantering. According to which diagonal is working together, the horse is said to be doing a right-lead or a left-lead canter. The sequence of steps in a left-lead canter is offside hind, followed by the right diagonal (nearside hind and offside fore) and finally the nearside fore. The opposite legs are used throughout in a right-lead canter.

The Gallop

The gallop is a gait in four-time, in which the forelegs are extended right out so that the gait is considerably faster than the canter. The sequence is near-hind, off-hind, near-fore, off-fore, followed by a moment of suspension.

It is generally a very comfortable gait to ride, but no novice rider should ever gallop a horse, as it is so easy for the horse to take over

Positions and aids for the canter

Most horses will naturally canter on the left lead, but it is the rider's aids which should determine the leading leg of a canter when a horse is being ridden. It is less important which leg is leading when a horse is being ridden in a straight line, than when he is being exercised in a circle. Then he should lead with his inside leg. Thus if he is cantering around to the left his nearside fore should be leading, and to the right, his offside fore should be leading. If he is allowed to canter to the left with the off-fore leading, this is known as cantering "false" or "counter-lead."

To ask a pony to canter on the left lead from a trot, the rider should adopt a sitting trot, sitting well down into the saddle, making sure his horse is well balanced and moving forward freely. Pressure should be applied with both legs, the left one on the girth and the right one slightly behind it. At the same time the horse's head is flexed very slightly to the left. This is known as a diagonal aid, as the main instruction comes from the opposite hand and leg. As the horse breaks into the canter, the seat should remain in the saddle while the upper part of

At the canter, the rider again sits well down into the saddle.

When a horse canters as described, be it on the left or right lead, he is said to be cantering "united." It is possible, for a variety of reasons, for a horse to get the sequence of legs wrong (perhaps because he was given the wrong aids or was thrown off balance as he changed gait), in which case he is "cross cantering." Then instead of a diagonal moving together, front and hind feet on one side move in unison. A cross cantering sequence would be nearside hind, followed by offside hind and offside fore together, and finally nearside fore. The result is a very rolling pace from the horse, which is ungainly to look at and uncomfortable for the rider. (Rider's aids and position at the canter are explained opposite, below.)

and the rider to completely lose control. Its only real use is during such sports as racing and polo. The position of the rider at the gallop is to lean right forward over the horse's neck with the seat straight out of the saddle. This position is accentuated by racing jockeys who ride with their stirrup leathers very short, enabling them to lean even farther forwards.

At the gallop, the rider's seat is out of the saddle as she leans forward.

the body should give and gently sway in rhythm with the horse's movement. A rider should sit upright at a canter, not leaning forward, which would encourage the horse to go faster. The suppleness of the small of the back is important as a stiff and rigid back results in the body bumping up and down in the saddle.

The walk, trot and canter, then, are the basic gaits of the horse. The positions and aids for each, with smooth transitions from one to another and back to a halt, should be learned and mastered before any thought is given to more progressive forms of riding. At all times learning and practicing should progress slowly, for this is the time when a rider's confidence, as well as ability, is being established. Every rider must, of course, face the fact that he is bound to fall off at some time – probably several times. All kinds of things can startle a horse, making it jump or shy and throwing it off balance. Even experienced riders get unseated at such times. By and large, few falls are serious. Those that are serious tend to be sheer accidents which can be likened to being knocked down by a car, falling downstairs, tripping – or any other similar accident.

Lunging and Exercising

Having learned the theory of the horse's various gaits in terms of movement, the rider's position and the aids, it is important for you to realize your initial aim as the novice rider. This is to strengthen your seat and consolidate your position while building up your confidence, as well as that of your horse in you. Only through developing a firm, independent seat and improving the balance and control of your body can you hope to develop sympathetic hands. There are a number of exercises you can do, both while the horse is standing still and while he is on the move, to help in achieving these ends.

First of all, try raising one arm and pointing it forward to touch the horse's ear. Then swing around with the same arm, keeping your seat in the same position, to touch near the tail. Repeat with the other arm, but make sure you keep your legs in the correct position. Do not let them move forwards or backwards according to which way your body is moving. Then raise your arms sideways and swing your body around from side to side, again keeping your seat correctly placed in the saddle. This will help to develop a supple waist. Try it again with your hands on your hips.

Exercises on horseback improve a rider's balance and position in the saddle. These are useful for all styles of riding.
Top: Lean over the horse's neck to touch the opposite toe. Repeat on the other side, maintaining the correct leg position.
Top center: With arms held level with the shoulders pivot to left and right from the waist, maintaining the correct leg position.
Lower center, far left and left: With legs in correct position, lean straight forward on horse's neck and then backwards on the haunches.
Bottom, far left: Practice posting to the trot without stirrups while stationary.
Bottom: Maintaining the correct position in the saddle, swing the leg backwards and forwards from the knee down.

Left: Circling the feet to the left and right (out of the stirrups) helps to develop supple and relaxed ankles.

Most exercises are best done under the guidance of an instructor. This is because your natural posture when walking will be echoed in the way you sit when on a horse. In assuming the correct riding position, you may have to adopt what is for you an unnatural position. This can easily lead to developing stiffness in your body instead of the overall relaxation which should be your aim. An experienced instructor will be able to recognize this and give you corrective exercises, which will help you overcome your particular problem. For example, if you tend to sit on the cushion of your seat instead of the seat bones (which will result in your being behind the horse's movement) try circling your arms forward so your upper body will be drawn forwards. This will help to correct the fault. If you were to circle your arms backwards, the problem would be accentuated.

Riding while the horse is being worked on a lunge can be a means of teaching and improving the rider. This has long been practiced in Europe and is now almost universally recognized as being the best way of training a rider. Its first and most important benefit is that a rider does not have to think about controlling his horse and can give his entire attention to the position of his body in the saddle. To be able to sit correctly while a horse is standing still is one thing: to maintain this position at all gaits is another, and a rider must first develop suppleness so that he can absorb the movement of the horse through his entire body.

Work on the lunge should be done at slow gaits. More exercises can be done to strengthen the seat. Ideally, a rider should ride without stirrups, which are crossed in front of the saddle (see illustrations on left and below). Many of the exercises you, as the rider, can do now will be aimed at controlling and maintaining the leg position, although you should first get used to the feel of the horse being lunged at a walk and a trot. A good leg exercise is to place both hands on the front of the saddle, raise your knees and then kick down, stretching your legs as far

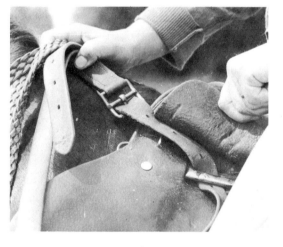

Right: In exercises with feet out of the stirrup irons, the leathers and stirrups should be crossed over in front of the saddle. As shown the buckle is pulled clear of the stirrup bar.

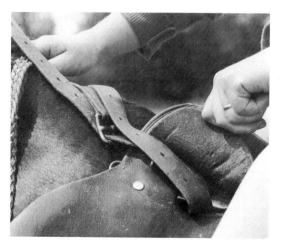

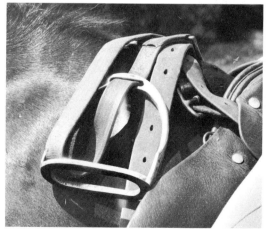

as you can. This will help to draw your seat into the saddle. After this, swing one leg forward and one leg backwards with the toes pointed towards the ground. Besides pulling you into the saddle again, the exercise will help in teaching you how to use your legs independently from the rest of your body.

Two exercises to try at the trot on the lunge are, first, to raise both hands above your head and hold them there while the horse is moving; and then, second, to fold your arms and work

at both the sitting and the posting trot. If you find your tendency is to lean forward, then fold your arms behind your back.

Working on the lunge gives you an opportunity to control your horse's gaits by your body weight and legs, helped by your voice, so that you learn that the reins are not as important as you had thought. The aim is for the horse to work well with you more in control than the instructor who is holding the lunging rein. However good a rider you become, working on the lunge is always good for you. Even Olympic riders are lunged during the course of their training, so how much more should we lesser mortals work in this way?

When you begin to feel more relaxed and secure and in harmony with your horse, enjoying pleasant rides together, you can work at improving your riding rather than going out for hacks whenever you ride. You will also find that it helps in developing a rapport between you and your horse if you work with an object in mind. At this stage, the object will be to improve the simple movements, to make good transitions up and down from the walk to the trot to the canter, and to try for correctness in turns and circles. Remember, too, that one of the most important factors in all good riding is to be able to ride a straight line. To achieve this, work in a field and pick out a tree or particular post. Then ride towards it, trying not to deviate from one side to the other. You will find it is not as easy as it sounds! When you get there turn around and ride back towards another

point. Work diagonally across the field, too – remember, a horse can get easily bored on schooling sessions if he is made to cover the same ground endlessly.

Work your horse in circles, making sure he works the circle with the whole of his body. Your hands will control the bend or "flexion" of his head and neck, while your outside leg controls the bend of his quarters.

Ask the horse to change the size of the circle, making it both larger and smaller, but always keeping the correct flexion and bends. The aids to increase the size of the circle are to apply pressure with the inside leg over the girth so that the horse is pushed over towards the outside, or indirect, rein, which is moved very slightly outwards. The inside hand and the outside leg, which is positioned just behind the girth, remain still. Keep the horse on the circle for a while and then reduce the size back to a smaller one. Remember to work evenly on both reins, going clockwise and counter-clockwise, so that you don't become more adept at riding on one rein or the other.

You can make sure that you are riding around the circle correctly by marking out a circle first with sawdust. If you ride the circle correctly, the sawdust should be kicked up by the horse's feet at every step.

Besides circling, position some posts or drums in two parallel lines (but not so they are right opposite each other) and ride in and out of these in a serpentine fashion. Remember that, in doing this, the movement of both your hands and your legs should not be exaggerated.

No schooling session should last much longer than 20 minutes at any one time, for both your own and your horse's sake. Always finish on a good note and make much of him to let him know you are pleased with what he has helped you to achieve.

Below: School work exercises should be varied and include riding in straight lines, circles and serpentines at all gaits.

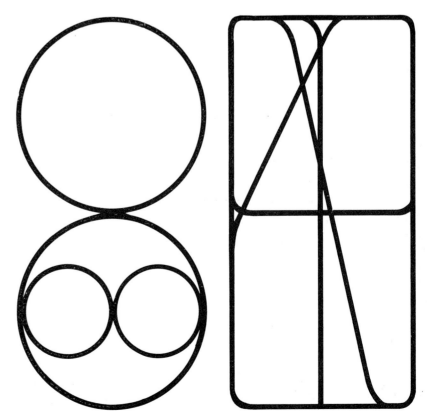

Jumping

At just what stage in people's riding lives they begin jumping can vary enormously. Some people may never show any inclination to want to jump at all – for them the enjoyment of riding may be just to hack pleasantly around the countryside with their horse never leaving the ground; there is certainly nothing to criticize in this attitude. To others, being able to pop over fences is an essential and integral part of horsemanship.

No one who shows any signs of nervousness should be pushed into learning to jump, until they really want to. On the other hand, if the new rider is very confident and appears to be at home and relaxed in the saddle in his first few lessons, I see no reason why the jumping position, coupled with some trotting over poles, should not be practiced – even at this early stage. It is not even necessary to have mastered the posting trot for this: the guidelines need only be that the rider has some natural balance and is eager to learn. Not only will it give a young person, in particular, an enormous sense of achievement to say he has jumped at an early lesson, but it also introduces jumping as a part of normal, everyday riding.

In my opinion, the position in the saddle for jumping should be learned, and the seat strengthened before a rider goes on to jump fences of any real height at all. So far the rider has had two different positions (albeit only very slightly different) in the saddle – that is, sitting upright on his seat bones for the walk, trot and canter, and sitting backwards on the cushion of his seat to halt. In the jumping position the seat is raised just above the saddle and the rider sits in a forward position, with his body leaning forward from the pelvis. It is easier to maintain this position if the rider takes hold of a lump of mane half way up the horse's neck. Try sitting at this position at a walk for a while to get used to it.

The next stage in learning to jump is to walk over poles laid on the ground, while sitting in this forward position all the time. Put three poles on the ground in a straight line, and when you have walked over them happily a few times, trot over them still sitting in a forward position. If all goes well, raise the final pole so that it is off the ground. It is a good idea for an instructor to be leading the horse when this is first done, so that you can concentrate on getting used to and maintaining this new position, without having to control the horse as well.

Some people would disagree with this method of teaching and learning, arguing that the rider should have control of the horse, but I would rather guard against the danger of a rider losing his balance and using the reins as lifelines to steady himself. This would not help to give

Below: Practicing the correct forward jumping position, while the horse is stationary. This should also be done at a walk, trot and canter, which will help to strengthen the necessary muscles.

come under him, he stretches his head and neck and begins to spring. When he is actually suspended over the jump, his head and neck are stretched as far forward as possible and his front and hind legs are tucked up underneath him. On landing, his head will come up as his front legs touch the ground and his neck shortens as he feels the impact.

Since the horse is continually altering the position of his head, by stretching it forward and bringing it back, you can see how important it is for you to have sympathetic or "giving" hands. These can only be developed if you have an independent and strong seat. Body weight during take-off and suspension is taken on the thighs and stirrup leathers. Ideally, the stirrup leathers should remain perpendicular to the ground throughout the jump, although a lot of riders, top-class ones included, do swing their legs backwards. At all times you should be looking ahead between the horse's ears, straight in front of you, not down at the jump.

After the poles on the ground, the next step is to progress to cavaletti work. Cavaletti are very useful pieces of equipment, comprising long poles attached at either end to two short, crossed planks of wood which rest on the

him confidence and would result in the horse's mouth being hurt as well. For the same reason, I think the best introduction a rider can have to jumping is by riding a horse on the lunge. The horse should be lunged at a walk, trot and canter, the rider maintaining the forward position throughout, as well as over the poles. This should all be interspersed with frequent rests for the rider, at which time he consciously relaxes certain parts of his body. For example, you can rest and relax your back by sitting upright again in the saddle. By taking your feet out of the stirrup irons, pointing your toes downwards and swinging your legs backwards and forwards, you will relax the thigh muscles. You can relax your ankles by circling your feet first upwards and outwards and then upwards and inwards. The ankles are particularly important in jumping as, in a relaxed position, they will work as shock absorbers for the rider when the horse lands after a jump.

It should help you to understand your position when jumping a little better if you know exactly how a horse moves over a jump. As he approaches a jump he lowers his head and stretches his neck. As he takes off he shortens his neck, allowing him to raise his head and lift up his shoulders and forelegs. As his hocks

Above: Jumping lessons begin with walking over poles. The rider is leaning forwards.
Below: A classic mistake is to look down at a jump instead of straight ahead.

ground. Again, three or four can be placed in a line and the horse trotted over them. Then the fourth one can be moved a little farther away, with another one placed on top to make a small jump. Do not put more than two together in this way, though – the practice of putting two cavaletti together with another one placed on top is extremely dangerous. I have seen a horse put its leg through the top one in such a case and turn a somersault. Its confidence and nerve were so impaired that it never jumped satisfactorily again.

When you are learning to jump, study all the photographs you can find of the famous top-class riders as well as watching them at shows. Analyze their positions: you can learn a lot from them. Read all you can, too. The theory should help your practical ability.

As your jumping progresses build some practice jumps in the field or paddock. These should not be fixed in one place, because you want to be able to move them around so they can be jumped from different directions. They should be about 2 ft. 6 in. (70–80 cm.) high and can be constructed from a variety of materials, painted in an assortment of colors. Use straw bales (again don't pile them up too high on top of each other), oil drums, old car tires suspended from poles, old doors (providing they have no nails or knobs sticking out of them) and so on. Put a pole on the ground in front of some of them to make a "ground line." Fences with ground lines are much easier to jump than those without. Continually change the positions of the fences so that you don't get used to one "course" and your pony doesn't get correspondingly bored!

Above: Build a variety of low practice jumps.

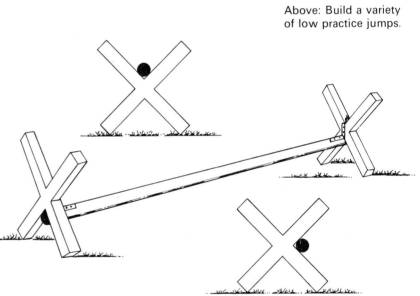

Above: Construction of cavaletti, showing their three different heights.

Left: Crossed poles make good practice jumps in the early stages. Try to jump in the center at the lowest point.

Practicing jumping without stirrups is a good idea, for you should not get to rely on your stirrups. Also, if you lose one in between fences, you should be able to continue jumping without it confidently and proficiently. Try jumping with one foot out of an iron, and then with the other foot out of the opposite iron. Finally, take both feet out of the irons and jump without stirrups at all.

You will find that each horse you ride differs a little in its length of stride and will need to be

Above: Compare the rider's position here with the picture at the bottom of page 71. It has greatly improved — she is leaning well forward and is looking straight ahead.

Trot

4–5 ft. (1.25–1.5 m.)

Canter

9–10 ft. (2.7–3 m.)

18–20 ft. (5.5–6 m.)

ridden at fences differently. But this understanding only comes with experience. By altering the positions of your practice jumps to make different, but easy combinations, you should get to know how many strides your horse will take between fences varying distances apart. A good jumper rider is one who sits still on his horse, helping when necessary, and instills the will in the horse to get over the fence. He will alter his riding to suit the horse. The jumping position I have described is known as the "Italian forward seat" and is generally and universally accepted as the most satisfactory. If you adopt it and work at it, it should help you to avoid the greatest fault of riders when jumping, which is to get left behind the horse's movement. This means you will bring your weight back into the saddle and onto the horse's back when he is in mid-air, which will result in his automatically dropping his hind legs, as the extra weight would not allow him to keep them tucked up. The knock that he will get against the fence will not only hurt him but will also shake his confidence in himself and in you as the rider. Confidence shaken in this way is not easily restored.

Left: Cavaletti positioned correctly for trotting exercise.

Below: An international show-jumper illustrates how easy it can be!

Care of the Horse

Most small riding ponies will live happily out in the open all the year round, but it is important that they have good grazing in a field that is securely fenced. In the winter, when the grass is poor and lacks nutritional value, you will have to supplement their diet with hay and probably some solid food.

When choosing a field to graze a pony, make sure the fencing is in good condition all the way around. Wooden posts-and-rails – although expensive – is the best type of fencing. Make sure the gate works properly – no broken hinges – and equip it with a padlock. Give the pony some kind of shelter – ideally a three-sided shed measuring approximately 30 ft. × 15 ft. (9 m. × 4.5 m.), which faces a strong hedge or line of trees. There should be a constant supply of clean water, either from a running water source, or in a large container which does not have sharp edges.

Grassland Management

Few people consider the subject of grassland management in any great detail, yet much can be done to get the greatest benefit from even a small paddock. Pastures can soon become "horse sick," because horses are selective eaters when grazing and will never pull the rough tufts of grass on areas where there have been droppings. This is one reason why it is a good idea to pick up droppings from the field each day. An equally effective way to keep pastures

Above: A sturdy wooden field shelter gives protection.

Above: Barbed wire fencing should be avoided. Water containers must not have sharp edges.

Left: Grass-kept horses should be visited every day and checked over for injuries.

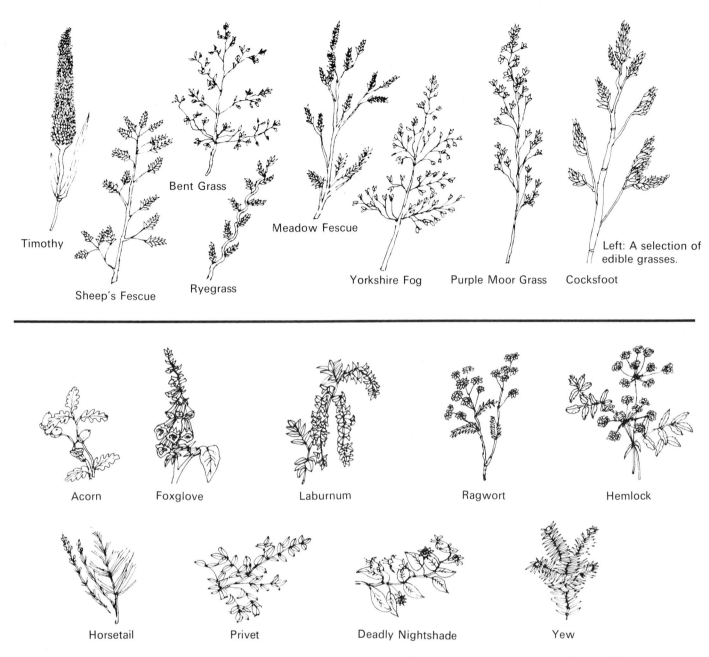

Timothy

Bent Grass

Sheep's Fescue

Ryegrass

Meadow Fescue

Yorkshire Fog

Purple Moor Grass

Cocksfoot

Left: A selection of edible grasses.

Acorn

Foxglove

Laburnum

Ragwort

Hemlock

Horsetail

Privet

Deadly Nightshade

Yew

Above: All these plants are poisonous and horses should not be turned out in pastures that contain them.

in good condition is to graze cattle (providing they are de-horned) either with a horse or when it is grazing elsewhere. This combination ensures that a pasture is evenly grazed and also reduces the worm infection of the field. The grass will benefit from cultivation after the cattle have been moved.

Horses that are grazed continually are very likely to suffer from worm infection. If you know the pasture is infected with worms, worm the horse every six to eight weeks. This makes it impossible for the female worm to lay fertile eggs, and so helps to keep the pasture as clean as possible. It is still a good idea to worm a horse every three to four months.

If the pasture becomes tufty, have it topped. The best way to do this is to ask a local farmer to trim the field at silage time, and take away all the worm-infected grass trimmings. Resting the paddock is another good practice, and is best done by fencing it off into sections. If all parts are rested in turn through the spring and summer, the grass will have a chance to recover. In the autumn, take down all the fencing partitions, and then towards the end of January, start fencing off a small portion. Manure this area with cow manure, if possible, or alternatively something like nitrate of chalk which can be spread by hand over a small area. This will ensure an early crop of grass.

Most grass crops or "lays" are at their best from one to four years, after which it is a good idea to plow up and re-seed. Should you consider doing this, it is advisable to plow, cultivate and generally work the land well before sowing. Young grass should be allowed to mature and should be grazed by cattle before horses are turned out. Cows do not graze as low as a horse, which tends to nip out the heart of clovers, for example, thus destroying the young shoots. If you are only able to graze horses, then it is advisable to cut a crop of hay in the first season, which helps in giving the lay time to get established.

Stable Management

The care of a horse kept inside in a stable is of particular importance, for he is basically being kept under unnatural conditions. It is also extremely time-consuming, for a stable-kept horse needs regular attention, regular feeding and regular exercise. When a horse is confined in such a small space he needs to be kept happy and amused.

First you should consider the actual construction of the stable, which should be roomy with as much light and air as possible let in through windows. These should be high up, out of reach of the horse, and must not provide drafts, which horses cannot tolerate. The door should be in two parts, so that the horse can look out during the day, while additional light and air is let into the stable. Flooring should be solid; in fact the best material is probably concrete, which is virtually non-absorbent and easy to keep clean.

All stables should have the minimum of fittings around them, as these provide potentially dangerous protrusions on which horses could injure themselves. Similarly, catches and bolts on doors and windows should be on the outside, and there should be catches on the outside wall to hold the doors back so they can't flap. There must be a convenient supply of fresh water and there should also be somewhere to hang up a haynet, if the stable does not have a hayrack.

As I have said, looking after a horse kept in the stable is a time-consuming business, for you must establish and stick to a daily routine. This will involve giving a small early-morning feed and cleaning out and refilling the water container, followed by that joy of stable management – mucking out. This means removing all the night's soiled bedding, either into a barrel or sack placed outside, stacking up the bedding in one corner of the stable and sweeping the floor down, before putting down a clean bed. Then at some stage during the morning or afternoon – or possibly both – you will have to exercise the horse. It is essential to exercise a stable-kept animal every day to keep him in good health as well as in top physical and muscular condition and, of course, to relieve boredom and monotony. In addition, he will need a thorough grooming (see under grooming, page 82), which is best done after the horse has been exercised. Ideally, you should incorporate tack cleaning into the daily routine, too.

A stable-kept horse really needs four feeds a day – a small one in the morning, one at midday, one in the late afternoon and one in the evening. Feeding is discussed more fully on the following pages, but assess how much your horse needs and keep to a regular feeding pattern. The daily stable routine should end with shaking up the straw and banking some up against the walls. Then make sure the horse is happy and comfortable and has a full haynet to see him through the night.

There is always work to do in a busy stable yard — hay nets to fill, stables to be cleaned, and, in the late afternoon, horses should be bedded unless they are wanted for evening lessons.

Stable Vices

The importance of keeping a stable-kept horse amused is well demonstrated in those horses that develop "stable vices." The majority of these bad habits are brought about by prolonged boredom, and lack of exercise.

The list of stable vices ranges from those that are little more than irritating or annoying to those that are more serious and may be classified as an unsoundness in the horse. Some of the irritating, but less harmful ones include such habits as upsetting water buckets, scraping bedding around or standing endlessly scraping the floor. Kicking at the wall is an annoying and very noisy habit and one which will be copied by other horses kept in adjoining stables.

Eating bedding or gnawing at the walls of the stable are bad habits which can lead to internal problems. Eating bedding can be discouraged by using sawdust, peat or wood shavings instead of straw, or by sprinkling it with disinfectant to make it taste unpleasant. In extreme cases, a muzzle may have to be fitted at night. Gnawing at the walls can be overcome by painting them with creosote.

The habit of swinging from side to side, putting weight first on one foot then on the other, is known as "weaving." Although they do not seem to put a strain on the front legs, many, though not all, horses that indulge in it constantly end up flawed, a problem if you want to sell the horse. Weaving is a hard habit to cure, but we have dissuaded horses from it by putting

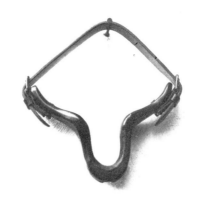

Left: A cribbing strap helps to stop horses indulging in the vice.

Below: Horse wearing a muzzle. The two holes allow easy breathing and the holes in the bottom allow him to drink, but he is unable to eat or tear his blankets.

vertical bars over the top half of the door, wide enough apart for them to look out, but not wide enough for them to weave without bumping themselves.

A cribber is one who catches hold of the door or manger with his teeth and then gulps in air or "wind sucks" at the same time. Some horses also wind suck just by bending their necks and gulping down air. The gulping in of air usually gives these horses pot bellies and bad digestions and results in loss of condition. These vices are very hard to cure even with the help of such devices as cribbing straps. Turning a horse out in a field on warmer days in a New Zealand Rug can often help to relieve the boredom that has led to many of these vices, although it may not help much with confirmed wind suckers and cribbers.

Right: A New Zealand Blanket offers protection to grass-kept horses and ponies in cold, wet weather. Stable-kept horses and ponies can be turned out in a New Zealand Blanket on warmer days.

Feeding

The subject of feeding a horse is a big one. Grass is his natural food, but in many countries of the world, grass does not grow all year round. That is why the grass in a horse's diet is replaced by feeding hay (which is dried grass) during the winter. Grass is at its best, providing the maximum nutrition, for only about four months of the year, in early summer. After this it begins to lose its nutritional value, or protein, and it will be necessary to supplement a horse's grazing with concentrated food such as corn, nuts, bran, etc. Even ponies need a small amount of grain or "short" feed when they are being regularly worked. "Man cannot live on bread alone" and working equines cannot live on grass alone! Certainly grass is an excellent subsistence ration, but real work, fast work, cannot be expected from a grass-fed animal. There is a high water content in all green grass which is inclined to make a horse fat and soft. If you want a horse to work, he must be in better condition than when he does little more than graze in a field.

One of the fundamental aims is to build up a horse's muscles so that he can perform the task asked of him more easily. When he is exercised he will use up energy, which uses up food. Fast work and sweating burn up more food than quiet work, which is why the food must vary according to the horse and his work.

There are many rules to be remembered in connection with feeding, but the two golden ones are:

1. Always give water before feeding. Water drunk in any quantity washes any food which is undigested into the bowels, and this may sometimes cause colic.

2. Feed little and often. Horses have very small stomachs for their overall size and they are by nature grazers. That is, they walk and eat and walk again, so they are eating almost continually when in the wild state. In cold weather particularly a horse needs to keep moving to keep warm and to find more food, since half his intake of food is burned up in the energy task of keeping warm.

The other rules of feeding are:

1. Feed according to the work required. This is common sense. You put gas into a car according to how far you want to drive.

2. Feed according to the type and temperament of the individual horse. As with humans, some horses get fatter than others. The worrying kind never get fat, while the more placid animal is easier and cheaper to feed (a point to bear in mind when buying a horse).

3. Feed plenty of bulk so that the digestion is as occupied as when the horse is grazing in his natural state.

4. Do not make sudden or complete changes in diet as this will upset the stomach. Adjust gradually to new foods. For example, when

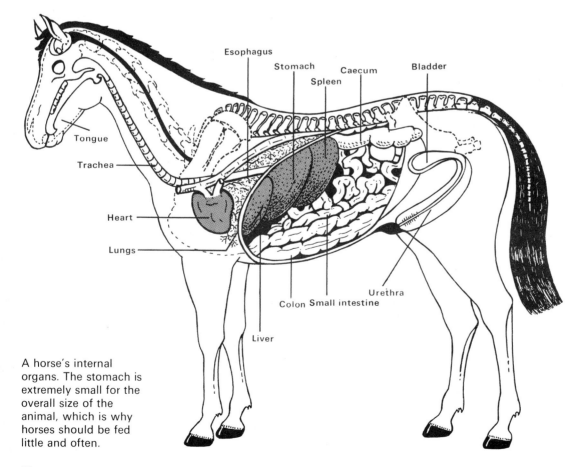

A horse's internal organs. The stomach is extremely small for the overall size of the animal, which is why horses should be fed little and often.

Mare and foal share a feed from an improvised food box.

When food is given in the field, use solid, heavy food boxes, preferably made of thick wood, so a horse cannot knock them over and so waste the feed. Ideally they should be creosoted which will discourage a horse from chewing them, as happened to the one pictured above!

bringing in a horse from pasture, start feeding him a little corn each day in the field beforehand. Dampen the hay when you first bring a horse in, as his stomach will be used to a high water content in the grass.

5. Keep to regular feeding hours. A horse gets used to having his food at certain times and his stomach will soon tell him when it is feeding time.

6. Do not feed immediately before or after strenuous work. A horse cannot work on a full stomach and should not be given a big feed until he has cooled down after hard work.

7. Try to feed something succulent every day to a stable-kept horse. He is deprived of green food and longs for something juicy to eat such as carrots, apples or turnips.

8. The quality of the food is very important. Try to feed the best – it is also the cheapest in the long run.

Types of Food

Hay. Hay is used as a supplement for feeding when the freshness of the grass disappears in autumn, or as a bulk feed when the horse is stabled. It may be brownish or greenish in color according to its type, but all hay should smell sweet and fresh, and it should be as dust-free as possible. Be sure to shake it out well before feeding it.

The two main types of hay are Seeds Hay and Meadow Hay.

Seeds Hay is actually a hard, coarse hay, so named because the seed is sown as a crop. Usually it consists of Red Clover and Rye Grass. Horses like the sweetness of the clover and the Rye Grass is rich in proteins. It is suitable for horses doing fast work like racing and eventing; it is not suitable for either old or young horses, as their teeth are not good enough to cope with the tough stalks. Alfalfa grass is an excellent grass both for grazing and for making hay.

Meadow Hay is a softer hay with a higher water content which makes it more fattening and more easily masticated than harder types, and thus more suitable for young stock and older horses. It has more leaf on it and is com-

Details of daily feeds should be pinned up in a prominent position.

A selection of clovers in hay makes it tasty and palatable for horses.

Under 12 hands 10–12 lb. (4.5–5.5 kg.)
12–13 hands 12 lb. (5.5 kg.)
13–14 hands 14–16 lb. (6.3–7.2 kg.)
14–15 hands 16–20 lb (7.2–9 kg.)
15–16 hands 20–30 lb. (9–13.5 kg.)
Over 16 hands 30–34 lb. (13.5–14.3 kg.)

In my opinion it is not good for a horse's wind to eat over 34 lb. (14.3 kg.) of food a day. I would rather my horses were a bit on the fat side – it is considerably easier to take a little extra off than it is to put it on. All owners will have their own ideas on how much grain to give their horses, so subtract that weight from those given above to gauge the daily hay ration. It is a good idea to get into the habit of weighing hay, and, incidentally, hay is most economically given in a haynet.

Besides bulk feed, most horses will need grain feeds. These are the more concentrated foods containing more protein- and energy-giving properties than hay.

Oats are the traditional and most important grain used for horses. They are one of the best energy-giving foods and a must for all horses doing hard work. They build the tissues of the body and are therefore important for raising young stock and also for feeding brood mares in all stages of producing foals – whether as a milking mother or as a pregnant mare. However, it is not always necessary to give oats to horses who are not really working hard, nor to children's ponies unless they are being asked to work over long hours. In general, they have a rather adverse effect on ponies, making them somewhat frivolous and over-exuberant.

Bran is another traditional food used for horses. Its purpose is to give the horse palatable bulk in his short feed. Fed dry, it is binding: fed wet, it is a laxative. The nutritional value of bran is determined by the the amount of wheat germ left in it. To test this, put your hand into the bran; it should come out white with flour dust on it. Bran is easily digestible and very useful fed as a mash in times of sickness. To prepare a bran mash, pour boiling water on to the bran and cover it with a double sack or towel. Leave to steep for some time before feeding. It may be flavored with anything that will encourage the horse to eat, should it be off its food – grated carrot, apple, a handful of oats or chopped grass will all help.

Barley is a fattening food which also produces warmth in the blood, making it best used in winter to maintain the horse's condition and to help him keep warm. Used more now than at one time, it is not as good a food as oats. It puts greater strain on the kidneys and it is also not such a good energy-giver. If you want to feed barley, do so in small quantities, boiled

posed of many different types of grass and weeds, such as dandelions, clovers, yellow trefoil, plantains – all of which are delicacies to the horse. This variety of tastes will encourage a horse to eat more. As long as it is not musty, the greener this hay is the better, as it indicates a high chlorophyll content and it also shows that it was made in good sunshine from young grass.

Whatever kind of hay you are buying, it pays to buy the best, but remember to watch the condition of your horse or pony so that you can assess whether the hay you are feeding it is what suits it the best. If the hay is really good, most grass-kept riding ponies can live very well on it alone, and they will then need just a supplementary small "short feed" when they are being worked.

How much to give?
The overall weight of hay plus grain given to a stable-kept horse or pony will vary according to the animal and the work it is required to do, as we have already seen. In general, the following approximate weights of food per day can be taken as a guide:

with linseed to make a hot mash in the proportion of six parts of barley to one part of linseed. It should be boiled for several hours – preferably overnight. Barley can be fed crushed or ground, but the kernel swells and, as it can cause colic, is dangerous to feed whole.

Flaked Corn has much the same properties as barley. It is a warming and fattening feed suitable for winter use and helps keep a horse in good condition. It should be fed in small quantities unless it is scalded and allowed to swell before being mixed with bran to form a hot feed on a cold night. Corn also swells when dampened and can cause colic if it is not soaked or scalded. Fed in small quantities, mixed with a feed of oats and bran, it is, however, very beneficial, and will be enjoyed by most horses.

Sugar Beet Pulp is a by-product of the sugar beet root and a residue after sugar has been extracted from the beet. Its sweet taste makes it palatable and liked by most horses. It can be useful for dampening the feeds of stabled horses, but must be soaked for at least eight hours because it swells when it absorbs water. Fed too soon, it can give severe colic. It must be renewed daily, and anything left over from the day before should be thrown away.

Linseed is very high in protein and helps to keep a horse's insides in good working order as well as to give him a shiny coat. It should be boiled for several hours to soften the seeds and to extract the full nutritional value from them.

Nuts are a commercially produced foodstuff which contain balanced quantities of all the major dietary requirements. Many kinds of nuts are available – varying from low protein bulk feed to high protein feed. They constitute an easy way of feeding and are most useful for children's riding ponies, since the nuts provide a balanced diet in themselves and no mixing is needed. A drawback to them is that unless they are fed fresh they lose a lot of their mineral and vitamin content. This means, of course, that you can't gauge exactly what you are putting into each feed, so it is hard to vary feeds according to the work and condition of individual horses. Nuts are readily eaten by most horses, however, and can constitute a pleasant change in the menu.

Molasses can be used in powder form as molasses meal or fed in liquid form diluted with hot water and used to dampen down the feeds.

Salt is a very important food constituent to any horse or pony. Just plain cooking salt added to the short feed is good, as it makes a horse thirsty and encourages him to drink water, which in turn will keep his kidneys clean and in good working condition. A lump of rock salt or a mineral salt lick can be fitted into holders in the wall of a stall for a horse to lick

A selection of feed stuffs.

Weeds (in hay and grass)

Oats

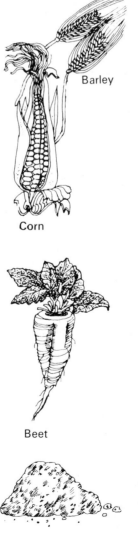

Barley

Corn

Beet

Bran

at whenever he feels inclined. These blocks are either white (plain salt) or pinkish red (when they contain minerals). Bigger blocks, with a hole in the middle through which a rope can be threaded and tied to a fence, are ideal for grass-kept ponies. Alternatively, large blocks of rock salt can be put in the field on a block of wood. Don't just put them on the ground – they will destroy the grass.

Chaff is chopped hay or a mixture of hay and oat straw and is used to add bulk to grain feeds as it stops a greedy horse from bolting his food. When he does this, he does not obtain the full value of his rations. I always use the best quality hay to be chaffed so that I can be sure the horse will enjoy, and therefore will eat, his feed.

Milk Pellets are useful to feed to mares and foals, and indeed any horse that needs a little extra nourishment to improve his condition will benefit from them.

Additives are such things as minerals, block salts, etc., produced commercially. Each is claimed to be the best, but it is trial and error to discover which suits your horse, which does most for him, and which he likes best. Those containing cod liver oil are good, but many horses don't like the taste. All additives should be introduced in small quantities to begin with so that the horse gets used to the new taste gradually, and thus does not reject them.

When a horse is too fat, he must be rationed for his own good. Conversely, when he needs building up he should be given as much as he can and will eat. Do not overwhelm a horse with food, though; too much will put him off and he is likely to actually eat less.

Feeding times may have to be adjusted to enable him to fit into the general schedule of your particular household. In a large stable where people are employed, a strict routine can be kept to. But in a smaller household, it may be better to arrange for the horse to be fed in the morning, and then turned out for the day in a New Zealand Blanket, bringing him in again at night, when he gets another feed. If he is going to be asked to do extra-long hours of work, he could have an additional feed at midday.

Looking after a horse in this way is ideal for a young person at school or college, and, providing a regular routine is established, a horse will quickly settle down and understand what is expected of him. Being creatures of habit, they usually adjust quite quickly to new conditions, although you should make allowances for some upset when you buy a new horse and bring it home for the first time. Such a change in routine and surrounding will often put a horse off his food, and you may need to indulge him with some patient coaxing with succulents you know that he likes, until he has become used to the new environment.

The grooming kit.

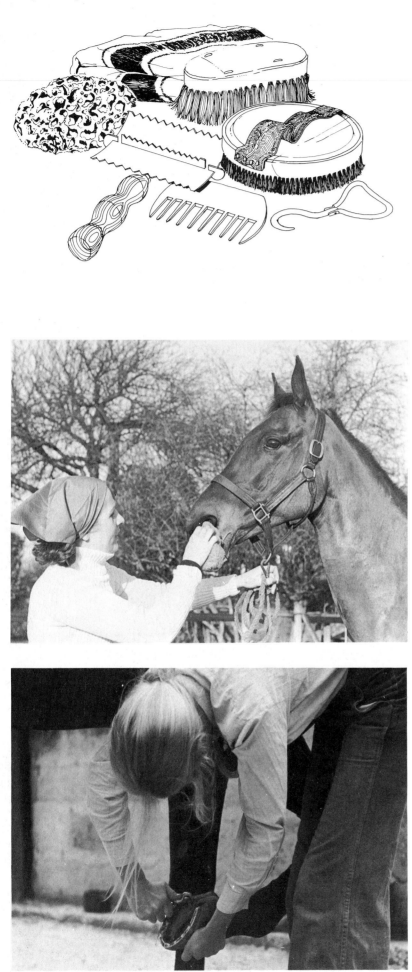

Grooming

The care of the horse's coat is important, whether he is kept out on grass and therefore groomed somewhat superficially, or is kept in the stable and groomed to perfection.

Ponies out on grass need to have their coats brushed with a stiff dandy brush occasionally, even when not being ridden. After all, the easiest way to inspect a pony thoroughly, to make sure he has no cuts or lumps, is to brush him over. If his mane becomes tangled, it should be brushed out. A knotted mane can be dangerous because a pony could get caught up in it when scratching his neck with a hind foot. A pony kept out on grass should not be groomed with anything other than a dandy brush, because the natural grease of his coat is needed to keep the rain from penetrating to his skin and making him really wet, cold and miserable. In fact, apart from removing the mud from his coat and legs, the only other grooming attention a pony on grass needs is to have his hooves cleaned out, and this should be done every day.

Cleaning out the hooves is done with a hoof pick and it makes sure the feet are kept healthy as well as giving you the chance to inspect the shoes – to make sure the clenches haven't risen, and that the shoes are not becoming loose or haven't slipped from their correct position. Hooves should be picked out before and after exercising.

The grooming of a stabled horse is a far more arduous business, for then he is usually kept in blankets and the aim is to remove all the grease from his coat so he looks at his shining best. Also, if you want to ask more from your horse than just gentle hacking, he is going to need special attention, and grooming comes into this category. Besides cleaning his coat, it stimulates the circulation, which is inclined to become sluggish when a horse stands in the stable for hours on end. It also massages the muscles, thus improving their development.

A horse will exude a certain amount of waste products from the pores of its skin in the form

Essential procedures in grooming a horse are:
Center left: Sponging the eyes and nostrils.
Left: Picking out the feet with a downwards flick of the hoof pick.
Top right: Brushing the coat the way of the hair from head to tail.
Center right: Parting the mane with a comb, prior to brushing between the hairs with a water brush.

Far right: Removing surface dust and shining the coat after brushing with a stable rubber. (Most people find it easier to groom the near side with the right hand and the offside with the left hand.)
Right: Oiling the feet to keep them supple and healthy and to give a smart appearance to the groomed horse.

of dust, grease and scurf. This should be brushed off with a flicking movement using a dandy brush so that the dust flies out of the coat. There are many kinds of dandy brushes available in varying sizes on the market, and you will find the job easier if you use one that is the right size for you. The bristles differ too, varying from nylon, which in fact do not wear well, to wire-drawn best bristle. Nylon bristles get closer together with use and do not penetrate the coat, whereas the best bristle will stay hard and parted for seemingly ages. There is also a type of dandy brush available called "Indestructible," which wear well but eventually go soft and become ineffective. If a horse is clipped out, or has a thin coat or sensitive skin, a hard dandy brush will irritate him, so use one of the longer-haired soft dandy brushes very gently.

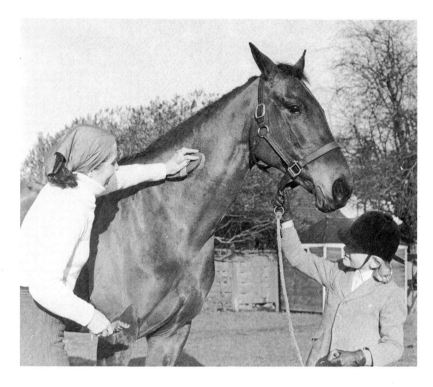

The next piece of grooming equipment you need is a body brush which gets the grease out of the coat and keeps the skin supple, so the pores of the skin can work well. If the horse has a healthy sheen on his coat, it is likely to mean he is in good health and that his digestion and all the vital organs are working properly. The body brush is the most important of all brushes to a stabled horse, and again there are many types available, from synthetic bristles, which are rather hard, to softer real hair ones. The backs may be plain wood or leather; I recommend the leather backed types as they are comfortable to hold.

The body brush should be used in conjunction with a curry comb, which is for cleaning it. The two main kinds of curry comb are the "Jockey" type, which has a webbing hand strap across the back, and the type with a handle. The brush is cleaned with sweeping movements downward on the curry comb, which is then knocked out on the floor to remove the dust (never on the door of the stable, where the dirt will then be rubbed off onto the horse's neck!). To get enough weight behind the movement of the brush over the coat, you should lunge your weight towards the horse by rocking from one foot to the other.

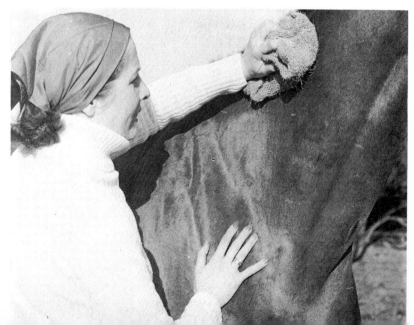

The third type of brush, the water brush, is essential to good grooming. The bristles of this must be hard enough to penetrate the hairs, but not too hard because then they do not remove the dirt so easily. Always leave this brush to dry out naturally after use.

A stable rubber is used to polish off the coat and give it a final shine. It is usually made of linen, although some people prefer to use a chamois leather.

I have already mentioned the item of grooming equipment which is perhaps most important: the hoof pick. In addition, you will need a mane comb and a sponge. A tail comb can be used on the tail, but I prefer to part the skirt of the tail (i.e., the full part below the bone or dock) carefully with my hands and then brush it in strands with a body brush.

There are several other pieces of grooming equipment that have appeared in recent years. For example, a leather pad is used in many stables instead of the traditional wisp of hay. Great stress was always put on wisping (working over his coat with a "wisp" made out of hay) a horse in olden days, and it was undoubtedly a good way to improve the tone of the muscles. Plastic curry flexes are another possible grooming item, good for use on muddy, thick-coated ponies. However, they do not wear well and, as they are made to work in one direction only, they also wear unevenly. Rubber curry combs are useful for removing surplus hair when the horse is losing his coat in the spring.

The procedure for grooming a stable-kept horse is to first sponge the eyes, nose and dock and then pick out the feet. Slip the head collar off the head and buckle it around the neck, turn the horse's head towards the light and groom his head behind the ears and over the poll quietly and gently with the body brush and rubber. Horses are very sensitive about their heads and ears and can be easily frightened by rough or quick movements. Replace the head collar, tie up the horse and remove or roll back his blankets. Groom from the head towards the tail, working the way of the hair. Use the dandy brush first in a circular movement to raise the dirt from the coat, then use a flicking movement to expel the dust. Next go over the coat with a damp water brush, not wet enough to make the coat wet as too much water merely makes for more work as the coat dries out. Again use a circular movement to take the dust from the hairs, and then brush the way the hair grows. Instead of the water brush, you can use an "Irishman's sponge" – a piece of sacking, dipped into some hot water, well wrung out and then rubbed over the coat. It is most effective on short coats, such as the summer coats of show horses or a horse that has been recently clipped.

Next brush with the body brush, cleaning it

with the curry comb after each stroke. If you are going to wisp the muscles of the neck, shoulders and quarters, do so with a rhythmical movement, making the muscles ripple under your strokes. Finally, rub the horse over with the stable rubber. In summer you can remove the blankets altogether during strapping, but in the winter it is best to groom both sides of the neck, shoulders and front legs; shake out one blanket and move it up onto the part you have groomed; groom both sides of the barrel of the horse from withers to quarters; shake out the other blanket and place it over the middle of the horse and finally groom the quarters. In any event, replace the blankets (summer sheet if it is hot weather) after you have worked the horse over with the stable rubber.

Finally groom the mane and tail with the

Above top: Few horses have their manes clipped off or "hogged" these days. If the mane is hogged, it needs regular clipping to keep it smart.

Above: The legs and fetlocks should only be clipped as part of a full clip if a horse is stabled. The hair gives protection to grass-kept ponies.

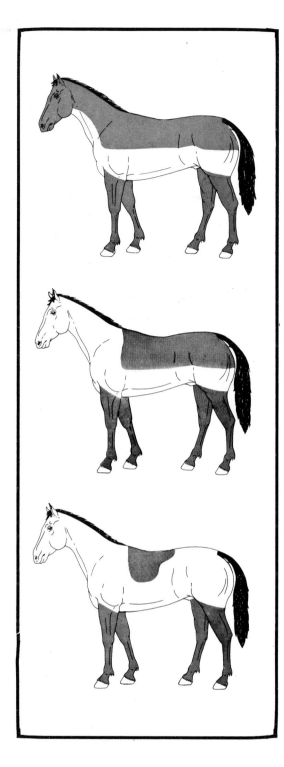

Left: Types of clip from top to bottom, trace clip, blanket clip and hunter clip. In addition, horses may be clipped entirely. Hunter clipped horses must be kept inside. Horses that are blanket or trace clipped can be turned out on warm, winter days in a New Zealand blanket.

Below: Stages in braiding a mane. As each braid is finished, the thread is taken up to the top of the braid at the back, taken back to the bottom and up again, so the braid forms a knot against the neck.

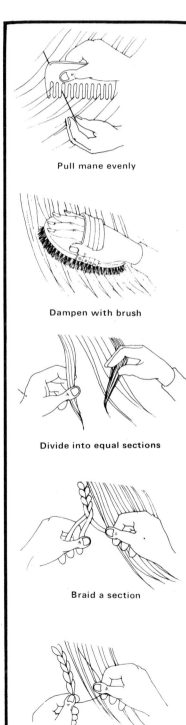

Pull mane evenly

Dampen with brush

Divide into equal sections

Braid a section

Secure end with thread

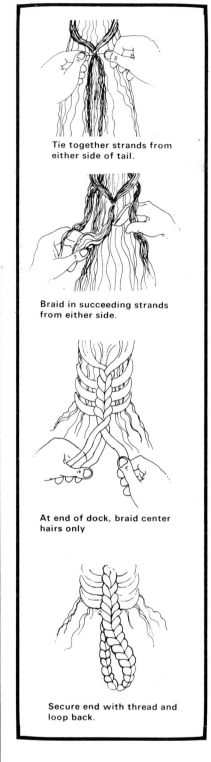

Tie together strands from either side of tail.

Braid in succeeding strands from either side.

At end of dock, braid center hairs only

Secure end with thread and loop back.

Above: Braiding a tail. It requires considerable practice to achieve a neat effect.

water brush and body brush, being careful to tear out as few hairs as possible. Damp the top of the tail and put on a bandage, keeping the hairs lying straight. Oil the feet, making sure you put the oil right up to the coronet band.

Horses that are clipped I have mentioned while talking about grooming. This practice of removing all or part of a horse's thick winter coat if he is kept in a stable is done for appearance, to save work and to make the horse who is being asked to do a lot of hard work more comfortable. The different types of clip are illustrated on this page. Clipping is a skilled job, which should be undertaken only by people who really know what they are doing.

The Health of the Horse

Every horse owner should keep a small collection of first-aid equipment in the tack room, comprising the following items:

A set of stable bandages · Cotton
Gamgee (for putting under stable bandages)
A spare blanket · A thermometer
Crepe bandages in various widths
Cough syrup
Animal lintex for poulticing
Waterproof material to cover poultices
A pair of scissors · A small bowl
Healing and soothing ointments
Mild disinfectant to wash wounds
Strong disinfectant for scrubbing out stables
A card with details of the horse, such as its date of worming, tetanus booster, etc.
Pencil and pad to write down vet's instructions

Once you own your own horse, your vet should become your personal friend and adviser, for you can never be sure when you are going to need expert help and advice. *It is always a good rule to ring the vet too soon rather than too late.* It is usually easy to see if a horse is not feeling well; he will hang his head and look generally dejected. If you find him looking cold and miserable, put an extra blanket on him and bandage his legs. Pull his ears to get them warm and give him a hot mash. If he refuses this, ring the vet. Treatment at the onset of an illness could well prevent your horse from becoming really ill.

Some common ailments

Colic. This is one of the most common complaints in horses. There are two main kinds – flatulent and spasmodic. Flatulent colic is caused by too much gas in the stomach and may be caused by eating too much too fast or from eating bad hay. A horse usually recovers from this quickly with little trouble, and it is far less serious than spasmodic colic. This may be caused by a disorder in the stomach, a blocked bowel causing constipation or something else causing acute pain. The main danger is of the horse being allowed to roll, when he might twist his intestine. This will be fatal unless the affected part can be removed by an operation. It is to stop the possibility of a twisted intestine that horses are walked around during an attack of colic. Symptoms of colic are uneasiness, pawing the ground, sweating, rolling, getting up and down, and groaning. It is best to call the vet at once, particularly if the horse refuses a bran mash.

Worms. There are many kinds of worms which live in and attack horses. All worms impair health in some way (some kinds cause colic), but some are considerably more damaging than others. The most deadly are the blood

sucking types, which can infect the horse's whole system by perforating the walls of the intestine. Other worms – such as the tapeworm, which feeds on the food in the stomach and interferes with the digestive juices, the Ascarid or milk worm found in young horses, the whip worm and the pin or threadworm – will deprive a horse of his nourishment or make him uncomfortable, but will not damage his body.

Infestation of worms is treated by giving the horse one of the worm powders or pastes available; it is best to obtain these from the vet.

Colds and Coughs. Horses will catch cold from getting wet and cold, from not being dried off properly if they are brought in sweating from exercise or from contact with another infected horse. The treatment is to keep them warm by putting on extra clothing and to give plenty of fresh air, but with no drafts. Wash out the nose continually and apply a cold cure to the nostrils. If a horse has a cough, treat him in the same way and give him some cough syrup. A horse with a severe cough should not be allowed to work until he has recovered. Strenuous exercise before the coughing has ceased can damage the lungs and impair the wind permanently.

Strangles. This is a highly infectious disease most often found in young horses. First symptoms are a runny nose and cough, but the nasal discharge is thick and yellow and there is usually a swelling in the upper branches of the jaw, which turns into an abscess. In addition, the horse will have a high temperature. The vet must be called and the patient isolated.

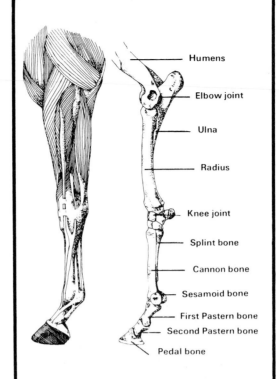

Left: The bones and muscles of a horse's foreleg.

Humens
Elbow joint
Ulna
Radius
Knee joint
Splint bone
Cannon bone
Sesamoid bone
First Pastern bone
Second Pastern bone
Pedal bone

Below: Every horse owner or equine establishment should keep a well-stocked first aid kit.

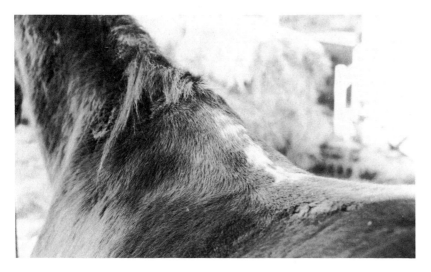

Above: The tell-tale growth of white hairs on a horse's spine indicates one-time saddle sores.

Below: Ailments and injuries that can occur to the lower part of the leg.

Leg Injuries

Capped Hocks and Elbows are caused by bruising or damaging these areas, which the horse can do in a myriad of ways. Lying down with insufficient bedding, resting hocks against the stable wall, being knocked about when travelling, lying so the point of the heel of the shoe rests against the elbow, and being carelessly groomed are just some of them. The area will look full and a hardening of the skin can be felt. If seen and treated in time, the swelling will not become serious. Protect the area with a hock boot or sausage boot and follow the procedure to give a mild blister (see under *Blisters*, page 88).

Bone Spavins are bony enlargements of the hock which can be caused by strenuous exercise, such as jumping from boggy ground. They may also result from bad conformation. The horse will usually drag the toe of the affected

leg and should be shod with a rolled or steel-tipped shoe.

Beside bony enlargements there are a number of soft swellings, also caused by strain, known generally as Bursula enlargements, and specifically as Bog Spavin, Thoroughpin and Windgalls. Pressure bandaging will help to repair the damage, and blistering may be necessary, but usually these swellings are merely unsightly, rather than being causes of lameness.

Lacerated knees are a stigma to any horse owner, as so often they are the result of careless riding over treacherous or stony ground, or on slippery roads. Remove all the dirt from the injury, wash it thoroughly and apply a soothing, antiseptic lotion. Keep the horse standing by chaining him, as lying down will open up the cut.

Sprains will occur when muscles are subjected to strain from blows, sharp turns at high speeds, awkward landing over jumps and so on. The result will be a swelling and heat in the affected area, coupled with lameness. Immediate rest is essential, and the application of hot and/or cold water helps to increase the blood supply to the damaged tissues. Bad sprains may require poulticing, but you should consult the vet. He may also recommend blistering.

Splints are in effect a small hemorrhage of the bone, most common in young horses whose bones are not fully calcified, and caused by blows, concussion or jarring. The affected area will be hot and the horse will probably be lame. Blistering and rest are the most effective forms of treatment for splints.

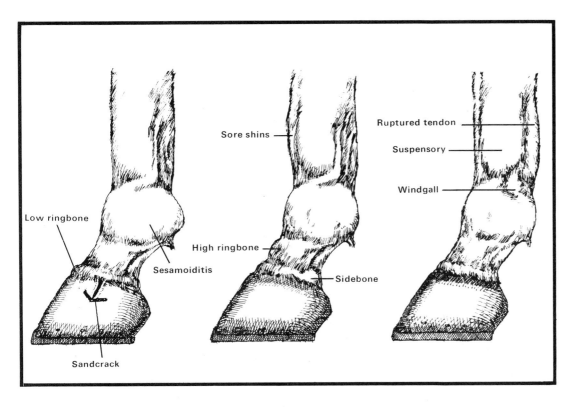

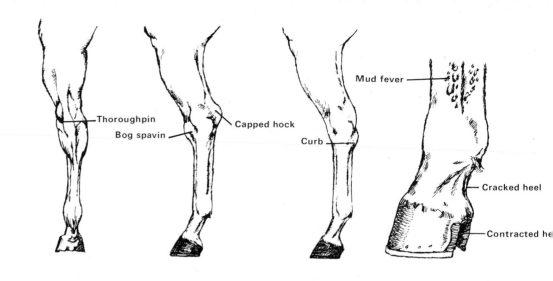

Ailments and injuries on the upper part of the leg and (far right) the heel.

Thoroughpin

Bog spavin

Capped hock

Curb

Mud fever

Cracked heel

Contracted he

Skin Complaints

There are a number of these, which are usually indicated first by the loss of hair. If neglected, this will be followed by broken skin and sores.

Sore backs and girth galls. The former occur from pressure on or around the spine, which may be caused by a badly fitting saddle, a rider who rises at the trot continually to one side and swings on the saddle so it constantly moves, or from continuous pressure in one place from a roller. Girth galls are caused by the girth rubbing behind the elbow, which often happens if the saddle is put too far forward on the shoulder blade instead of behind it, or if the skin is not smoothed out under the girth, or if hard or dirty girths are used. The treatment for all these complaints is to first heal the skin with a soothing antiseptic ointment and, when the scab has gone, to harden the area by rubbing it with salt and water, or methylated or surgical alcohol. Thereafter make sure you remove the cause of the sore!

Sweet Itch is caused by attacks from a particular gnat, which is most active just before sunset and at sunrise. It occurs on ponies more often than horses, and is concentrated on the mane and just above the tail. The resulting irritation makes the pony rub these areas until they are raw. Stabling from late afternoon until after sunrise helps minimize attack, but affected areas can be treated with a diluted chemical, Benso-Bensoate, obtainable from most pharmacies.

Ringworm is a fungus which is usually caught from cows. It is highly contagious and may be transferred from one animal to another through rubbing on a tree or fence. The hair comes off in small, round patches which have small, raised scabs. It may be treated either externally with an ointment or internally with a drug called Fulcin, obtainable from a vet.

Cracked Heels are a winter complaint that can affect stabled and grass-kept horses. Stabled horses suffer from them when they are brought in wet from exercise and their legs are not properly dried off. Horses kept in fields with deep mud in the gateway or around their water

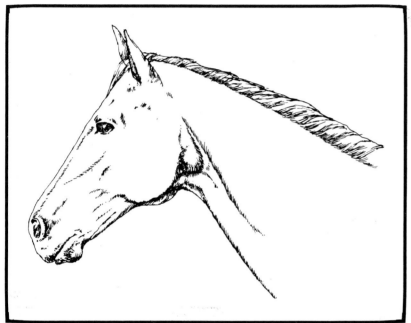

Strangles is an unpleasant disease that occurs most usualiy in young horses. Its symptoms are dullness and apathy, a discharge from the nose, red – as opposed to pink – mucous membranes of the eye, a high temperature, and swollen, hot, tender glands beneath the throat. It is highly contagious and horses with the disease must be isolated.

Blisters are frequently recommended as a form of treatment for various lamenesses. They are a counter-irritant, themselves producing a severe form of inflammation but having the effect of drawing the blood to the affected area. This helps to speed the process of repair. There are three main kinds:

The mild or working blister, induced by the use of various embrocations. Providing there is no lameness, a horse can still be ridden when these are given.

The non-irritant blister is slightly more severe. It is usually greenish in color.

The red blister is the most severe and should be used only on a vet's advice.

To prepare a horse to be blistered, clip away the hair, and then wash and dry the skin to remove the natural grease. Rub in the blistering embrocation for the required time, and then smear the area around it with vaseline to prevent any further blistering. A bandage with gamgee underneath, put on over the blister, stops the air getting at it and drives it inwards instead of outwards. This appears to render the blister more effective.

trough or shed are likely victims. Prevention is better than cure in both cases – use lots of stable bandages or straw bandages on the stabled horse when he comes in wet; try to ensure there is no deep mud in the pasture of horses wintered out. In any case put grease in the heels to stop muddy water from penetrating and affecting this area.

Cracked heels will result in lameness. Keep the horse on a laxative diet and heel the cracks with ointment, using sulphanilamide powder first if they are running.

Cuts and Wounds. First-aid rules are the same for these as when they occur to humans. Stop the bleeding, dress the wound and, if it is severe, call the vet to have it stitched. Cuts and wounds often used to result in the deadly disease tetanus, which happily is less common now than it used to be. This is mainly thanks to the present-day inoculations, which can give constant protection, and horses should be given these each year. Even so, if a deep cut or bad wound is incurred, an extra tetanus "short term" injection should be given for extra protection during the two or three weeks it will take for the wound to heal.

Although Tetanus is a deadly disease, if it is diagnosed early enough, it can be cured. The symptoms will be an odd stiffness about the body, with the head held in an unnatural position. One of the most decisive symptoms is the appearance of a small membrane, known as the third eyelid, in the corner of the eye. This may even extend to cover part of the eyeball. The sufferer will be nervous and any sudden movement will cause a contraction of his muscles. As the illness worsens, the horse will adopt a stiff, stretched-out position with its tail held

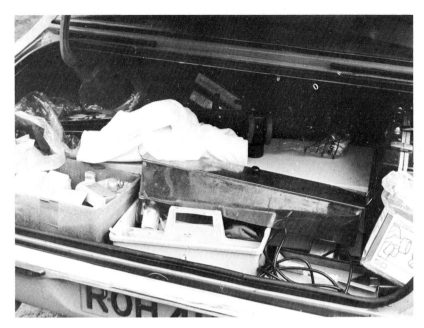

There's little room for luggage in the trunk of a horse vet's car!

high and its abdomen tucked-up and taut. Eventually its jaws become locked so it cannot eat – hence the old-fashioned name "Lockjaw."

If the wound can be located, which is not always easy as it may be just a small puncture, it should be treated in the same way as any open wound. The vet will give daily injections. Small feeds of bran mash with added laxatives should be given several times a day. It is essential to keep a horse suffering from tetanus in the stable – make sure it always has a very thick straw bed, hang a sack over the door to keep the place quiet and in semi-darkness as well as free from drafts, and remove the droppings after each feed. It is a good idea for anyone working constantly with horses to have regular tetanus injections to protect themselves.

One of the first symptoms of tetanus is the appearance of the membrane extending over the eye. The horse becomes generally stiff in all limbs and stands in an unnatural, outstretched way, with taut muscles. Tetanus can be cured if it is recognized and treated early enough.

Care of the Feet and Shoeing

The care of a horse's feet is perhaps the most important aspect of horsemastership. The old horsy adage "No foot, no horse" is very true, for without good feet, the horse cannot work.

The wall of the hoof protects a complex of small bones which forms the foot, and it needs constant care to keep it supple and in good condition. Just as under the human nail there is a sensitive quick, so inside the wall of the hoof there is a sensitive lamina (see page 92). When a horse is turned out to grass, the natural dampness in the pasture keeps the wall of the foot and the coronet band in a healthy condition. But when a horse is stabled, the outside of the hoof becomes hard and dry, which is why it needs oiling every day.

The most important parts of the hoof to oil are the coronet band and, particularly if the horse is stabled, the inside of the hoof. Rubbing the coronet band with an old toothbrush helps to stimulate a healthy growth of the wall of the hoof. Oiling inside the hoof helps to protect the foot from contracting *Thrush*, which is an unpleasant disease of the frog. It can be detected by a most objectionable smell which you will notice when you are picking out the feet, and is caused by constantly standing in manure and urine. This penetrates the cleft of the frog, eating it away and forming a black, molasses-like substance. Hoof oil should also be applied to the frog occasionally to provide a waterproof protection.

I have already mentioned, when discussing grooming, the importance of picking out a horse's hooves each day. Stable-kept horses should have their hooves picked out two or three times a day – before they go out to exercise or are turned out in the field, when they are

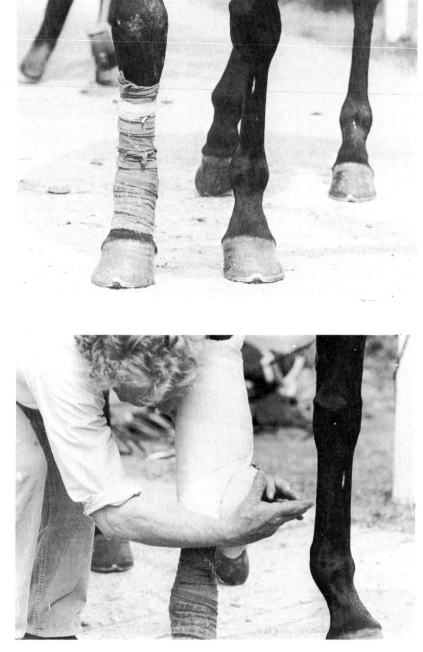

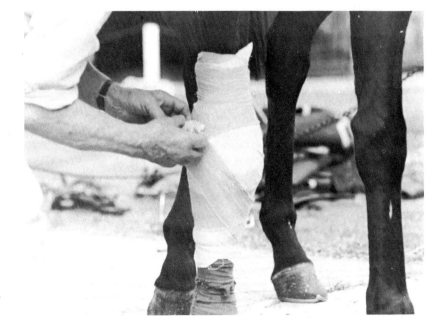

Right: Poulticing and bandaging a swollen knee.
Top: an ordinary stable bandage is applied beneath the swelling. This will help to hold the top bandage in place.
Center: The Poultice is applied using animal lintex, and the knee is bandaged with a crepe bandage secured in a "figure-of-eight" application.
Bottom: Finally a colored stable bandage is applied over the crepe bandage.

brought in from exercise, and then again before they are put up for the night. The most important time is when a horse returns from exercise, during the course of which he could easily have picked up a stone, piece of glass or even a sharp piece of metal, which could bruise or penetrate the sole of the foot.

I do not think it is necessary for the average rider/owner to know all about the bones that constitute the foot, although a rough idea could be helpful. It is necessary, however, to understand the structure of the hoof as you look at it while holding up the foot. The outer wall should be even, with the frog making a well formed "V." This is the foot's natural shock absorber and helps the planter system to work properly as it pumps the blood back up the horse's leg. A poor frog means more strain placed on the heart as this system is not working well, and there is also more chance of concussion to the feet and legs, which could lead to splints and other disorders.

Right: A neck cradle prevents a horse from reaching down to rub an injured or blistered leg.

The procedure for poulticing a quitter (a sore on the coronet), is shown in this sequence of photographs. Top right: The foot is washed and the quitter is cleaned. The leg is bandaged with an ordinary stable bandage. Center left: The poultice (bran and salt mixed with boiling water for example) is put in a piece of linen and placed over the wound. Center right and bottom left: This is covered with waterproof material, and sacking is placed on over the top. The poultice is held in place with an extra bandage. Bottom right: Note that a good support bandage is put on the good leg to help support the extra weight it will be taking off the bad leg.

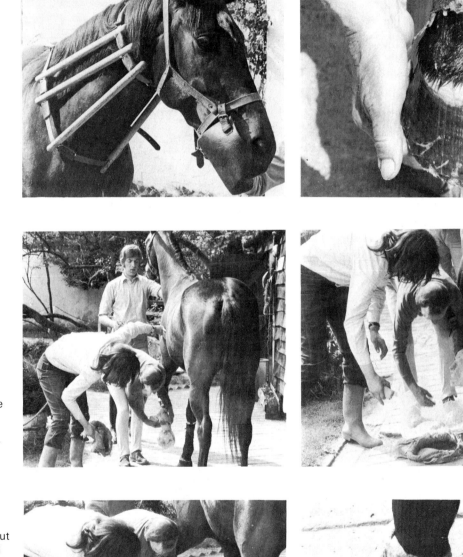

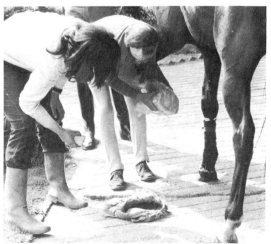

91

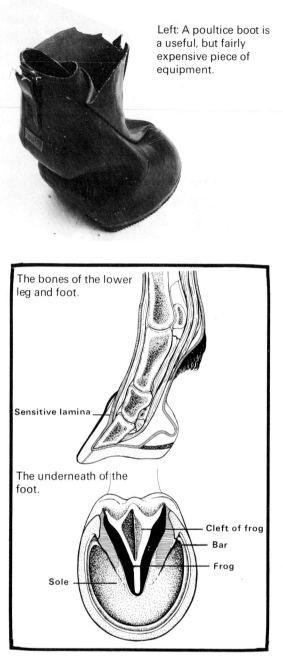

Left: A poultice boot is a useful, but fairly expensive piece of equipment.

The bones of the lower leg and foot.

Sensitive lamina

The underneath of the foot.

Cleft of frog
Bar
Frog
Sole

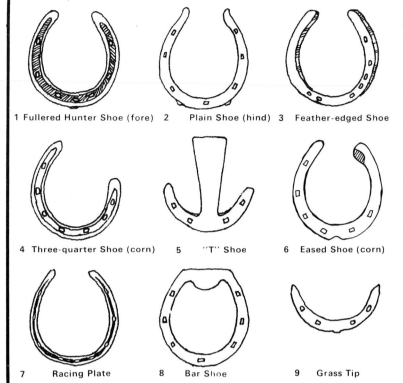

1 Fullered Hunter Shoe (fore) 2 Plain Shoe (hind) 3 Feather-edged Shoe

4 Three-quarter Shoe (corn) 5 "T" Shoe 6 Eased Shoe (corn)

7 Racing Plate 8 Bar Shoe 9 Grass Tip

The white line inside the wall of the foot is the sensitive lamina. This is particularly tender, for if it becomes inflamed (during the disease laminitis, for example) or if it is pricked when the horse is shod, the inflammation cannot spread like most swellings, as it is confined in space by the pressure of the wall of the hoof.

The sole of the foot is a hard layer of a leathery, scaly substance, but it can be bruised if a horse is ridden hard over rough and stony ground. Slight discolorations, which you should notice when you pick out the feet, will be bruises. As in humans, slight bruising is of no great consequence, but should it be bad, the horse will go lame. It will then be necessary to remove the shoe and poultice the foot. In very extreme cases, the vet may have to open up the bruise to let out an excess of blood. The sole then has to be covered with a leather protective pad and the horse rested and asked to do no work until the new sole grows.

Should you need to poultice a foot, you need the following equipment:

Cotton

A stable bandage

An extra bandage to tie on the poultice

A piece of waterproof material

A piece of linen for the poultice

A square of sacking

Whatever poultice you choose to use

The procedure for poulticing is explained in the photographs and captions on page 91. A bran poultice is one of the easiest and cheapest to use. To prepare the bran, put a small quantity in a basin or large cup and add a teaspoonful of salt and boiling water. Wrap this in the linen and proceed with the poulticing.

Foot Disorders and Diseases

Laminitis, Founder or fever of the feet, is the most common disease to affect the feet of the pony population kept out at grass. It occurs when ponies which were bred to live on poor land are brought to lush meadows. The excess of rich grass causes an inflammation of the sensitive laminae. The feet become very hot and the pony becomes lame and in pain. He should be put on a laxative diet of bran mashes mixed with Epsom salts, and in bad cases the vet should be called. He will give cortisone injections to relieve the acute pain.

Seedy Toe is a separation between the sensitive and the insensitive laminae. It is not a great cause for alarm, but if it lasts for a long time the blacksmith should be asked to cut out the cheesy-looking substance which forms in the

Above: A selection of shoes. Their uses are as follows:
Top row – (1) Good grip is provided by the grooved surface. (2) The smooth surface affords less grip, preferred by some people. (3) For horses that brush slightly.
Center row – (4) For horses that brush badly. (5) For horses with contracted heels or corns. (6) For horses with corns.
Bottom row – (7) Made of steel or aluminum. Has no side or front clips, so doesn't lame a horse if it is wrenched off in a race. (8) Same use as "T" shoe. (9) To prevent feet cracking when horse is turned out to grass and is not being ridden.

cavity. This cavity is then cleaned out and stuffed with cotton and Stockholm Tar. Any infection will soon die down and the wall of the hoof can be filed down normally.

Sand Cracks appear on the wall of the hoof and usually run from the coronet downwards. Often the crack does not appear immediately beneath the coronet band, but shows as it reaches the part where the hoof thickens and the foot widens. It is caused by generally neglecting the feet or by some direct damage to the coronet band. Treatment is to fill the opening with Stockholm Tar and to get the blacksmith to run his file across the wall of the hoof to stop the crack from running further. In severe cases a chip can be set in the foot. Very much akin to a sand crack is a *False Quarter*, which means that, as a result of a formerly badly damaged coronet band, the hoof never grows properly. This is unsightly, but does not often cause lameness.

A Quitter is an abscess on the coronet band, usually caused by a piece of gravel or grit working its way under the shoe, or by too tight a nail driven into the sensitive lamina. Although the swelling may appear on the coronet band, the source of the trouble could be at the sole, but the wall of the foot is too hard for the poison to travel any way other than upwards. Once the abscess has formed, it should be poulticed to encourage it to burst.

Corns are usually caused by neglected shoes which were due for removal slipping inwards at the heel. The seat of the corn is situated between the bars of the foot and the wall at the heel where the sole of the foot is thin. Have the shoe removed, and the corn pared out before re-shoeing with a three-quarter shoe.

Nail Binding sometimes occurs when a nail is

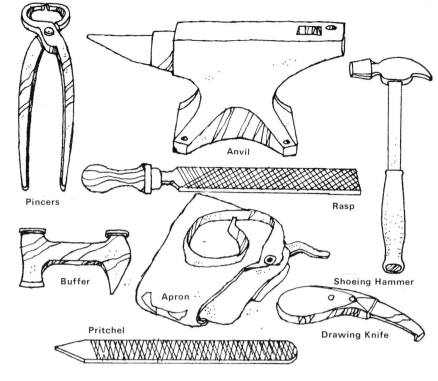

The blacksmith's tools.

Below: The blacksmith at work. A good and conscientious blacksmith is invaluable to a horse owner.

driven in too high or too close to the sensitive lamina. Check for this if the horse goes lame immediately after shoeing. If it is the cause of lameness, it may be possible to remedy the situation by merely removing the offending nail. More usually, the shoe has to be removed and the foot poulticed.

Shoeing

It can be seen from many of these disorders and problems that shoeing and how it is done are of paramount importance. As with your vet, your blacksmith should be a personal friend, although nowadays it is considerably harder to find a careful, good, skilled blacksmith than it was in the days when horses were the main form of transportation.

Obviously, shoeing is the blacksmith's job, but you should know both what he is doing and why, and what to look for when he has finished. Generally a horse needs a new set of shoes about once a month, although this will depend on how hard you are working him. In any event the feet should be looked at once a month in case they need trimming.

A good blacksmith makes it a rule to interfere with the feet as little as possible during shoeing, which means making the shoe to fit the foot and not the other way around. A shoe should lie evenly and level on the hoof. The blacksmith will file or clip the horn of the foot to cut back the growth that has occurred since the last shoeing.

There are various types of shoes (see diagram, opposite page). These all have specific purposes – for example, *Feather-edged Shoes* are sometimes used on horses which are inclined to brush the inside of their legs against each other. The inner part of the shoe is narrowed from the toe to the heel, and it slopes inwards.

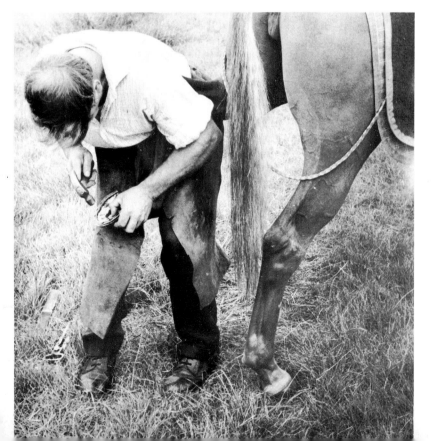

Tack and Equipment

There are many pieces of equipment which the horse or pony owner needs, and equally as many which are interesting to know about, but quite unnecessary to own!

The first essential is to have something with which to catch the horse if he is kept in a field, so as to lead him and tie him up. A halter or head collar and rope are used for this purpose. The halter is strong and cheap and has its own rope attached, but if it is lost in the field it will rot. A head collar may be made from leather or nylon, and varies enormously in cost according to the type of material used and the degree of elaboration. In my opinion, the most service-able, if not the smartest, is the chrome leather head collar. It is both weather-resistant and long lasting, and as it is soft it will not rub a horse's head.

Ropes on head collars vary from homemade braided pieces of baling string to expensive colored ropes with spring hooks on them. If a pony chews its rope, you should use a rack chain, of which there are also several types. The best type is the old-fashioned kind in which the chain is slotted through with a self-fastener. A horse will not hurt himself if he takes the chain in his mouth.

Above: Headcollars should always be strong and well fitting.

Parts of a bridle.

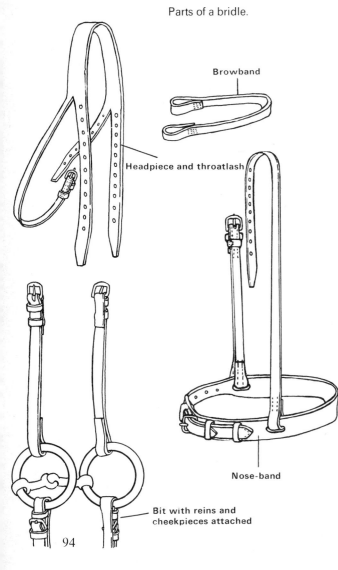

Browband

Headpiece and throatlash

Nose-band

Bit with reins and cheekpieces attached

Bits and Bridles

There are two main types of bridle – snaffles, and those that have a curb pressure. These are commonly known as double-reined bridles, although the curb bit, the Pelham, when equipped with a rounding attachment, can be used with a single rein.

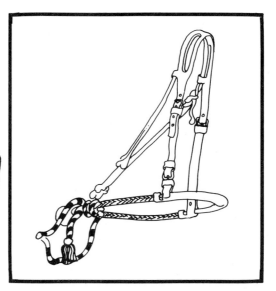

Left: A western type bitless bridle with a bosal nose-band.

94

The snaffle bit is the most used bit in the world, and, in fact, nobody has improved on it in principle since the pre-Christian era. There are endless variations of this one piece of metal, rubber, plastic or vulcanite which passes through the horse's mouth, as there are also of curbs and Pelhams, but I think the accepted rules of bitting are the same the world over. The aim is to control the horse. This can be difficult: temperaments vary and so do the demands made on horses by their riders. That all horses are born with delicate mouths is certain, but to make and keep a good mouth once riding has begun is another matter.

In an impetuous horse which has to be held firmly the bars of the mouth may soon become worn and insensitive. But the first rule must always be to use the mildest form of control possible, to keep the horse's mouth as sensitive as possible. Books as long as this one could be written just on the subject of bits and bitting. But for our purposes it is enough to know the rules about the severity of bits and to understand the old saying, "There is a key to every horse's mouth; the trouble is to find it!"

Horses have different-shaped mouths: some will have more rounded jaws than others and some will have larger tongues (this often applies to horses with Arab blood). Some horses go well in the bitless bridle or Hackamore, which has become very popular in recent years. Its severity can be varied by using an ordinary lip strap, covering it with lamb's wool or using a chain instead.

The mildest bit of all is the rubber snaffle, which as a safety precaution has a chain running through the center. This is followed by the vulcanite snaffle, and then the metal mullen or half-moon mouthpiece (a straight-bar mouthpiece gives more tongue pressure). The jointed

Above: A bridle correctly dressed. The throatlash is crossed around the cheekpieces and buckled. The noseband is put outside the cheekpiece.

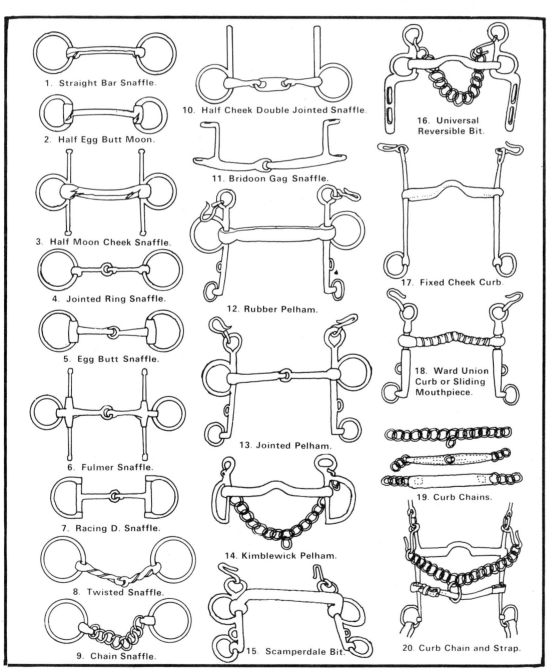

1. Straight Bar Snaffle.
2. Half Egg Butt Moon.
3. Half Moon Cheek Snaffle.
4. Jointed Ring Snaffle.
5. Egg Butt Snaffle.
6. Fulmer Snaffle.
7. Racing D. Snaffle.
8. Twisted Snaffle.
9. Chain Snaffle.
10. Half Cheek Double Jointed Snaffle.
11. Bridoon Gag Snaffle.
12. Rubber Pelham.
13. Jointed Pelham.
14. Kimblewick Pelham.
15. Scamperdale Bit.
16. Universal Reversible Bit.
17. Fixed Cheek Curb.
18. Ward Union Curb or Sliding Mouthpiece.
19. Curb Chains.
20. Curb Chain and Strap.

Left: A selection of bits and curb chains. Note the use of the lip strap, threaded through the ring of the curb chain to keep it in place (bottom right of picture).

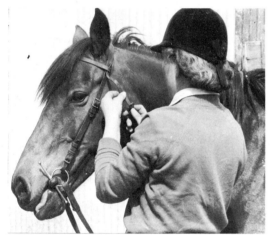

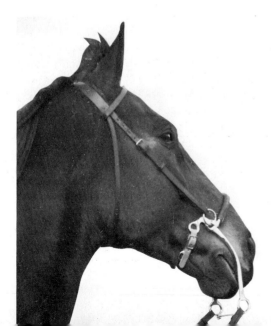

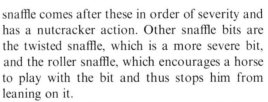

snaffle comes after these in order of severity and has a nutcracker action. Other snaffle bits are the twisted snaffle, which is a more severe bit, and the roller snaffle, which encourages a horse to play with the bit and thus stops him from leaning on it.

The true double bridle is composed of two bits – a snaffle bit called a bridoon, which is usually smaller than the snaffle used as a single bit, and a curb bit. There are two main kinds of curb bit, the fixed mouthpiece used for steady head carriage in dressage and show horses, and the sliding mouthpiece which allows more movement in the horse's mouth. The severity of the curb is governed by the length of the cheek piece and the size of the port. The length of the cheek piece above the bit gives poll pressure, while the length below the bit gives curb pressure.

The width of the port gives tongue room while the height of the port puts pressure on the roof of the mouth. A narrow, high port is thus very severe while a thick, wide port gives tongue room and is mild. Ports ask for the flexation of the horse's head, from the poll.

Above: Example of a bitless bridle. This one is far less harsh than the Hackamore.
The small picture shows the position of the bit correctly placed on the lower jaw.

Above left: Bridling a horse.
Top: The mouth is opened and the bit slipped in.
Center: The headpiece is put over the ears.
Bottom: The throatlash is buckled, allowing room for at least two fingers' width to be inserted between it and the horse.

Left: The German Hackamore. This bitless bridle is very severe.

The Pelham bridle comprises a single bit, which has cheek pieces, and can give curb pressure. Purists despise this bit, and it is not permitted to be worn in dressage events. However, many horses go very well in Pelham bits, preferring a single bit in their mouths, so they cannot be disregarded by the every-day horseman. Again, there are many different types of Pelham, ranging from the jointed Pelham to the really severe ones which have huge long cheek pieces and high ports. The curb chains that are worn with double bridles and Pelhams may also vary in severity. The mildest type is made of broad elastic and has two or three rings on each end and one in the middle for the lip strap. Also quite mild is the leather curb chain. Then there are the curb chains comprised of steel links: the smaller the link, the more severe the pressure. All curb chains must be worn with a lip strap; rubber covers can be fitted over any curb chain so that it lies more comfortably in the chin groove.

It is a fact that the Pelham bridle is preferred by many horses. Hack championships have been won in such bridles and Pelhams used with roundings are often very useful for head-strong, small ponies, who may be too strong to be controlled in snaffles by young riders.

Nose-bands can also be a help in controlling a horse, although many are worn purely for ornament. The *plain Cavesson nose-band* is often used to break the line of a long face and it will improve the look of a large-headed animal for the show ring. A smaller version of this nose-band, probably stitched and padded, would look better on a neat-headed horse. The Cavesson nose-band should lie two fingers' width below the projecting cheekbone and should be buckled so that two fingers can be inserted behind the jaw.

The Dropped nose-band is used to keep a horse from opening its mouth and thus evading the bit. The fitting of this nose-band is of particular importance (see caption for details), for it must not interfere with the breathing in any way. If the horse makes a noise through its nostrils the nose-band must be raised to relieve the pressure.

The Flash nose-band essentially allows for a standing martingale to be used with a Dropped nose-band, as the martingale is attached to the Cavesson part.

A Figure Eight or Cross-over nose-band has much the same effect as a Flash nose-band, but pressure can be brought higher up on the nose. It is useful on a horse who tends to cross his jaw and pull.

The Kineton nose-band fits behind the bit in the mouth. By adjusting the buckle at either end of the nose-band, the bit is kept forward in the mouth to prevent the horse from getting his tongue over it, so the rider loses control.

Below: The cheekpieces of this type of snaffle bit fit into loops in cheekpieces of the bridle to keep the bit correctly placed.

Left: A dropped nose-band should be low enough to ensure the bit does not wrinkle the corners of the mouth. It must not be too low or it will interfere with the horse's breathing.

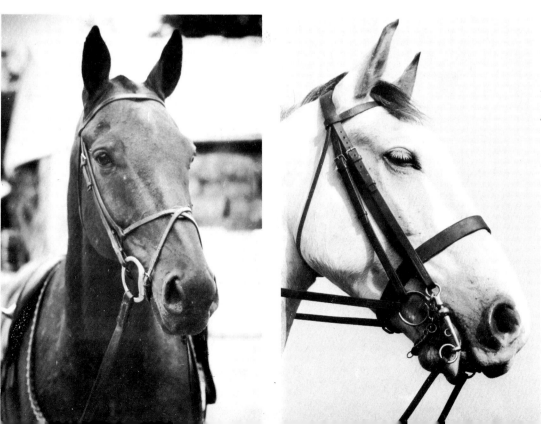

Far left: Cross-over or Figure Eight nose-band.

Left: Cavesson nose-band worn with a double bridle.

97

I have not attempted to describe the several racing nose-bands, but I will mention two of the more common ones. These are:

The Sheepskin nose-band, which is an ordinary Cavesson nose-band, bound with sheepskin. It became fashionable some years ago as it was supposed to stop a horse from seeing the shadow thrown by its feet when galloping.

The Australian nose-band has the same purpose as the Kineton; that is, to keep the bit forward in the mouth. This it does by the use of two rubber rings which go around the bit and are held in place by more rubber pieces, which are joined to go up to the bridle head between the ears.

Reins are a very important part of the bridle and there is a wide range to choose from. Leather reins vary in width and may be plain, laced or braided (which give a better grip). Rubber-covered reins are particularly popular for racing. It is usual to use narrower reins on a double bridle than on a snaffle, and the curb rein is narrower than the bridoon one. This makes distinguishing one rein from the other easier. Then there are many kinds of reins, used mostly for jumping, such as string and nylon braided ones, cotton reins with leather straps and reins made of webbing. Reins will vary in length, too, from short ones for small ponies to very long ones for side-saddle riding. It is important to use reins that are the correct and comfortable length. They may be stitched to the bit or attached by studs or buckles (in the latter case they are said to be billeted).

Above: Three types of leather reins – braided, laced and plain.

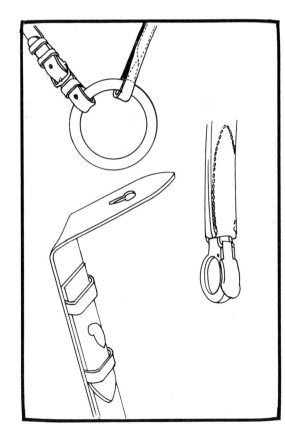

Left: Reins can be attached to the bit rings by buckles or stitching (top), stud fastenings (left) or springs (right).

Saddles

Our earliest pictures of men riding horses show them to be bareback. Then a simple form of pad appeared, followed by stirrups or rests for the rider's feet. As saddles bearing close relation to those we know today came into existence, they tended to be built up in the front as well as the back so as to keep the rider in the right place. This tendency has been retained in several types of saddle in use today – the best examples being the *Western Saddle,* which has a horn in front and has a raised back, and, to a lesser extent, the modern *Show Jumping Saddle.*

It was the need for a saddle which fitted the horse's back without pressing on its spine, yet at the same time provided ventilation and gave as much protection as possible, which led to the production of the saddle as we know it today. All saddles are constructed on a frame called the "tree" which comprises an arch over the withers. This is known as the pommel and is joined by the waist (the middle part of the saddle) to the cantle at the back. Trees used to be constructed of beech wood, but now lamina-

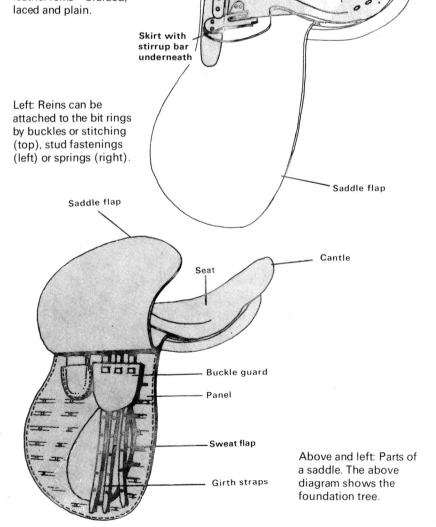

Pommel

Waist

Skirt with stirrup bar underneath

Saddle flap

Saddle flap

Cantle

Seat

Buckle guard

Panel

Sweat flap

Girth straps

Above and left: Parts of a saddle. The above diagram shows the foundation tree.

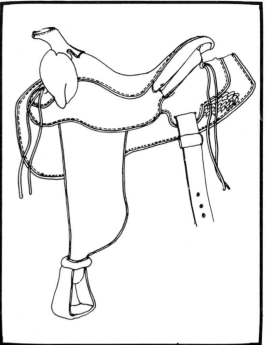

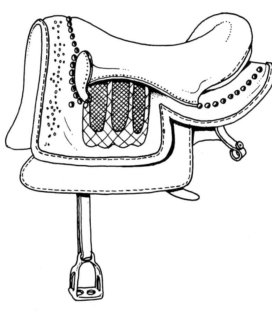

ted woods and plastics are used instead as they are lighter. Recently a very strong tree has been constructed out of fiberglass. Some years ago, "spring trees" were introduced, which means the tree is inset into the waist of the saddle, giving "spring" to the seat. The tree of the saddle is usually made in three fittings – narrow, universal and wide – to fit the withers. The length and size of the saddle are determined by the size of both horse and rider.

Saddle flaps and stirrup bars are attached to the tree, after which the panels are constructed. These may be either full, with the padding reaching down to the end of the flap, or short so there is only a half panel reaching to the knee. Some variations are found in the *Saumur Saddle*, which gives a slight indentation for the rider's knee, and the *Continental Saddle*, which has a sweep down the whole length of the panel. The short and Continental panels were designed to get the rider closer to his horse and this is also a feature of the *Dressage Saddle*, in particular the *Cavalier Saddle*, which has no panels at all. In this saddle the girth webs come off the tree and are enclosed between two thicknesses of pigskin. Every movement of the horse may thus be felt. Some saddles have a point strap fixed to the end of the point of the tree, designed to keep the saddle down in front and thus prevent it from moving forward.

The most popular saddle today is the *General Purpose Saddle*, which is a cross between a forward-cut jumping saddle and the old hunting saddle. It retains the wider seat of the hunting saddle, but does not have quite such exaggerated knee rolls nor such a deep seat as the jumping saddle. As its name suggests, it can be used for anything – everyday riding, jumping, even

dressage – but being such a "Jack-of-all-trades," it probably won't suit the specialist. The flat-race jockey, for example, needs a very forward-cut saddle, while the steeplechase jockey needs a rather bigger saddle with forward-cut flaps. These allow the jockey to put his knees on the flaps when riding with very short leathers. Racing saddles are made of different weights, as many jockeys prefer to use these than burden their horse with the "dead weight" of a weight cloth.

The Forward-cut Saddle is supposed to have developed in recent years to meet the demand from riders who have adopted the modern Italian forward style of riding and jumping. On looking through old pictures, however, one can see Polish horsemen of Rembrandt's day adopting much the same position in the saddle as today's riders in their modern saddles.

Above left: The underneath of a side-saddle.

Above: A typical Western saddle. Note the high pommel, and the stirrups which are made of leather.

Left: An example of a saddle used by officers in the United States Army in about 1770.

99

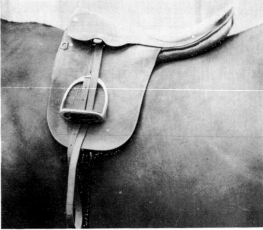

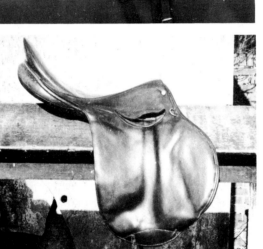

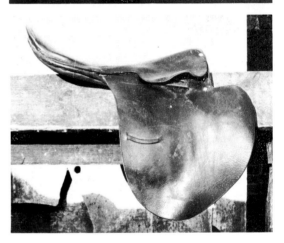

The more exaggerated forward cut jumping saddles tend to keep the rider well forward and are not less comfortable for ordinary riding.

The English Show Saddle is used only for showing. It has straight-cut flaps and the stirrup bars are set back to allow the rider's leg to be kept straight. The idea is to show off the horse's shoulder to the best advantage. As this saddle is also positioned well behind the shoulders, it usually has four girth straps, one on the point to keep the saddle steady (necessary on a fat, round-withered horse).

The Dressage Saddle is centrally seated in rather the same manner as the Show Saddle, but it is not quite so straight-cut and has a slight roll for the knee. It is a short tree'd saddle and usually has a gusset to allow for added stuffing under the rear of the saddle. This helps to keep the rider in the center. The girth straps are longer than usual, and are attached, as with the Cavalier Saddle, to a two-buckled girth. The Dressage Saddle allows a rider to ride with longer stirrup leathers than a Forward-cut Saddle and, having a very short panel, the rider's legs are closer to the horse's body.

Today it seems we have as many types of saddle on the market as are needed to meet the demands of riders. The old hunting saddles of 50 years ago are still in use, and their central and large seats make them particularly suited to older, well-proportioned riders! In general, modern spring tree saddles are more comfortable for the average rider, and sometimes for the horse, as they are lighter than the older saddles. However, they do have a tendency to perch on a horse's back and to swing when the riders get tired. A wider-backed saddle, which distributes the rider's weight over a larger area of the horse's back, is more suitable for long distance riding.

Far left: An all-purpose saddle.

Left: An old side saddle hanging on a Spanish farmhouse wall.

Above: Girths are buckled to the two outside girth straps.

Before the Second World War, it was customary to have a saddle re-stuffed at regular intervals and to fit each saddle to each horse at least twice a year. Then the lining of a saddle was usually linen, although some were of serge and a few of leather. Leather was the least popular as it encouraged the horse to sweat under his saddle. Today, nearly all saddles are lined with leather, as it is the easiest to keep clean – a factor that merits more consideration than the comfort of the horse! Now there are so few working saddlers about that saddles are not usually fitted individually to a horse's back. Instead we have overcome the problem with the universal use of Numnahs, which 20 years ago would never have been seen in the show ring and, indeed, would have been frowned upon in all branches of horsemanship. They would have indicated that the horse had a sore back, because of either bad riding or a badly fitting saddle!

Most modern saddles have two-girth straps, as it is usual to use a double-buckled girth. Many saddles, however, retain the old-fashioned three-girth straps, originally intended for use with the Fitz-Williams wide-webbed girth and a smaller girth which was used in the center. If there are three girth straps and a double-buckled girth is being used, saddlers will tell you it is best to use the first and third straps.

As with all saddlery, there are many types of girth, too. Narrow girths have largely replaced the wide ones popular in years gone by. They may be made from any material, the most usual being leather, webbing, candlewick, string and/ or nylon. Some are made with a definite object in mind, such as the string and nylon girth, which although it does not wear all that well, is supposed to be cooler than others and less likely to rub. However, any girth will rub unless the wrinkles are taken out under the elbow. To do this, run your hand down the horse's side, inside the girth, or, better still, pull each front leg forward in turn, thus smoothing any wrinkles that may have been there. It is the top of such wrinkles which will rub against the girth and result in a girth gall. If the girth slips forward it causes discomfort and may restrict the horse's movement.

Right: A selection of girths.

steel. Nickel ones are cheaper as nickel is a cheap metal, but it is a false economy to buy them for they will bend easily, and even break. Buy stainless steel and choose heavy irons so that they will always fall downwards into position should a rider's feet slip out of them at any stage. Irons should always be slightly too big rather than too small for a rider's foot, because it is very easy to get the foot caught and wedged in too small an iron.

There are a number of different types of stirrup iron available.

The *Kournakoff Iron* is slanted both backwards and sideways to encourage a good position of the foot. It also helps to keep the weight on the inside of the foot, thus ensuring that the knee and thigh are carried into the saddle and the heel pushed downwards.

The Bent Top Iron, as its name implies, is bent so that it will not rub the rider's boot if he rides with his foot right "home" (with his instep rather than the ball of the foot resting on the iron).

The Racing or Cradle Iron is a rounded iron, often made of aluminum for extra lightness.

There are also several types of *Safety Iron*, the best known being the Peacock, which has a leather and rubber attachment designed to pull off if the rider's foot gets caught as he falls off and is in danger of being dragged along. However, they do not always work as well as they might. *The Clog* is an old-fashioned "stirrup," although perhaps it is not strictly correct to classify it as such. In any event, I think it is far and away the safest stirrup for children and also for disabled riders. Besides giving a small or handicapped rider a great sense of security, it encourages the foot into the right position by keeping the weight on the ball of the foot and pushing the heel down.

Left: Three types of stirrup bar for side-saddles. In the center picture the stirrup leather is shown attached. In the bottom picture the catch or "bar" is open. When the leather is put on, this will be closed to secure the leather in position.

Below: A selection of stirrups. From left to right, top row — Peacock safety iron, leather clog (ideal for young children). Front row — ordinary iron with rubber tread (to prevent foot slipping), Kharnikov iron with tread; Bent iron with tread, and children's ordinary iron.

Stirrup leathers and irons

Stirrup leathers are threaded through the bar at the top of either side of the saddle and their function is, of course, to support the stirrup irons. They may be made of leather or webbing, the latter usually being used for racing as it is lighter. Stirrup leathers may be made of cowhide, which does not stretch, rawhide, or buffalo hide, which is strong but will stretch and, as it is a soft, supple leather, can be awkward to put on the stirrup bars. My feeling is that rawhide leathers are the best as they are more or less unbreakable. All stirrup leathers are available in a variety of widths to suit individual requirements.

Stirrup irons are usually made of nickel or

Martingales

In an ideal world, the horse would be so trained that martingales would be unnecessary! However, there are factors, not the least of which can be conformation, that contribute to a horse not always carrying his head where one might hope he would. Thus, a variety of martingales exists to make sure, for example, that a rider is not likely to be dealt a painful blow from the tossing of his horse's head. A horse that tosses his head can also get the reins over his ears, causing the rider to lose control. In fact, tossing the head in a horse can be a mannerism, or it can be caused by pain from the bit or from bad teeth. So if you find you need a martingale to check this habit, first make sure that your horse's teeth do not have sharp edges, which are causing pain.

The Standing Martingale is attached from the girth, running up between the front legs to the Cavesson nose-band – never to a Dropped nose-band, unless specially designed (see page 97 under Flash and Crossover nose-bands). It should be measured to a length just below the top of the wither (see illustration overleaf), at which length a horse can jump without restriction. If it is tighter than this, there must inevitably be some restriction of the horse's neck. If you are riding a rearing horse or one that drives into his bridle before taking off and running away, it may be necessary to impose such a restriction. In such cases, however, I would rather re-school the horse than resort to a restricting length of martingale.

The Running Martingale is used to hold the reins down, so that the bit works on the bars of the mouth. It should be fitted in such a way that the reins run in a straight line from the bit to the hand. If it is too tight, the reins will run down to the martingale rings and then upwards to the rider's hands.

In horsy circles, it is often said that a Standing Martingale is for the horse's head and a Running Martingale is for the rider's hands!

The Bib Martingale and the *Irish Martingale* are both used to keep the reins on either side of the horse's head and both are used by racing stables, particularly when two and three year olds are ridden out in a string (that is in a line, one following behind the other).

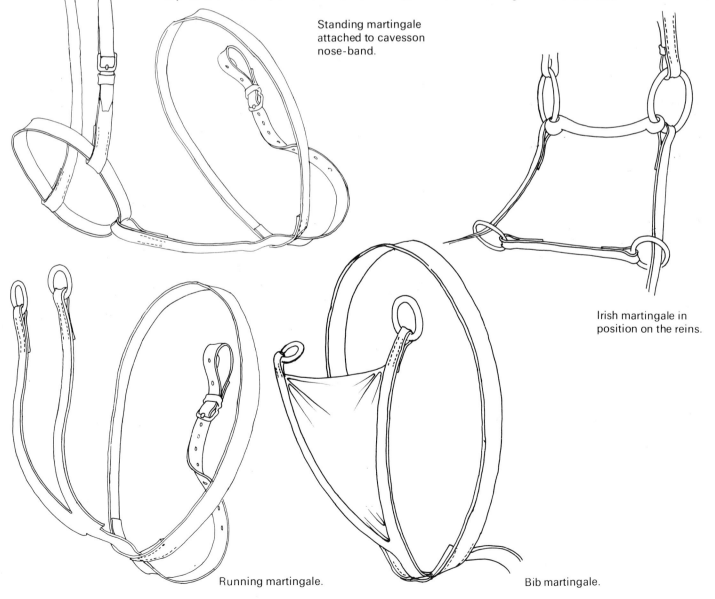

Standing martingale attached to cavesson nose-band.

Irish martingale in position on the reins.

Running martingale.

Bib martingale.

lowers the horse's head, at the same time making him use his back muscles and encouraging him to stretch forwards and downwards towards the ground.

Both the Cheshire and the Chambon Martingales, and indeed any of the other schooling martingales, should be used only by an experienced person, thoroughly conversant with their aims and correct use. If you feel they might help your particular horse, take a lesson with a really experienced instructor and ask to be shown how to use them properly. Otherwise it is very easy to get into a real muddle with them, which can do a great deal of harm.

Above: Measuring the length of a standing martingale. The strap, which will be attached to the nose-band, should just reach the withers when the other end is attached to the girth and the neck strap is buckled in position.
Above right: A cheshire martingale.
Far right: This horse is equipped with running reins which run from the girth, through the bit rings. They are held by the rider.

The Cheshire Martingale controls the head by the use of two reins which run from the girth through the rings of the snaffle and back to the rider's hands. This is a severe type of control and should be used in a similar way to the curb rein in a double bridle, so the greater pressure is taken by the ordinary snaffle rein. A Cheshire Martingale tends to lower the horse's head, forcing him to flex. In fact, it works in much the same way as drawing reins, which run from the girth straps, making a straight line from the bit to the girth, before running through the rings of the bit back to the rider's hands.

The Chambon Martingale, of French origin,

Care of Saddlery

"All leather needs feeding" is a quotation taken from a pamphlet issued by the Master Saddlers' Association. In other words leather needs care to keep it supple and to prolong its life. When used for saddlery, that is for saddles, bridles and harness of any kind, leather comes into contact with sweat from the horse, as well as with rain and mud, all of which tend to make it hard. In time it will crack, become brittle and then be unsafe to use. Tack should therefore be cleaned after each time it is used, in order to keep it in good working order; but I fear this is sometimes neglected!

Far right: After washing over the outside of the saddle with a damp rag, saddle soap is applied with a sponge.

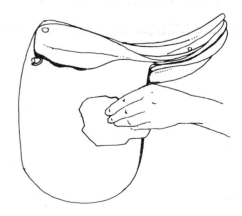

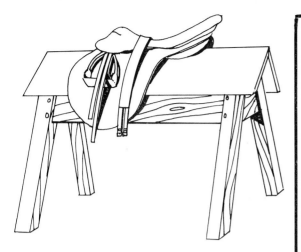

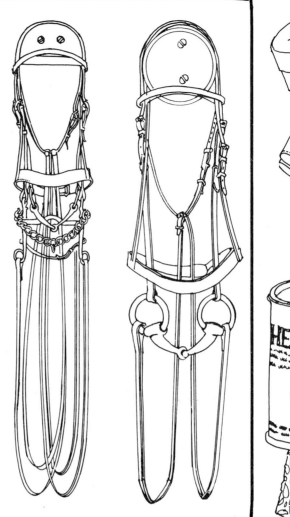

After a ride or exercise or schooling session, the parts of the saddle or bridle that are soiled should be sponged off with warm water and a damp rag to remove the dirt. Then they are soaped with saddle soap. There are two distinct sides of all leather – the flesh side and the grain – and about once a month, even if the leather has not gotten wet, the flesh or rougher side should be oiled with Neatsfoot oil to keep it in good condition. Each time the leather gets really wet, through a horse being ridden during a rainfall, the bridle and saddle needs to be stripped down (including unbuckling each strap) and cleaned and oiled. All new leather should be oiled and then soaped before use. Hard leather will rub a horse's skin, and will soon result in galls or sores, which can take a long time to heal. All metal parts of the tack should be cleaned and kept polished. The mouthpiece of the bit must be washed each time it is used, in order to prevent any saliva hardening as it dries.

All saddlery should be kept in a dry room. If your tack gets very wet – when you are exercising in the rain, for example – always let the natural air temperature dry it out. Don't try to speed the process by hanging a damp saddle or bridle over a radiator or heat source, because the intense heat from this will certainly dry out the leather's natural oil, thereby causing it to get hard and to crack.

Above: Saddles should be kept on specially constructed saddle "horses" in order to keep their shape.

Right: A neat, well-organized tack room

Above center: A double and snaffle bridle correctly hung after cleaning.

Above right: Tack cleaning equipment.

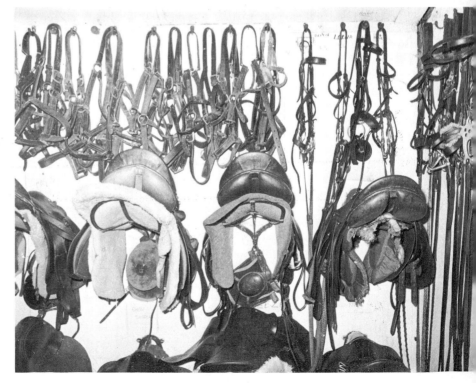

Leg Protection

Besides the equipment necessary to control a horse when riding, there is a host of ancillary equipment designed for protection or warmth.

Sausage Boots protect the elbow when the horse is lying down in the stable, (see page 87 – *Capped Elbows*).

Knee Caps protect the knees, either during transit or when exercising on slippery roads. In the latter event a skeleton knee cap is usually used which has an elastic strap above the knee for comfort.

Hock Boots protect the hocks during transit and can be used for those stabled horses that scrape away their bedding and are then liable to "cap" their hocks on the floor.

Brushing Boots give protection when a horse brushes one leg against another. They can vary from long protective boots to just a rubber ring that fits around the coronet.

Speeding Cutting Boots are well padded from the knee or hock to the pastern on the inside, instead of downwards over the pastern as in an ordinary Brushing Boot.

Polo Boots reach well down the leg on forelegs and cover the coronet on hind legs. They can be useful for ordinary exercising as well as during polo.

French Pastern Chasing Boots run from just below the hock to the fetlock and give added protection to horses when racing.

Over-reach Boots are worn by horses which tend to strike their forelegs with their hind legs during jumping or galloping. There are various types available.

Bandages are probably the simplest form of protection when travelling and are taken from just below the knee or hock down to the coronet over a piece of cotton or gamgee. Exercise or working bandages, which are made of a more elastic material than stable bandages, should also be used with gamgee, and these bandages should be run from just below the knee to just above the fetlock.

Right: Fitting leather and felt-lined fetlock boots to prevent brushing on the fetlock. Far right: Sausage boots.

Right: Hock boot in position. Far right: Two types of knee cap. The type on the right is generally used for exercising.

Right: The night cap helps to warm the ears. Far right: The hood must be carefully fitted so it does not cover or hurt the horse's eyes.

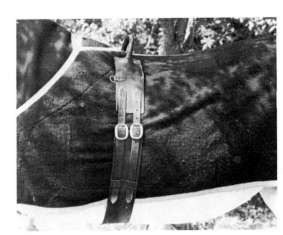

The many different blankets available for horses all have specific uses.

Far left: Horse wearing an anti-sweat blanket. Worn with a light blanket on top, this helps to cool a hot horse, but stops him from catching cold.
Left: A woollen checked day blanket in position. It keeps a stable-kept horse warm and clean.

Far left: The hood in position with a headcollar on top to keep it in place.
Left: Horse wearing a Lavenham night blanket.

Clothing for Warmth

The Hood is a shaped covering for the head and neck. It reaches to the shoulder and is buckled under the jaw and tied in place under the neck.

The Night Cap is a small version of the hood, ending just behind the poll. It should be kept in place with a well-fitted head collar.

The Night Blanket is the most essential of all blankets. It is made of canvas or jute, and may be half-lined or fully lined with a woollen blanket. It is available with or without surcingles attached, or can be used with a roller.

The Day Blanket may be made of heavy woollen material known as livery cloth, or a lighter woollen material more suitable for use on a cool summer's day. The first type is really better, as the lighter blankets do not provide any warmth at all. Day blankets are far from essential pieces of equipment, but they can be useful when a horse comes in a little too warm from exercise.

The Quarter Sheet was designed to be worn over the saddle when race horses parade before a race. It is also useful to put under a saddle to keep a horse's loins warm when exercising in the winter.

The Mackintosh Sheet is useful in most European countries to keep horses dry when they are waiting to compete in racing, eventing or showing. They may be a simple blanket made of waterproof material, or they can be more elaborate and lined with a woollen material. They should always be worn with a fillitt string to prevent the blanket blowing up in the wind.

Summer Sheets may be made of any light material, usually cotton or linen, bound with a

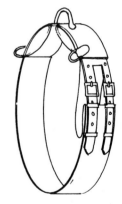

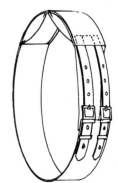

Left: The Arch roller in place.

Below: Two types of roller. The Arch or Anti-cast roller is illustrated top.

bright color. They are sometimes known as Fly Sheets, because of their use in summer on stabled horses to keep off dust and flies.

The New Zealand Blanket is made of sailcloth or waterproof cloth, lined with wool. It may be kept in place with surcingles or leg straps, although the well shaped, true New Zealand Blankets have only leg straps. New Zealanders devised these blankets to enable horses to remain out in the fields through the winter.

Rollers, of which there are many different kinds, are designed solely to keep blankets in place. It is essential they put no pressure on the spine, especially on a horse with prominent withers. For this reason, the Arch or Anti-cast roller is popular with most people, since there is no chance of any pressure falling on the spine. Leather rollers are the most expensive, but the easiest to keep clean and the longest lasting. The cheapest type is the plain jute roller which has one or two straps. Those with two are preferable for keeping blankets in place.

Buying a Horse

If it seems strange to discuss the business of actually buying a horse or pony after we have already talked about their care, it is as well to remember that horses are valuable, living animals which need a lot of knowledgeable attention. No one should own their own horse or pony until they are thoroughly conversant with all the ins and outs of that attention. Having said that, I would go on to say that there are more pitfalls in the buying of a horse than in anything else connected with our long-faced friend!

The personal-relationship aspect is very important when buying a horse. Not every animal gets on well with every person, and yet it is difficult to assess this in a short space of time. A horse that pleases you initially may not come up to your expectations when you spend more time together.

The physical side is important, too, for there are many ways here in which a horse can be defective. He could well have some problem of which, in all honesty, the owner or breeder has no knowledge. However, horses have to be bought and sold, and the fact that none of us is infallible means that many of us learn the hard way – by our mistakes. The perfect horse, like the perfect person, just doesn't exist and we have to accept that all horses will have "ifs"

about them. An "if" is a horsy term meaning a fault! "*If* he were a little bit faster, he would be a really super horse!"

In the days of grooms and gardeners, the realization of almost every child's dream – to own their own pony – relied on little more than the depth of Father's pocket. Nowadays there are more points to be considered. Can a pony be fitted into a school routine? Is there someone who can look after it in the event of sickness or vacations?

If a prospective owner has little or no horse knowledge, I would advise him to seek expert advice when buying. In any event, two pairs of eyes are better than one. In addition, get a vet to look at any horse you are thinking of buying. The vet should be a horse vet, and not one who specializes in small animals or birds. He will know immediately what to look for and will be able to check and report on the condition of the heart, lungs, feet and eyes as well as to tell you about any basic flaw.

Where to go to buy a horse is always difficult. For the less knowledgeable, auctions should probably be avoided and in any event you are unlikely to want to buy an unbroken youngster.

So first decide what sort of animal will be suitable for the demands you will be making on it. It is no good buying a Thoroughbred or Arab type if you mean to keep it out on grass. In that case, you need a horse which has a thick, protective coat. Decide on the size of horse or pony you are looking for and the age – and then try to find this animal! Don't discard the possibility of going to a dealer. I have found, on the whole, that dealers are no more dishonest than private owners. After

Below: Prospective buyers and sellers survey the horses at a market in Spain.

Below right: The age of a horse can be told by his teeth – by how long they are, how much they slope and the marks on them. The lips should be parted and the teeth viewed from the side to check the angle of the slope.

all, they have a reputation to protect; their trade will depend on recommendations, whereas the one-horse owner is more interested in getting rid of his present incumbrance – that is, a horse he does not want to keep. Alternatively you could try buying a horse from the advertisements in local papers or horsy magazines. But be prepared for journeys to end in disappointment. The most perfect-sounding horse may fall far short of expectations when you see him!

There are many points you should look at, whatever horse you are planning to buy, and possibly the first of these is the feet. They should be well rounded and open, as opposed to narrow and donkey-shaped. This ensures that there is enough room for the bones of the foot to work within the case of the protective wall of the hoof.

The soundness of the heart is important, although this is a point for the vet to check. Lungs are important too, as they govern the athletic ability of the horse. That horses can live and do light work for many years with slightly defective lungs, resulting in some unsoundness in the wind, is true – but there is no point in buying trouble.

Always visit the stable or field where the horse you are thinking of buying is kept, and try to determine if he is easy to handle. Beware of the horse that is all tacked up and ready for you, or that has obviously been recently exercised. If he is kept on grass, arrive in time to see him caught. Don't rush over your inspection of the horse; stand back to look at him first and consider his type and shape. Does he please you? Is he the type of horse you had in mind? Does he stand firmly and squarely on his legs, and do they look capable of carrying you as well as him? Don't just buy a pretty picture.

It is difficult to offer hard and fast rules about conformation, because again so much depends on the demands you will be putting on the horse. Study the chart on the next page and then look out for the following general points. The pasterns should be slightly sloping, but not too long, which denotes a weakness. Upright pasterns jar the whole leg and give an uncomfortable ride. The neck should be strong (but not heavy looking), so that it is able to support the head. The back should not be too long. This is where the horse's strength lies, so avoid a horse whose back resembles a suspension bridge slung between the front and back legs, giving the impression of needing support in the middle! The hind-quarters are essentially the horse's "engine." Powerfully developed quarters indicate that the horse really uses his hind end. If you do not want to show the horse, I don't think it matters if the

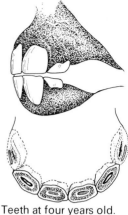

Teeth at four years old.

Teeth at ten years old.

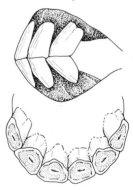

Teeth at fifteen years old.

Left: Tavistock market, the main center for buying and selling Dartmoor ponies.

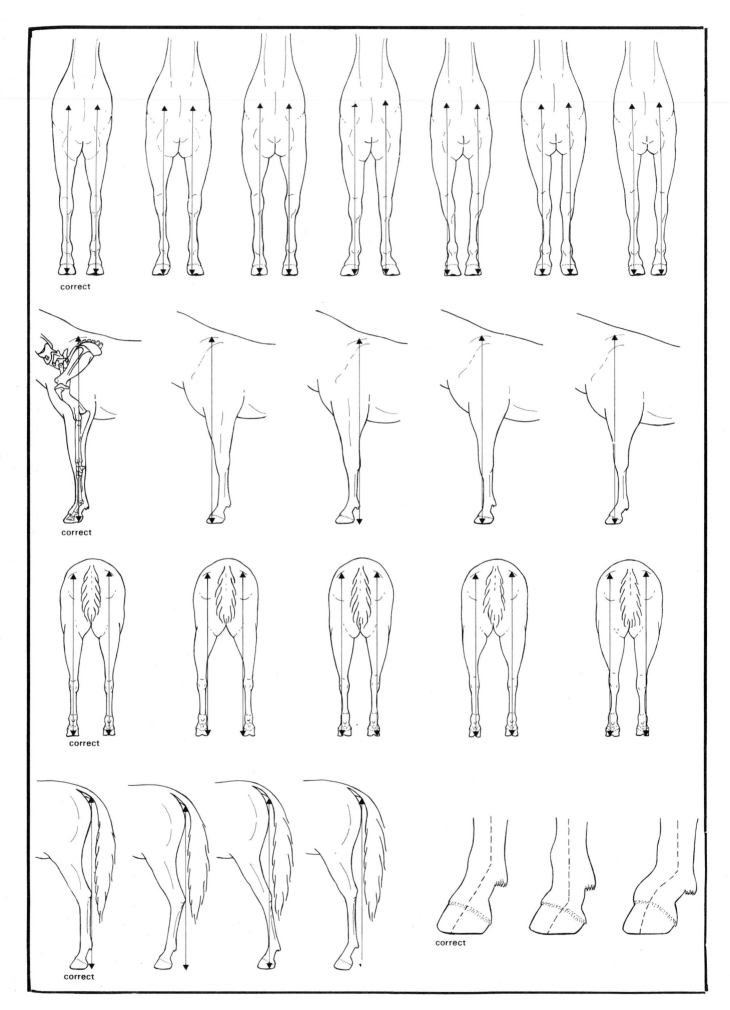

correct

correct

correct

correct

correct

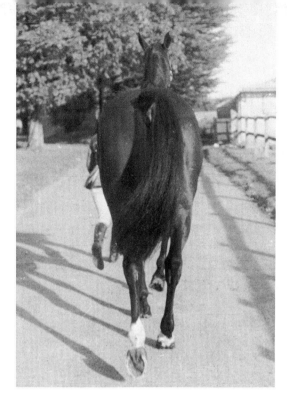

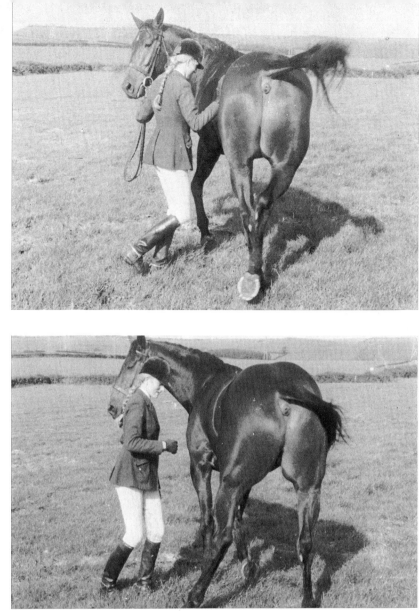

quarters slope slightly towards the tail, as usually this shows some ability to gallop, particularly if it is coupled with a good length from the pin bone to the hock.

Look at the horse's head, in particular his eyes. They will give you the best clue to his character. They should be large, open and kind. If they are small and mean and show lots of white around the edges, don't buy the horse – he will have a mean streak. The head itself should look slightly small in proportion to the rest of the body, and should be well set on the neck. A big, heavy head puts a horse off balance easily and tires him quickly.

When you have completed your inspection, assess whether what you have seen pleases you, and whether you think you would enjoy spending time in this horse's company. If so, ask to see him walked and trotted in hand. Stand right behind him and watch to make sure that he moves his legs in two parallel lines. Note that the feet do not cross over the path of each other, so brushing the fetlocks. This will certainly cause lameness at some stage and in time the joints will enlarge and rheumatism will set in. It is in cases such as these that modern drugs make a horse's life easier, but the purchaser's more difficult, for they could easily mask lameness. Try to make absolutely sure, therefore, that pain killers are not being used for any reason.

Never ride the horse yourself until you have seen him ridden. Then try riding him away from his home, not just around a field he knows well. For the same reason, if you want a horse specifically for jumping, don't just put him over his home fences – he will know them all too well. Ask if you can alter the course or, better still, ask to try him at the next local show. Likewise, prospective eventers need to

be tried across country, and especially through and over water. A calm temperament is particularly necessary for eventers, and is more important than good looks. Temperament is important too in a dressage horse, but then it must be combined with impressive carriage. Driving enthusiasts will be looking for a placid horse if they want to go for quiet country drives; one with a bit more courage and "presence" for competition work.

Any horse nowadays must be quiet in traffic, so ask to see him ridden out, preferably on a fairly busy road. Don't do this yourself until you are sure he is safe. Never rush a decision to buy a horse, and if at all possible take the horse on trial. At one stage this was fairly common practice, but people are rather less willing to allow valuable horses out on trial nowadays. However, any reasonable trial of riding or handling of the horse by the prospective buyer at the owner's premises should be allowed.

The price is obviously a personal question, but remember that the breeder should get a reasonable payment for his efforts and that breeding, rearing and training horses is very expensive. You will get what you pay for!

Above: When buying a horse watch it being walked and trotted towards and away from you on a level surface so you can check its action is correct in either case. Also watch it being turned to see that it moves its hindquarters fully and correctly.

Conformation Chart
Opposite: The pictures on the extreme left show the correct conformation in each case. All the others have obvious faults. Of the three small diagrams on the bottom right, the one on the left is again correct.

Riding for Pleasure

Preparing a pony for a ride is all part of the fun of riding and horsemanship.
Far left: He is collected from the field and led to the stable in a head collar. Left and below: Grooming begins with picking out the feet and sponging the eyes.

Opposite, top left: The bridle and saddle are put on, and he is ready to be ridden.

Hacking and Trail-Riding Vacations

Many people who ride do so just for the sheer pleasure and enjoyment of being on top of, and at one with, a horse. It may be that, having always wanted to ride, they did not have an opportunity to learn until later in life, and so competitive riding has never really interested them in the way it does others.

If you ride just for pleasure, there is no point in riding in bad weather. You cannot enjoy yourself in the cold or wet when you come home frozen half to death or wet through. After all, why make yourself a martyr to something which is supposed to be enjoyable? There are, of course, times when horses have to be exercised in bad weather. Stable-kept horses must be taken out each day, regardless of rain, winds or icy cold, although nobody except the horse is going to enjoy it very much. However well we humans wrap ourselves up in layers of warm clothing, we can still get cold and miserable on horseback. But a horse needs only a light covering or plenty of exercise to keep himself reasonably warm. Covered riding schools have done much to make life pleasanter for "fair-weather" riders. In good weather, however, there is nothing nicer than to go for a two- or three-hour hack, seeing the countryside and building up a partnership with your horse. My favorite time is early on a summer's morning when everything is silent and peaceful and most of the world has yet to awaken to begin the new day.

Whether you are catching a horse from a field or exercising it from the stables, there are certain preparations that have to be made before going out for a ride. The horse's feet must be picked out and ideally his eyes and nostrils will be sponged out too. If you are catching him from the field, catch him in a headcollar so you can tether him while you do these things. A grass-kept pony may need a brush over with the dandy brush before saddling him, to remove patches of dried mud. A stable-kept horse is best groomed or strapped after exercise, when the dust will have risen to the

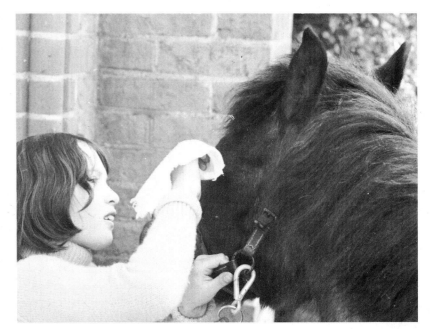

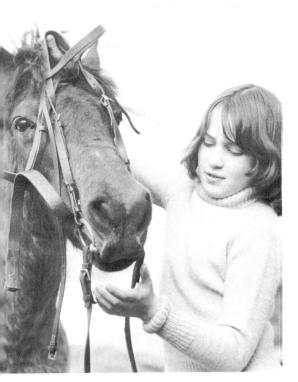

surface of his coat. Once he has been saddled and bridled, the horse will be ready for your ride.

Plan where you are going for your ride before you go, and always start off slowly, ideally at a walk. Remember to check the girths after five minutes or so; they will probably need tightening. If the horse is very fresh and frisky, a good, long, firm trot will steady him down, better than trotting in short bursts, every now and then.

Those of us who live in places where we can ride over farmland or through woods are particularly lucky, for this undoubtedly makes for the most pleasurable hacking. But there is a code of manners which should be strictly adhered to by such riders. If the bridle-path goes through a field of sheep or cattle, just walk quietly, guiding your horse carefully so that he does not startle the stock. That might make one of them move in a hurry, and the others would all start to run, too. Always shut all gates behind you. The damage and trouble you can cause by not latching a gate properly is enormous. Suppose a bull escaped on to the roads, or a herd of cows trampled through a cornfield. Not a happy thought! When you meet other riders, always slow down and be courteous. They may have young animals with them, which would be upset if you dashed past. In any event, it's good manners to pass the time of day – and one day you may be glad of one another's help. Likewise, slow right down if you pass people out walking – don't spoil their enjoyment by galloping past.

Always be particularly careful and thoughtful when riding along the road. Particularly on main roads (which it is actually best to avoid if at all possible), it is advisable to go no faster than a walk. Their hard surfaces make them especially slippery and the vast amount of speed-crazy traffic has made them unpleasant places to be with horses. When riding along the road, keep your horse well under control and ride on the same side as the on-going traffic. If cars do slow down when they go past, thank the drivers. It may encourage them to repeat

Above: Hand signals should be given clearly from horseback when riding on roads, to warn motorists of intended action.

Below: Riding with others is companionable and pleasant.

113

their kind action to other riders. If riding with others, ride in single file along the road. You should give clear hand signals if you mean to turn left or right on the road just as if you were riding a bicycle.

Riding with other people is fun and companionable, but choose the people you ride with carefully. After all, you will both enjoy it more if you want the same things from a ride; if you want a gentle, pleasant hack, don't ride with people who want to gallop and jump all over the place. Riding on your own is equally pleasant, however, although it is wise to leave word with someone at home as to which way you are going, just in case you meet with an accident. If you need help, and no one knows where you have gone, it could be a long time before you are found.

Don't bring back a horse dripping with sweat. Walk for some way at the end of a ride to cool him down first. If you are going to turn the horse out in the field, and he is slightly warm, providing it is not a very cold day, he will probably get down and roll and then dry himself off naturally. If you bring a horse wet into the stable, either from sweat or from the rain, he must be dried off either by rubbing him down or covering him with straw and putting a blanket on top. Remember that is a sure way for a horse to catch cold if he is just left to dry off in a stable, where he can't move around to keep warm.

Some people have had their first introduction to riding by going on a trail ride. Many trail-

riding establishments use safe, reliable horses, often of sure-footed, native breeds. As the idea is to explore and enjoy the countryside, and many of the riders are novices, the pace is slow and steady. Most establishments give some basic instruction in horsemanship, and many encourage riders to help look after their horses. Trail rides are usually conducted under the supervision of a group leader, who ensures that everyone is comfortable and happy on their horse. To me these outings mean long, slow rides through glorious open country with wonderful views, interspersed perhaps with

Above: A stop for a chat with a companion.

Below: Riding by the sea and in the shallow waters is enjoyable for horse and rider.

shady rides through beautiful forests and woodlands.

For those who want a bit more dash in their riding, there are many establishments operating on flatter country, where the going is safer for faster gaits. At these places the rides will not be so long, for, if ridden faster and harder, the horses get correspondingly more tired. Many establishments specializing in riding vacations plan a busy curriculum of "horsy" interest. Besides hacking in the countryside, many offer lessons and clinics in the morning or afternoon as well. Or you may be expected to help look after the horses. There may be brood mares and foals to help with or to watch being handled. In any event, there is so much to learn about horses that there is never a dull moment in a busy stable – whatever its particular specialty may be.

Riding vacations have become an excellent way for us all to explore other countries, for there are many places in the world where they are now well established. In the British Isles, "trekking" vacations are popular in such places as the Scottish Highlands, the Welsh Mountains, in Ireland, Exmoor and Dartmoor and across the superb north-country moors. The US and Canada have summer camps from which riders go out all day to explore the Rockies, perhaps, or one of the national parks. There are many

Left: When riding with others, keep a reasonable distance between you and the horse in front.

Below: On vacation in a horse-drawn carriage on the peaceful roads of the Jura Mountains in Switzerland.

other vacation riding camps in the US too, in particular for children, where both Western and European styles of riding are practiced. Competitions are arranged within the camp or are sometimes arranged with another camp that is close by.

Most vacation camps have superb facilities for other sports, too, such as canoeing and swimming as well as a wide variety of popular games.

Many countries in Europe offer marvellous riding vacations. France, Belgium, Hungary, Italy, Austria, Switzerland, Spain, Luxembourg, Germany and Bavaria, and the countries of Scandinavia all advertise riding holidays of various types. Iceland runs trail rides using their hardy little native ponies throughout the country – in their own words, "on the fertile hills of the west, the wide open spaces of the interior, to see the boiling pools of Geysire and Hveravellir, on the great lava fields, or by

Below: A cross-country pony ride in Austria.

Above: Riding along a beach in Tunisia.

the extraordinary rock formations at Myvatn." They stress both the variety of holidays available, from day rides to genuine camping trips when you can ride for several days, and also the extremely relaxed and easy-going atmosphere that prevails over all.

Denmark's specialty in riding holidays is to offer trail rides combined with accommodations at local farmhouses. In addition, there is an organized center for western riding which is in Jutland.

Vacations in Switzerland and Austria are also particularly interesting. In Switzerland riding schools all over the country offer a variety of activities, from short guided hacks to all-day trail riding, and from elementary instruction to advanced courses in dressage techniques. In addition, the Automobile Club of Switzerland runs trips through the Swiss Jura in horse-drawn carriages. The trips last eight days and the nights are spent at comfortable inns en route, where the horses are looked after, so the "gipsies" can set off fresh each morning. Although these trips are very carefully planned, with pre-selected routes that are signposted, the vacationers spend their days driving along on their own, unaccompanied by any official guide.

Austria also offers a wide range of holidays in the saddle, including trail riding or lessons at one of their many riding establishments. They have the added attraction for the horse lover of being the home of the Spanish Riding School in Vienna, where public performances are given regularly throughout the tourist season. Visitors can tour the stables where the horses are kept and also attend the training sessions, when the magnificent Lippizana horses are taught their intricate and advanced paces. It is also possible when in Austria to go to one

of the Federal Studs, such as the one at Piber where the Lippizanas are raised, or the Federal Stallion Center, where more than 100 stallions of such Austrian breeds as the Haflinger are kept. The markets, shows and sales, organized at a number of places by Austria's Norik-horse breeding association, are also of interest to the horse-loving tourist.

Riding outings are organized in France throughout the country, from the craggy coastal area of Brittany to the wild mountains of Savoie. Riding establishments in the Camargue use the famous white horses of the area as their mounts. The famous haute école Cavalry School, the Cadre Noir, at Saumur is open to visitors in a similar way to the Spanish Riding School of Vienna.

In Belgium and Luxembourg most riding establishments are in the lovely Ardennes, and in Germany the main areas for riding are the Black Forest, Bavaria and the Rhineland.

Vacation riding opportunities are in no way neglected in Spain and Portugal. In Spain the visitor can ride the magnificent Andalusian horses in the region of Andalusia, or enjoy riding along the beaches of Catalonia and the Costa Brava. There are various establishments in the Algarve in southern Portugal where horses may be hired for rides by the hour or by the day, and Lisbon has a few riding schools that specialize in tourist arrangements. It is also possible in Portugal for one to visit some of the State-run studs and horse sales, which are particularly interesting.

Below: The snow-capped mountains provide a superb backdrop to riders in Switzerland.

Below: Riding through the sun-lit trees in Belgium.

One of the most enjoyable and exhilarating places for anyone to ride is along the beach by the sea. Besides the pleasure of being far away from roads and "civilization," it is also an extremely beneficial place for a horse to be exercised. Hard sand makes the going easy and pleasant, and, if you include splashing through the shallow waves in your ride, the sea water is very good for a horse's legs.

Riding or indeed plodding along in a horse-drawn carriage is not the only way of spending vacation time involved with our equine friend. Many people further their interest in some particular aspect of equestrianism by attending one of the many special courses available. You could learn to ride western style, or side-saddle or have instruction in how to break-in horses or how to drive them. You might want to go to a farm and learn about working with Heavy Horses, just because their power and magnificence have always fascinated you. You might have a new pony that you wish to show, so one of the showing classes would help you, or you could go to a breeding course if you want to get your mare in foal. All sorts of courses are available in countries all over the world to those who want them. You can discover more about these courses by writing to the National Horse Organization of the country you wish to visit.

Left: Riding across England's rugged Dartmoor country.

Below: A welcome respite for these tough little Icelandic ponies.

Pony and Riding Clubs

One of the best ways to further an interest and learn more about all aspects of horsemanship is to join a nearby branch of the thousands of pony and riding clubs in existence. It is also a congenial way to meet people with a similar interest and thus to make new friends.

The Pony Club movement has spread all over the world with flourishing branches in England, Australia, New Zealand, the US, Canada, France, even Zambia, to name just some. It was begun initially in England many years ago by a group of "horsy" people who ran it on a volunteer basis. The idea behind it was to help and encourage farmers' children in their riding, out of gratitude to the farmers for allowing the various Hunts to ride over their land. The help was then extended to any other children who wanted to ride, but whose parents were either too busy or not sufficiently interested to assist them. The children were taught how to care for their ponies and school them over fences, and a number of adults volunteered to look after the children out hunting. That is how each Pony Club chapter in England became affiliated with a Hunt.

From this small beginning, the Pony Club grew into a large and highly organized institution, which has accurately been described as one of the world's great youth movements. It publishes an excellent book on equitation and pony care which is compiled by a group of eminent riders and which is continually being revised. I have old copies which are a quarter the size of the latest edition.

Above and left: The Pony Club exists in countries all over the world. Young riders get together for lessons, games and social gatherings.

The best way to describe the motives and aims of the Pony Club is to quote verbatim from their pamphlet. It says: "It is represented in no less than 22 countries and has a membership exceeding 75,000. Its object is to encourage young people to ride and enjoy all kinds of sport connected with horses and riding. To provide instruction in riding and horsemastership and to instil in members the proper care of their animals. To promote the highest ideals of sportsmanship, citizenship, and loyalty, thereby cultivating strength of character and self discipline. Its membership is open to anyone under 21 years of age. Ordinary members consist of boys and girls who have not attained the age of 17 years. Associate Members are those over 17 years. Membership terminates on attaining 21 years."

The Pony Club runs a series of proficiency tests for its members, beginning with the "D" standard and progressing up to the "A," which is very advanced. These tests are universally recognized and must be conducted by qualified examiners. Members are tested both on their riding ability and their practical knowledge of care of their pony and stable management. But perhaps even more important as the mainstay of the Pony Club movement are the clinics sponsored by each chapter regularly during school vacations. At these, riders are given instruction by volunteer teachers and, provided of course membership fees to the chapter have been paid, there is no extra charge. In

addition to the tests and rallies, the Pony Club organizes a number of other events – gymkhanas, films, demonstrations, lectures, visits to some of the large horse shows, and in most areas there is also a one-week summer camp to which Pony Club members may take their ponies for seven days' fairly intensive instruction, not to mention a great deal of exciting fun and games!

In the US, as well as a thriving Pony Club, there is also a horse section of the "4 H," which stands for Health, Heart, Hands and Head. Just like the Pony Club, it encourages young riders by running sessions on stable management

Above top: A riding club receiving instruction on a course at the riding school in Stoneleigh, England.

Above: Members of the Pony Club practice a balance exercise.

Right: Pony Club mounted games.

Right: Pony Club mounted games.

and riding, as well as giving demonstrations and lectures on anything connected with horses. It is all very informal and friendly, and although they do have some competitions, the competitive element is kept to a minimum. Quite popular among 4H members is what is called "the back yard pony." It is almost invariably well cared for and often kept in the yard behind the house! Interest often seems to be a family affair and parents and children will go off on their horses or ponies for daytime excursions and adventures. The Pony Club, incidentally, was introduced into America by Mrs. Barbara Bristow Taylor, an amazingly energetic lady who loved horses and people.

As membership in the Pony Club terminates when riders have reached the grand old age of 21, most areas also have Riding Clubs. These are almost an extension of the Pony Clubs and are run in much the same way, with meetings catering to all types of riders. Besides instruction in riding, their calendar of events includes such things as picnics, general outings and "get-togethers," visits to Hunt Kennels, horse shows and dressage events. Then there are also evening "socials" comprising lectures, films, shows, inter-club quizzes, talks by equestrian personalities, parties and dances. Most Riding Clubs hold their own horse shows or other competitive events, such as hunter trials. In general these events are not of such a high standard nor are they as keenly competitive as the open shows, which of course makes them more fun and also more encouraging to those people who are basically riding for enjoyment and their love of horses.

Gymkhanas and Mounted Games

Gymkhanas, with the myriad of fun-games played on horseback, are often thought of as typically English, but not only are they an equestrian event that takes place in many other countries, the origin of mounted games goes much further back than the staging of the first gymkhana. Mounted games in various forms have been part of man's riding life for thousands of years and probably began as a means of both testing and improving his skill and accuracy

Below: Pony Club members are taught practical stable management as well as riding technique.

121

in hunting and warfare. Nowadays, mounted police and cavalry still practice various mounted games and include a number of them on such occasions as the famous Royal Tournament held in London. The aim is to show the rider's accuracy at performing unusual tasks on horseback and his skill at controlling his horse throughout these somewhat unconventional maneuvers. This is precisely what is displayed at gymkhanas, too. Just as the fastest and most accurate combination of horse and rider will win at the Royal Tournament, so the most proficient child with the most aggressive pony will win at gymkhana games.

Gymkhana events and mounted games have been included in this chapter rather than under "Competitive Riding" for they are, and always should be, more in the realm of fun than evoking any great feeling of competition. Of course, there is an element of competition – winning is bound to be more rewarding than losing. But even if the events themselves first came about through training for more serious matters, they are now primarily intended as pleasure, relaxation and entertainment.

Any pony can be trained to play gymkhana games. Some ponies love it every bit as much as their riders. Others are more unwilling starters, but can be useful for teaching a somewhat more anxious child and giving him confidence. I have had great fun with children and ponies at gymkhanas and enjoy nothing better than seeing those happy, laughing faces. An ideal gymkhana pony will be one that is small and aggressive. Very many ponies do not have the second attribute, but with patience can still be taught to compete more than adequately. It is important, though, that the pony is small enough to vault on (although this should not be attempted initially while the pony is moving fast). The best way to train a pony for gymkhana games is to begin with the commonest of all games – the bending race. This means weaving alternately to the left and right of five or six poles placed in a straight line, turning around the end one and weaving back again.

To begin training, place five or six posts or upturned buckets in a line, about five strides apart. These act as markers. Begin by walking the pony down the line, keeping as close to the markers as possible. Talk to him, use your legs and weight correctly and give with your hands. Turn him as closely as possible around the end marker and pat him when you get back to the beginning, as a reward. Do this about six times until he begins to understand what is required of him. Then start slow trotting along the line, sitting well into your saddle so that you can use your legs and hands to the greatest effect. Press against the pony's side with your legs, con-

An energetic start to a race at a gymkhana.

tinuously, but gently. Make much of your pony – a few nuts in your pocket offered as a reward can help considerably in making a pony understand what it is you want him to do! When you are trotting happily up and down the line, try quickening the pace to the finishing line. Take several days for this training, and don't try going any faster until you really feel the pony is virtually doing it on his own, with you acting as little more than a passenger. If properly trained, most skilled gymkhana ponies will enjoy themselves as much as their riders.

I suggest that you practice two or three gymkhana games a day for no more than half an hour. Some of the races will cause trouble initially – games which involve carrying water, for example, as most horses hate having cold water slopped down their shoulders! The sack race can be another problem one. It involves a rider jumping along in a sack while leading his pony and, understandably, some ponies get very apprehensive at this strange, legless thing bobbing along by the side of them. When doing this race, remember to bunch the sack well up around your waist. If you let it trail behind you on the ground, your pony may step on it, in which case you are extremely likely to fall flat on your face!

Training ponies for gymkhana games is no different from any other kind of training, in

Above right: A good turn in a gymkhana game. The rider is riding without stirrups for speed in mounting and dismounting, but is in perfect balance with the pony.

Right: The Prince Philip mounted games – finales of which are held each year at the Horse of the Year Show in Wembley, England.

123

that you should progress slowly and quietly all the time, always showing him that there is nothing to fear, and never doing one thing for so long that he gets bored. The more slow practice a pony has, the better, because it allows him to get the idea of it all and also helps in maintaining his balance and perfecting his turns. Too much kicking, pulling and shouting on the rider's part will only worry a pony and soon takes his mind off his work.

The highlight of the gymkhana season in England comes about with the Prince Philip Cup at the Horse of the Year Show, held each year in October. This first began in 1957 after HRH Prince Philip had suggested that inter-branch Pony Club gymkhana games should be run. Competitions were held in defined areas and the first two teams from these went on to regional semi-finals. The four winning teams to emerge from these competed for the supreme award at the Horse of the Year Show. It is an event which always stirs up tremendous excitement in the spectators, who realize it to be of a more frivolous nature than the rest of the Show. Since its inception, The Pony Club teams that reached the finals have twice been sent to give exhibitions in Paris and Amsterdam, where they have been greeted with the same enthusiasm from the crowd.

Gymkhanas in general, and the Prince Philip Cup in particular, have come in for much adverse criticism. People say that the riders' aids are too rough; that many of the children are far too big and heavy for the ponies they

ride. Of course, over-excitement and disappointment on the part of the young rider can lead to adverse handling of the pony, but I would say this is an exception rather than the rule. On the point about the ponies being too small, it must be said that most gymkhana ponies are tough little animals, which are often descended from hardy native breeds. With such blood in

Above: A cossack leans right off his horse to retrieve something from the ground.

Below: Mounted police participating in a tent-pegging competition.

their veins, they can carry much more weight than their size would suggest.

It always gives me great pleasure when I see these little ponies being exercised around the outside rings at the Horse of the Year Show, trotting impudently alongside the grand show horse and pony and the big international show jumper. Of course, at this level the whole thing has become more competitive, and it is important to choose the right type of pony for the riders. In my opinion, the really light-boned ponies are not suitable for they would not be able to stand up to the rough and tumble of sharp turns and quick stops. It is fair to say that gymkhana ponies should resemble miniature polo ponies, for much the same demands will be put on them as those in polo playing.

These games certainly do promote great pride in the various branches of the Pony Club. And a place in the final teams can give parents some reward for all the time and effort they have put into transporting children and ponies to practices. It gives a child with an average pony a chance to show himself as an important member of his Pony Club chapter and can also turn a not-so valuable pony into a more sought-after animal. I would agree with some critics, however, who say that not enough attention is paid to the slower work needed for perfecting turns and training the pony properly, and I believe that all new games should be taught slowly and patiently. A very great amount of the groundwork should be done at the trot, even after a team has been picked and all the riders are fairly experienced at the many different gymkhana games.

With the spread of the Pony Club into so many countries of the world, the popularity of gymkhana games has spread too, but, as mentioned earlier, mounted games are practiced at a number of other times and events. In South America, where ponies have long been of prime importance for work on the ranches, mounted games have been played for centuries as a form of relaxation. It is no coincidence that the best polo ponies in the world are bred and trained in South America, where precision turns and the ability to stop and start at a moment's notice are all part of a rancher's daily demands on his horse. Polo is itself a mounted game that has been played all over the world for years, and I shall talk more about it in a moment. There are, however, various more light-hearted versions of it, such as "cushion" polo, which should nevertheless only be attempted by fairly competent riders. Two teams take part and a cushion or similar object is passed from one to another, while the opposing team attempts to take possession of it. In some countries, a game similar to polo is played except that it could be likened to "horseback Lacrosse" rather than "horseback hockey." Players carry sticks with nets on them in which the ball is scooped off the ground and then carried, or passed on to another player. Theoretically, the ball is kept in the air rather than on

A cowboy ropes a calf in the standard event of calf-roping held at rodeos.

125

the ground as in polo. This is popular in Australia and the USSR, particularly in Georgia, where it is known as Tskhenburti. It is much less demanding on the horses than polo, as it is not so fast and exacting and is also played in a smaller area.

Another kind of mounted game which originated in Russia is that of pushball. It involves pushing a huge soft ball over the goal line of an opposing team, which tries to stop it. Pushball is a game that is very popular in various other countries, the Netherlands in particular.

Polo is a very old mounted game that originated in Persia and spread to China and India. It was popularized in England during the nineteenth century by cavalry officers who had played it in India. It is now popular in many areas of the world – the US and Argentina in particular – and mention has already been made of the superb polo ponies produced and trained on the Argentine ranches.

Polo enjoyed particular popularity in England in the early part of this century, one of the centers of play being the English Polo Club at Hurlingham. This club brought in a ruling that no pony should measure more than 14.2 hands high. There were many people who made a business of breeding polo ponies. The usual practice was to breed small Thoroughbred stallions to heavier type pony mares, not necessarily native breeds – often "milk-float" ponies would be used. These were sturdy ponies which were able to pull the milk wagons from the farm down to the road for collection by the milk trucks, and their strength and stamina, when mixed with the fineness and speed of the Thoroughbred, produced all the right qualities for a polo pony. When teams began to come over from the US and Argentina, however, the British-bred ponies proved no match for their superior mounts, and it became fashionable to import Argentine-bred polo ponies. After the Second World War the height limit was dropped, but the popularity of the Argentine ponies remained, as indeed it still does today throughout the polo-playing countries of the world.

Another of the standard events of a rodeo is bronco riding. A cowboy has to remain seated, usually for about ten seconds. Marks are awarded for the rider's style and according to how hard the horse bucks.

Polo is credited with being the fastest team game in the world, which in part accounts for why it is so expensive to play competitively. The traditional time for each full game makes it essential to have at least two ponies per person per game, for one could not maintain the gruelling pace. In fact, in some instances two ponies are not enough, for the game is divided into short periods known as "chukkas" and it is generally considered that no pony can play more than two chukkas a day. In most matches there are four chukkas, but the larger contests have five or six.

The essence of the game is to hit a small ball with a long bamboo mallet while sitting astride a galloping pony, with the aim of scoring goals. Two teams participate with four players on

Above: A modern mock jousting tournament. Here a rider, his lance held out parallel to the ground, charges at the quintain, an object mounted on a post.

Left: Polo is a popular mounted sport the world over.

each side. Each player's role is defined according to the position in which he plays, but basically a team works together to prevent the opposing side from scoring. There are a variety of recognized strokes, which have to be well mastered before anyone can attempt to play competitively.

The rules of the game of polo have been devised with safety as the most important factor and any infringement of them results in a penalty.

Success inevitably depends on good teamwork and co-operation. As may be imagined the skill and horsemanship of the players, combined with the great speed of the game, make polo an extremely exciting and exhilarating game to watch.

Mounted games of various types are "played" or undertaken in the rodeo competitions held in North America and Australia, and often a number of typical "gymkhana-type" games will be included in the program of events. Most of the events at rodeos test the day-to-day skill that the cowhands or ranchers employ in their regular work on the ranches. These include such things as riding wild, bucking horses; roping steers; riding bulls and "bulldogging" – a dangerous "sport" involving galloping alongside a steer until the rider hurls himself from the saddle, gripping the steer's horns as he does so, and trying to wrestle him to the ground. Australian rodeos also include an event known as camp-drafting, which means a rider separating a steer out from a large herd and then galloping it around a marked course, using his horse to keep it going in the correct direction. Rodeos are extremely colorful and exciting spectacles that capture the unique atmosphere of everyday life as still experienced on the huge cattle ranches.

Training a Young Horse

As we have seen previously, the role of the horse in most societies around the world has changed over the years. Where once it was the main form of transportation and an important aid in agriculture, it is now used mainly for pleasure. But even in this capacity, a horse must still be trained, for, like a dog, or any domestic animal, it must be kept in its place and taught who is master. Most animals can size up the humans with whom they come into contact and will take advantage of them whenever they get the chance. A horse is no different, and yet if you consider how little time we spend with our horses during the course of the day, and then compare this with the great deal more time domestic dogs or cats spend in human company, it makes the fact that they work and cooperate with us at all even more remarkable. A horse therefore has intelligence – not a great brain, perhaps, but a wonderful memory, and it is because of this and his association of ideas that we can train him to obey our commands.

By and large, when training horses for riding, in whatever sphere of equestrianism, it is generally and universally accepted that the best way to go about it is following a carefully planned, patient and progressive procedure. Some people tackle the job in a different way, maybe for reasons of speed or expediency. What could be termed the "Western style" of breaking, for example, appears to aim at making a horse obey his human master by breaking

Above: Foals should be handled from a very early age to get them used to their human masters.

Below: A mare and foal standing peacefully in the stable.

his spirit. The cowboys, gauchos or stockmen (depending on which part of the world they come from) will single out a horse from a herd with a view to using him to ride. First he is tied securely to a post and, being used to roaming free, he obviously tries to free himself. He is left to fight it out, until he eventually stands still through sheer exhaustion. Then a saddle and bridle, usually of the bitless type, are put on him. The rider mounts and the battle commences again, as the horse is let loose. He is encouraged to gallop away so that he becomes even more tired. But he is pushed on and ridden hard, until he acquiesces to his rider's command because he is too exhausted to do anything else. We are told that after three days the horse will be quiet enough to ride.

I tried something along the lines of this method when breaking an old, wild, unbroken Welsh pony. We were able to hold her while we put a Western saddle on her back (Western saddles are easier to sit into on a bucking horse than conventional European saddles). My daughter got up – cowboy fashion – and "bucked" her. We did this for three days running, at which point I could see no improvement, so we abandoned the idea and broke the pony by the usual methods.

There are other rather crude methods of breaking, such as driving a horse or pony into a bog and mounting it there so that it can't do much except flounder about, thus exhausting itself. Quite apart from the fact that one would have no hope of keeping a sensitive mouth in a horse with such methods, there can be no hope of building up mutual trust and respect, which must be done if a happy partnership is to occur and remain in the future.

Following the more widely practiced methods, then, if we know the background of the young horse we are about to train, it will help a lot in understanding him and his reactions. A nervous animal is more difficult to handle than a placid one who has a confident outlook. Interestingly, these attitudes can lead to different situations. The nervous animal will probably be more sensitive and will develop quite remarkably when correctly and kindly handled, while our confident friend may develop an obstinate streak showing wilfulness and even defiance.

There are two main categories into which young horses fall, although there are marked variations within each category. There are:

1. Horses that have been handled from birth as the result of planned breeding.

2. Horses that have run wild, having been bred as nature intended. These have probably been herded only at intervals during their lives to change pastures, to be weaned or to be sold.

Early Handling

Early handling of the first group to start building up confidence is discussed earlier. By the time you are ready to start their training they should be quiet enough to handle and lead in hand. The second category have to be taught to be handled and gentled because their only reaction to humans will be one of fear. The first step will be to gain the horse's confidence sufficiently to put on a head collar at least, so that there is some way of controlling its movements. This animal will presumably have been delivered to you in a truck or trailer and will be very frightened. With a few people to help, you will have to more or less herd it into a box stall, before work can commence in earnest!

There are many ways of taming a horse. In

Above: A halter can be placed on a "wild" pony by using a crooked stick. The rope of the halter is held in the other hand.

Below: One way of putting a head collar on a nervous horse. The nose of the collar is inside a bucket of food. As he puts his nose into the bucket, the strap is pulled gently over his head and buckled.

my opinion, the slower the better from every point of view. The ideal would be to spend at least three hours a day in the box stall with the newcomer just standing, talking quietly, offering grass from the hand, and trying to touch the nose, neck and quarters. (Remember that the animal is probably on the defensive and its hind legs can flash out with lightning speed and force.) Even supposing you have this amount of time and patience, progress may be very slow, so it may be necessary to revert to firmer measures to speed things along.

First withhold all water, except that offered by you in a bucket. Stand flicking the water with your hand so that the horse knows it is there if he can pluck up enough courage to come to you for it. To him, you are a two-legged monster who has taken him away from all the things he knew and understood and instead plunged him into new and frightening surroundings. However, his instinct for survival is stronger than his fear. Hunger is not so pressing as thirst, so water is more important than food, but you can also tempt him with fresh grass or leaves, which he will have been used to and will recognize as being tastier than hay. The first snatch of food or drink taken from you is the first step won. From there, keep progressing just as slowly and quietly, until you can touch and stroke his forehead and neck as he drinks from the bucket you are holding out to him.

When you are able to touch his head and rub behind his ears with him offering no fear or resistance, you can think of putting a head collar on him. This is best accomplished by putting the nose of the head collar inside the top of the bucket of water. Then carefully, while talking in a soothing voice and caressing his face, work the strap of it up behind his ears.

Balance the bucket (with very little water) on your knee or get the pony used to drinking from a bucket on the ground. Be prepared for it to take several attempts to get the head collar accepted. Once this is achieved, try leading him about, first in the stall, then outside. After this training, the next steps are the same for both our categories of animal.

Of all the virtues a trainer of horses must possess, besides patience, the greatest is foresight or intuition, so that he can be "one jump ahead" and anticipate the next move of his equine pupil. In addition he must have kindness, firmness and, not least, self control. Horses can be exasperating, but it is essential that respect and confidence are not lost by outbursts of temper. Horses have highly developed memories and consciences and, given sensible handling and training, will know when they have transgressed. Correction by the voice is usually enough to bring them into line.

The *Breaking Cavesson* now takes over from the head collar for actual breaking and schooling. This is a strong piece of equipment, to which a lunge rein may be attached. It is built to withstand the sudden plunges that any youngster "worth his salt" will make either from the sheer joy of living or from trying his strength against his trainer's control. Having gained his confidence, however, it is essential for us as the trainer to teach the horse that it is we who have control, and that however much he wishes to free himself we are not going to let him get away. It helps to begin this stage of schooling in an enclosed space, so that the horse has a feeling of being confined. This will diminish his desire to pull away and, even if he does get free, he won't be able to travel far.

Lessons on the Lunge

Now the horse must be taught to *lunge*. The object of work on the lunge is to teach him three main things:
1. To answer the trainer's voice.
2. Self Control.
3. Free Forward Movement.
   Let us look at each in turn:
   The Voice, as previously discussed, is one of the aids of riding, the importance of which is not always recognized. A rider's hands and legs can be contradictory if wrongly used, but the voice can never err. Nobody is going to say "walk" when they mean "canter." Thus a horse can depend on the voice and its instructions throughout his life.

The breaking cavesson.

Above: The breaking cavesson in position on a horse's head.

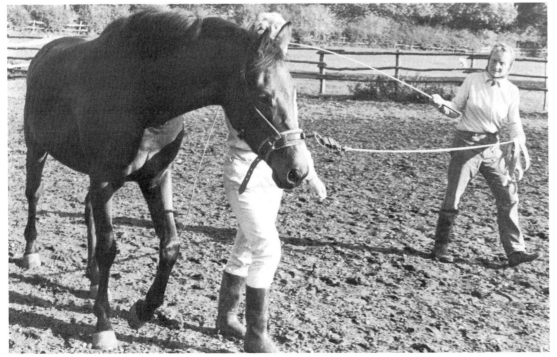

Left: Early lessons on the lunge. An assistant at the horse's head leads him around, while the trainer stands in the middle giving clear instructions.

130

Self Control could also be described as obedience to the wishes of the trainer on the ground and later to the wishes of a rider. It means curbing a horse's natural desire, particularly at this stage, to think of other things or to play at the wrong time. We do not want a cowed horse, who has no interest or pleasure in his work and no zest for life, but we must aim to have a controlled one who works in harmony with his rider.

Free Forward Movement means developing a nice, swinging movement of the back at all gaits. Suppleness of the back may be recognized by the swing of the horse's tail. Free Forward Movement is a term that one hears used much more today than when I was young, which may possibly be a result of riding in more enclosed spaces now. In the old days, horses moved forward naturally, the open surroundings encouraging them and making them less bored with schooling work. Riding has always been done on the continent of Europe in enclosed spaces, such as covered schools, but these have existed in England only in recent years. To my mind, this is why dressage expertise in England is behind that of other countries.

Undoubtedly the best way to teach a horse to go forward is on the lunge. He is taken to the schooling area and then worked in a circle around the trainer. It helps to have an assistant at his head leading him, while the trainer stands in the middle of the circle. Instructions are given by the trainer at all times.

The trainer holds the lunge rein in the leading hand (i.e., if circling counter-clockwise, in the left hand), and a long training whip is held high in the other. The whip follows the quarters, helping to position the horse on the circle. Its use is all important, for the horse should respect it, but not be afraid of it. Should he stop, it can be used to touch his tail; and if he comes in towards the trainer, so cutting the circle, the whip can be shaken at his shoulder or given a slight flick. Similarly, the voice commands the

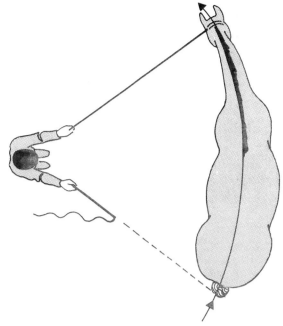

Left: The correct bend of a horse on the lunge moving in a circle. Note the V-shape formed by the instructor's arms holding the lunge rein and the whip.

same respect but also encourages, and each individual trainer will have his own favorite words to give the horse instruction and encouragement.

First lessons on the lunge are best given in the corner of a corral or ring, as two sides of the work area are then fenced. Although a really small area – say about 11 yards × 11 yards (10 meters × 10 meters) – may be fenced on all sides, it will be too small after the first few lessons. If we are trying to teach Free Forward Movement, there must be enough room to move freely! More space will give a horse the impression of freedom and the desire to move forward when encouraged to do so. When the horse will walk, trot and stop at your command with your assistant at his head, you can dispense with the assistant and begin to increase the size of the circle. In fact, as you develop obedience from the horse on the lunge, it is a good idea to work in an open field, weather and the state of the ground permitting. Be sensible, though; no good can come of plowing through deep mud, which will only tire man and beast, and

Below: Still early in the training. The assistant has been dispensed with, but the trainer is lunging the horse in the corner of the field, using two sides of a fence to confine him.

Above: The breaking roller is introduced as a preliminary to a saddle. Elastic side reins are attached to the side rings of the cavesson and the dees of the roller to start getting the correct position of the head.

puts far too much strain on a young horse. Working around an open field makes it somewhat harder for the trainer to keep control, but then we are eventually going to ride the horse outside the enclosed space, so it is necessary practice.

As you feel you are getting the horse's attention and have established a reasonable amount of control on the lunge, you can introduce a roller – or, if you prefer, a saddle – onto his back. Let him first inspect the object well. Let him smell it and investigate it. Then pull it on his neck near his withers, just putting it on and taking it off several times. Finally slide it back into position just behind the withers. The next step is a controversial one. I personally always attach a breast plate around the horse's chest (a piece of string will do equally well) to keep the roller forward in case I do not get the girth tight enough to keep it in place. Should the roller be allowed to slip backwards into the horse's flank, he is likely to get really frightened. In fact, he can become so distraught with fear that you may well lose all control, and even in the small, confined space of a covered school he can hurt himself. The other train of thought on this matter, however, is that a breast plate can be dangerous should the roller slip and get tangled in the horse's legs. I have never found this to happen, while I have often seen the roller slip backwards.

I like to have the assistance of one other person when first putting on the roller. One person holds the head, taking and patting the horse to reassure him, while the other puts on the roller and does up the girth fairly tightly. Then the horse is asked to walk on. Some will accept the tight feeling at the walk, but will buck at a trot or canter. Others will explode at once, trying to rid themselves of this nasty pressure around their rib cage. A few arch their backs, lowering their heads and swinging from

side to side, being what was called "saddle proud" in the old days. If the horse is already used to wearing blankets, he will probably take it as a matter of course. I must say I like to see a horse put up a bit of a fight. One feels he has a little bit extra about him – courage, maybe, but then I was brought up with the idea that one day the horse will test his strength against that of the trainer. One day he would inevitably say, "Why should I?" and as the old breakers would say, "Better to have the fight sooner than later!"

As a saddle is more difficult to keep in place, I usually use a roller. I would also be loathe to risk a good, expensive saddle on a horse who might fall on it and break the tree or damage it in some other way. A lot of people feel that a horse has to wear a saddle sooner or later, and he might as well learn at this stage. Yes, I agree, but after two or three days. I do have an old saddle known as "the breaking saddle." It is a pony type saddle which, when I am working with an awkward animal, I often leave on his back during a night in the stable. I don't mind if it is chewed, rolled on or generally abused in any other way.

Bitting

Once the saddle has been accepted at all paces, the horse then has to learn to accept the bridle. Introducing the bit for the first time is never easy, but of course it must be done. There are several methods of "mouthing" a horse – which means getting him used to having a bit in his mouth and answering to a light touch on the

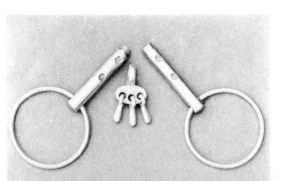

Left: A mouthing bit.

reins as a means of guiding and control. The old-fashioned way was to put a jointed key bit in the mouth, with side reins attached tightly to the girth, and to leave the horse like this for three days. The theory was that at the end of three days he had mouthed himself. I look back in horror now on the first horse I broke this way, and yet I cannot remember him having a bad mouth as a result. However, I feel it was an unthinking way to go about what must, at least initially, be an unpleasant experience for the horse.

Nowadays I alter my method according to the horse I am training. There is an old theory which says "the thicker the mouthpiece, the milder the bit." But I feel a small pony cannot possibly be comfortable with a big thick bit in its mouth, since it is bound to force its mouth too far open. In this case I feel it is better to wrap the bit in a piece of rag and then dampen it with diluted sugar. This gives the pony something to chew on, which encourages him to move or play with the bit. Playing with the bit is necessary in order to develop a sensitive mouth. If the horse is big and has a large mouth, I have found that either a straight bar bit with keys or a jointed bit with keys is suitable. The keys encourage the horse to play with the bit so that he learns to accept it. The bit illustrated on the left is based on the design of a French snaffle with keys hanging from the central ring. I have used this on big horses for only about two years but I have found it most successful. They seem to like it and will play with it.

One training stable I know mouths its horses by using a small half-moon cheek bit and putting it in for ten minutes at a time, during which the horse can chew at its hay. I'm always a little frightened that the horse may develop the habit of putting his tongue over the bit if it is left in too long and gets uncomfortable. I prefer to introduce the bit for not more than five minutes at a time, while I'm grooming, perhaps. I let the horse get the feel of the bit on several occasions through the day but only for this length of time. Then the next day he can start to have the bit in his mouth while he is being lunged, with the rein still attached to the Cavesson. The Cavesson helps to keep the mouth closed and gradually the horse will keep the bit on his tongue without fuss. Do be careful, though, to see that he never puts his tongue over the bit, by stopping frequently to check if you have any doubts. Putting the tongue over the bit is a very annoying and trouble-making habit, which must be avoided.

If a horse persists in putting his tongue over the bit, it may help to use a Wilson snaffle with a straight bar. It has two spare rings (other than those which take the cheek pieces) with an adjustable piece of leather joining them together

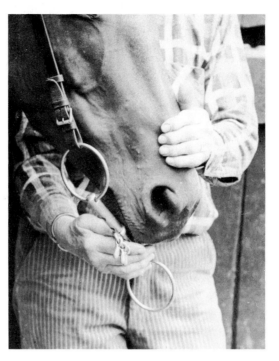

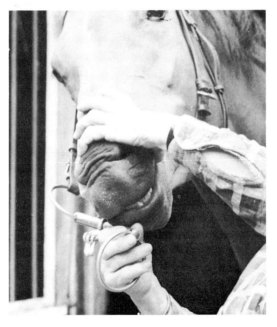

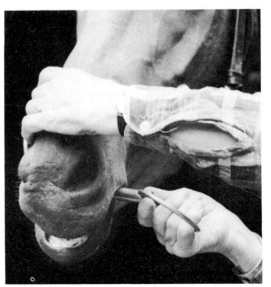

Stages in introducing a bit into a horse's mouth for the first time. Left: With one hand on the horse's nose, the bit (attached to one cheek piece only) is held by the horse's mouth. Center: The horse's mouth is opened gently. Bottom: The bit is put in with care not to knock the teeth.

133

over the bridge of the horse's nose. This means the bit is kept forward in his mouth, thus giving the minimum of pressure on his tongue. After

a few weeks of this, horses can usually be put into another kind of snaffle bit, such as an Eggbutt.

When putting a bit into a horse's mouth for the first time, great care should be taken so that he is not hurt or frightened. Pain can be caused by pinching his lips and he will immediately associate this with the bit. The best way is to put the head piece on over the head and then, with one hand over the nose to prevent him from throwing his head up, to attach the bit to the right cheek piece. After that it can be eased very gently through the mouth and attached to the left cheek piece. To remove the bridle, place your left hand over the nose, ease the head piece forward over the ears. Open the corner of the mouth with your left thumb so that the bit can drop out of the horse's mouth without getting caught in his teeth. If it does get caught in this way, he will get really frightened.

Side Reins

The progression now is to start using side reins, which are fixed to the girth on either side and which begin to introduce the feel of control from the reins. These can first be attached to the rings of the Cavesson and after that work can begin with loose side reins attached to the bit. There are two main types of side rein –

elastic ones and fixed ones. Both have their uses and, at the time of writing, I am using both types on the five animals we are breaking and schooling. In general I prefer to use elastic reins on any horse that cooperates well, as I feel the give in them can be likened to the movement of a good horseman's hands – that is, gentle and giving. They also allow more movement of the horse's head, neck and back than fixed reins. But should a horse lean on the reins and put his head down against them, I would use fixed reins. If he persists in bucking when being ridden, which usually happens when one is reschooling a horse, I would use fixed side reins crossed over the withers in order to prevent his getting his head down. In my opinion this could then be termed a corrective rein.

Above: Side reins shown attached to the bit and the girth. The saddle has replaced the breaking roller.

Below: Side reins shown attached to the stirrup bars. The head is thus held in the position it would be if a rider was holding his hands low on the horse's neck.

A great many people use fixed reins when schooling a horse for the first time, with very good results. I agree that it makes for steady head carriage, but I also feel that it introduces a certain restriction of movement of the head and neck and, indeed, of the whole body. On the other hand, I find better head carriage can be achieved from a heavy-headed animal if he is lunged with fixed side reins. It is apparent therefore that the trainer must have an idea of his aim. When starting to use side reins, it is usual to attach them so that they run in a straight line from the mouth to the girth or roller-dee, maintaining a very light contact between these two. One expects a horse to carry his head about level with his withers in the initial stages. As training progresses, the reins should be raised, so that after a while they will be attached to the dee of the saddle or the stirrup bars. The reins are then very nearly in the position they would be in if a rider were keeping his hands low.

Besides the question of whether to use fixed or elastic reins, the other controversy about

side reins is whether the inside rein should be shorter than the outside one when working in a circle. Those people who argue in favor of having a shorter rein on the inside say that we ask for a bend from the horse when riding in a circle, so we should do the same when lunging. This makes sense to me. The other school of thought says that both reins should be the same length, as this will control the swing of the quarters. I think it really boils down to the fact

that the trainer of the horse must keep a constant watch on the whole body and be guided accordingly, making his own decisions to alter the length and position of the reins to correct the horse's head, neck, quarters and movement. In this connection I can only repeat what Count Robert Orsich once said: "You look at the head, you look at the leg and in the end you either know or you don't know. It's no good talking!"

Above top: Still in the corner of the field, the horse is being lunged with the lunge rein attached to the bit.

Above: Lunging in an open field introduces the feel of space to a young horse.

135

Backing

Work continues on the lunge all the time to improve the general behavior of the horse – his balance and his obedience to the trainer's voice. Soon the time will come when the trainer feels the horse should accept the rider. This is known as "backing." First the horse must become accustomed to a person putting pressure on his withers, which you can do by just pulling on the withers with your hands. Then jump up and down, holding onto the withers. This can be done in the stall to begin with. Take the roller or saddle off and, with someone at his head to pat and talk to him, just jump up and down beside him, until he accepts this movement. With someone still at his head, either stand on a bale of straw or get a leg up so that you can lean over his shoulder. Repeat this many times. This is how a horse is first taught to accept the weight of a rider on his back.

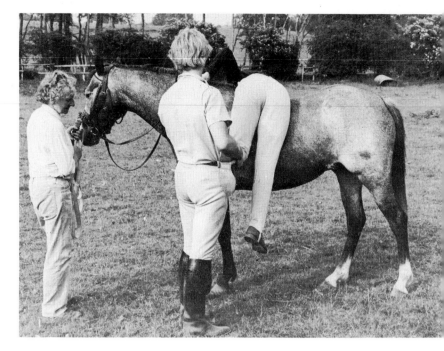

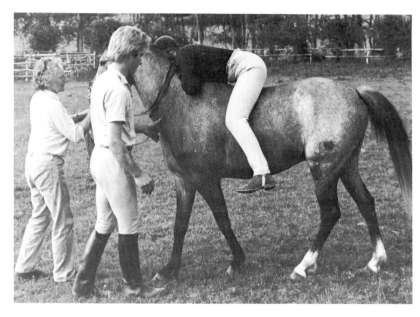

The first steps of introducing a rider onto a horse's back.
Above: Leaning over a horse's back. Note the trainer stands at the horse's head to reassure him, while an assistant holds onto the rider for safety.
Left: The rider astride the horse leaning forward on the horse's neck so he is not frightened by the shadow or the feeling of someone towering above him.
Below left: The trainer leads the horse with the rider sitting upright. An assistant walks alongside to keep the rider steady.

Some people back a horse in the stall. I personally prefer to have more room, as I feel the walls of the stall are a little too close to my head. Some people back with a saddle in place on the horse's back, but it can move or squeak as it takes a rider's weight, which will frighten a nervous animal. A rider's body is softer and warmer, which I feel makes it more acceptable to the horse.

Once on the horse's back, encourage him to walk a few steps with someone leading him. Halt and make a fuss over him. Then walk on again. When he will lead quietly, carrying a rider at the walk, you can try the same exercise with the saddle in place. It is important to think of all eventualities. It will help, for example, if you have lunged the horse wearing a saddle, on which the stirrups were swinging and touching his sides. Then later, when a rider loses a stirrup and it bangs against the horse's side, it will not be a new experience, resulting in bucking. Our main aim now is to keep the rider on the horse, for once a young horse learns he can get rid of the rider, he will do so again and again and will quite possibly develop a permanent vice. So proceed slowly until the rider's weight is really accepted, without meeting any resistance.

How soon a horse can be backed depends on when it has learned self control and natural balance. I can quote as an example a small three year old pony I was using for demonstrations during a course on how to start breaking a pony. So far she had only been led in hand. After petting her and jumping up and down beside her, I lay on her back and then put my leg across her. In a matter of ten minutes I was being led around the indoor ring – but what had I achieved? I had shown you can get on top at a very early stage, but until a horse has been taught self-control and natural balance there is really no point in sitting on his back. In fact the weight and presence of the rider just disturb his concentration at this stage, and certainly make it difficult for a horse to maintain his natural balance and stride. Some of the older trainers would not allow a young horse to trot for several days after it had first been mounted. This is because until a horse has become accustomed to balancing the extra weight of the rider on his back, he will shorten his stride in an endeavor to carry the extra weight. This could spoil his trot for the rest of his life.

Long Reins

The subsequent procedure is for the rider to ride the horse off the lunge rein, with the trainer on the ground encouraging and controlling with his voice and using the whip to position and help forward movement. I think this stage of schooling is much easier if the horse has been worked in long reins – a method of schooling I have not yet mentioned. As its name suggests, it employs the use of two long reins which can initially be attached to the two side rings of a three-ringed Cavesson. It used to be practiced a lot at one stage and then it went out of fashion, partly because, except in the hands of an expert, it can be dangerous. A theory evolved that work on the lunge with side reins was sufficient to make a horse bridle-wise – that is, educated to the indications of the reins. I have found, however, that without teaching the aids of the reins from the ground, my progress was slower when I began mounted training.

It is indisputable that there are faults which can develop when a horse is long-reined inexpertly. If the reins are attached to the bit and not the Cavesson, the bars of his mouth are likely to be damaged in the same way they would be if a youngster were shown in hand with the rein or control coming directly from the bit. It is also easy to get the wrong bend when working in a circle with two reins, but neither of these adverse things need happen. To avoid injuring the bars of the mouth, the reins are attached to the side rings of the Cavesson, or if it has only one ring, they are

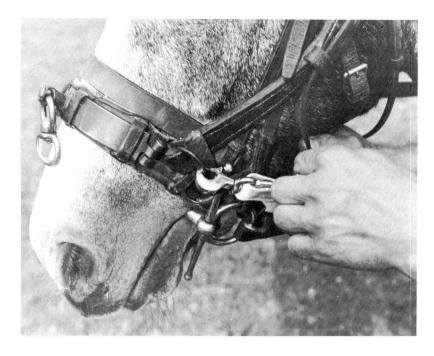

Above: In long reining, the reins are initially attached to the side rings of the cavesson.

Right: Stirrup irons are tied to the girth to keep them in place. Long reins will be threaded through them.

Below: Providing an expert is in control, long reining can be done later with the reins attached to the bit. It is still more advisable to attach them to the rings of the cavesson, however.

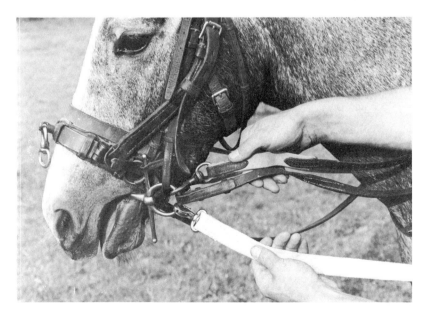

buckled to the nose band in front of the cheek pieces. The horse is held by an assistant and led on a lunge rein attached to the front ring, while the trainer takes the long reins. To avoid getting the wrong bend on a circle, I would advise that a trainer who is not very experienced with long reins should work mostly in straight lines, with turns to both sides and halts. As he becomes more used to these "driving" reins, he can begin circular work with a trained horse. In fact no one should learn how to use long reins on anything but a schooled horse, which thus becomes the teacher.

In these days it is very important that a young horse should get used to traffic on the road. If he has been taught to long rein, it is a useful way to take him walking on the road, although you must have another person with you. Choose a quiet lane to start with and, to safeguard his mouth, have the reins on his nose in case anything startles him. Often a young horse will be frightened just at leaving the security of its familiar surroundings, and will be ultra-sensitive to any strange noises or objects it sees. So with someone to talk to him and reassure him, while leading him from a lunge rein on the center ring of the Cavesson, the horse is driven from behind on the long reins by the trainer and thereby is able to become used to traffic.

Should the horse not have been long reined,

he should be ridden out with a quiet horse in front to give him confidence. Then gradually he can be asked to go in front of his companion. But keep lunging and riding him in your school area, too, to improve his general way of moving. Ask for halts and turns when out riding so he is doing some school work while out hacking too. Your aim should be to bring him back from each ride going better than he went out.

It is essential at this stage of the horse's education that the rider should be confident and have a good independent seat so that his

Above: The horse is long-reined, at first with an assistant at his head to lead him.

Below: Later the trainer works alone with the horse, walking in a straight line.

hands and legs are still. The horse is thus allowed to move forward freely, without being muddled by badly applied aids.

Teaching the Aids

As soon as a horse has become used to having a rider on its back, it must be taught to recognize and respond to the specific aids which are used to ask it to change gait and direction. By this time it will be thoroughly used to its trainer's voice, which will have been used constantly from its earliest training. It will also become automatically used to the aids as soon as it begins to move with a rider on its back – that is, the weight of the rider and the position of his seat as he sits in the saddle. For this reason it is essential for the rider to be extremely sympathetic, and to sit correctly but in a relaxed manner with his legs still, not banging against the horse's side. It is imperative to instill in the horse's mind that the weight on its back, the contact with its mouth and the legs hanging on either side of its stomach are all harmless factors and that they will not hurt it in any way whatsoever.

If the horse is being lunged with the rider on top, the instructions to change gait will come from the trainer on the ground by using his voice and the whip. As the horse is being controlled by the trainer, the rider can let the reins remain loose and concentrate on getting the

Above: A horse being long reined in a circle. Note the inside rein threaded through the stirrup iron, and the position of the outside rein above the hocks.

Right: Long reining a horse (with an assistant at his head) is an ideal way of introducing a horse to the rigors of the road.

139

horse used to feeling the body and leg aids as he changes gait. As the trainer gives the command to move from a walk to a trot, the rider confirms the command by applying the aids – i.e., pushing with his seat and applying very slight pressure with his legs. As the command is given to canter, the rider again applies the aids. In this way, through constant repetition and feeling the aids as he moves, the horse naturally begins to associate the change of gait with these specific commands. Once off the lunge, the rider uses the aids as he wishes his horse to change gait or direction, thus taking over from the trainer.

As the young horse begins to really understand the aids given by the body and legs (which you should continually try to perfect), you can begin to think more about the contact through the reins to his mouth. He should begin to feel this contact, too. Be consciously aware of the position of your hands, together with the weight, the openness and the position of the thumb needed to get free forward movement. The aids given to a horse to encourage it to move forward freely come from the elbows, which cannot work unless the thumb is held upwards. This allows the elbows to be relaxed and therefore to work with the movement of the horse. Should the thumb be allowed to turn downwards, then the elbow becomes stiff and the corresponding pressure through the hand and the rein does not allow forward movement. A very good tip I once learned from Brian Young when he was National Instructor was that the thumbnail should hold the rein onto the first finger. It gives a very light touch, and light, sympathetic hands are so very important. Without them the rider can only be half as good as he might otherwise be, and he can easily ruin a good horse before it is half trained.

In asking a horse to turn a corner, the rider first echoes the training the horse has received on the lunge. Keeping up the pressure from the seat, the rider moves his inner arm sideways

and forwards, so that he effectively leads the horse in a fairly wide arc. The outer rein is kept straight. As the horse becomes used to it, these aids should be replaced with the active, diagonal aids. This means applying slight pressure with the inside leg (i.e. the side in which you want him to move) on the girth and stronger pressure with the outside leg just behind the girth, while gently easing the inside rein and giving slightly with the outside rein. His hindquarters should follow his forehand in a correct bend.

Should he fall into the circle, use your inside leg against the girth to push him out again, easing the outside rein outwards very slightly. At the same time you must keep the direction of the circle with your inside rein, which, in fact, should be motionless once the horse is set on

Right: When circling, a horse must remain accurately on the circumference of the circle all the time. A trainer on the ground can help to judge this.

140

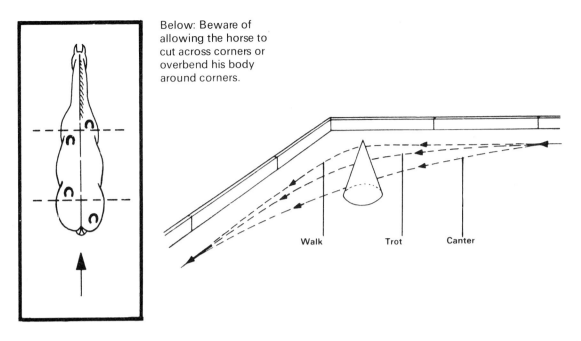

Right: Hoof prints should fall in exact line with one another on the left and right side, with the horse's weight equally distributed.

Below: Beware of allowing the horse to cut across corners or overbend his body around corners.

Walk   Trot   Canter

the right course and the right bend has been achieved.

All the work at this stage is aimed at teaching the horse to thoroughly understand the four natural aids – voice, weight of the rider's body, legs and hands – and to move forward freely with an easy rhythm at all gaits. He should be able to bend correctly and be obedient to the leg. Practice in straight lines up and down and diagonally across the schooling area, and in circles of various sizes. Frequent changes of gait and direction, as well as your place of work, if possible, will help to keep the horse interested. Never school anywhere for long periods of time. Short and frequent sessions will achieve much more. Work evenly on both reins, so that a tendency is not developed to work better on one side. Ask for advice from other people. Get an experienced person to watch you and your horse at work. No one can work unaided all the time; faults creep in unrealized. The evenness of the bends may differ on the left or right rein and often it is easier for such things to be noticed from the ground. It will help, too, if you take lessons on horses that are better schooled and more advanced than the one you are training, so that you learn the correct feel of various movements from a horse that really knows them. Learn from different people's methods, for each horse is different and, as he progresses, will need slightly different treatment. Some horses need coaxing, others need persuading, and some need a bit of bullying before they respect you. It is, after all, very important that you impress your horse with your own superiority over him. This has to be done right from the start and maintained thereafter, without ever losing the all-important rapport between horse and rider.

Work at trying to improve the horse's gaits too. The best way to do this is to find a slightly sloping, but smooth surface. Trot downhill, pushing strongly with your seat as you ask him to lengthen his stride. He will have to stretch out his legs to reach the receding ground, and after a time you will find his strides will lengthen automatically. He will begin to enjoy pushing out his legs and using his shoulders, and again he will naturally come to learn the aid for lengthening his stride. Always show that you appreciate his trying to please you with a patting and a "good boy." Then relax on a loose rein. Or get off and loosen the girth and give him a tid-bit – some grass, some horse cubes or

Below: Trotting downhill is useful in teaching a horse to lengthen his stride.

anything, just so he knows you are pleased with him and you finish on a good note.

Although it is important for a horse to learn to keep his body straight by a coordination of the rider's legs and hands, schooling work should be aimed at suppling his back for more advanced work. This is mostly done by working in circles in the early stages. At this stage of his training, a horse should be a nice amiable ride. He should show a certain amount of natural balance by cantering on the correct leg on either circle. His gaits should be even and his transitions should be smooth, but his outline will still be rather long and his head will be held lower than we ultimately aim for. It is from here that we must decide what he is going to do in the future. To me he will be the sort of horse that could be advertised as "going quietly, ready to school on."

Schooling on is more advanced work for both horse and rider. Of course there are going to be days when the horse will be a little frivolous after he has had a day off. Then it is wise to start working on the lunge and let him settle down, working through his nonsense to calmness. In fact it is best to continue to work on the lunge combined with riding all through his life, whatever stage his training has reached. Should you wish to work on long reins may I advise that, although the side reins are on the bit, most of the work is done with long reins on the rings

of the Cavesson? A horse can over bend so easily with long reins on the bit.

There is so much open to owners of horses today in the competitive field. There is dressage, combined training involving both dressage and jumping, jumping, endurance riding and showing. For the latter, the conformation must be good. In the other fields the horse's own ability will direct you. Even so, a horse with good conformation will tend to train more easily, helped by the natural balance which comes from having a well proportioned body. Whatever direction *you* wish the horse to go, his ability may be different, as I discovered after looking for a jumper. The young horse I selected jumped 45 fences faultlessly at the first show, and I felt sure that with this horse I had found a jumper at last. But I had not. She proved to be too hot and excitable for show-jumping.

Remember, too, that at this stage in his training a young horse should not be ridden by more than two or three people at the most, and only then if they really know what they are doing. It certainly should not be shown, for the galloping of other horses in the ring might excite it. A Hack or Riding Horse class would be more suitable since the emphasis is on manners. Only a lengthening of stride is asked for from a riding horse, although it does also have to jump a small fence which is about 3 ft. 4 in. (1 m.) high.

Constant exercise to supple a young horse is important in early training and schooling.

Jumping

Although from here on the training of a horse will vary according to the future plans you have for him – that is, whether he is to be a show horse or an eventer; a show jumper or general-purpose riding horse – most people like their horses to be able to jump over low fences at least. There are some people who disapprove of very young horses jumping early in their training. I must admit that I like to try a youngster over poles on the ground, to see how clever he is naturally and whether his foot work is good and tidy.

The poles that you use for this must be really good and heavy; if they are flimsy and the horse kicks them, they will roll about. Start by walking him over just one on its own, and then as you add more make sure you place them the correct distance apart to suit his stride. When he walks over them naturally and easily without kicking them, try him over them at a trot. This will help to improve the balance as well as the natural rhythm of any horse. After a while move the poles so that there is a different number of strides between them, to see how he copes with this new situation.

The next step is to try him over a raised pole of about 1 ft. (30 cm.) with a solid ground line made with another pole. In my opinion, including these exercises as part of a young horse's training cannot harm any young horse.

Below: Here the horse has become too exuberant and is jumping the cavaletti instead of trotting calmly over it.

Left: Teaching a horse to back up. The trainer pushes gently on his nose and shoulder to encourage him to take one step back.

Below: A horse is brought parallel to the gate in order to open it.

Top right: The quarters are brought around as the rider keeps hold of the gate.

Center right: The rider makes sure the gate is properly open before walking through

Bottom right: The horse is turned around to face the gate again, so the rider can latch it.

Backing Up

Teaching a horse to back up is an essential part of his training. It is important that he can move backwards as well as forwards, so that, for example, his rider can open, walk through and close a gate without dismounting. Just when this movement should be taught arouses some controversy among trainers. It is best left until the principles of free forward movement are firmly established in the horse's mind, and if a horse is encouraged to back up too soon, this can develop into a run backwards when halting. The back up should never be a run, in which, inevitably, the horse will move back in four-time, each leg moving independently. Instead it should be a pace of two-time, opposite diagonals moving in unison, and a horse should never be asked to take more than a few steps back in a reverse direction at any one time.

A horse is first taught to move backwards without a rider on top, by the trainer standing on the ground. The trainer places one hand on the horse's nose and the other on his shoulder and then gently pushes him back for one or two steps. As soon as the horse has taken a few steps back, he must be led forward again immediately. This is very important, and indeed a horse should always be asked to move forward immediately after he has moved backward.

The action can then be repeated with a rider on top giving the aids, while the trainer again pushes the horse back with one hand on his nose and the other on his shoulder. The aids for the back up are to put the body weight on the seat bones and close the legs slightly, while flexing the head by a slight feel on the reins. As soon as the horse understands these aids, the rider can ask for the back up without the trainer's assistance.

When the back up has been thoroughly taught and understood, it can be incorporated into the action of opening and closing a gate, without the rider dismounting. To open a gate,

144

bring the horse parallel to it, so that you, as the rider, can unhook or unlatch it. Say, for example you have unlatched the gate with your left hand, you should continue to hold it open with this hand, as you ask for the back up, thus opening the gate as you move. Still holding the gate open, use your left leg to push the quarters around. Then walk forward through the gate, being careful not to let it swing shut on the horse's quarters. Once through, turn around, and bring the horse parallel with the gate again so you can latch it.

An important aspect to remember throughout the procedure for opening and closing a gate is to stand parallel to the gate, as opposed to perpendicular to it, particularly when you are opening it. Inexperienced, young horses have been known to attempt to jump a gate from a standstill, because the rider's legs have swung back and the aids have been misinterpreted.

The Future

The overall training of any horse is a long process. Like a human being, a horse goes on learning all his life to accommodate himself to his surroundings and some are more adaptable than others at learning self-control. Some horses are just full of fun and cannot concentrate. This is when keeping lessons short and frequent becomes even more important.

Whatever time of year you begin the breaking-in and training of a young horse it is a good thing to turn him out to grass for one or two months after about three months' work, unless it is wintertime. If so, slacken off the work and turn him out during the day in a New Zealand Blanket, bringing him in at night to the warmth and comfort of the stable. This helps to make sure a horse does not get bored and "stale," and when the rest is over, work can begin again slowly. Do some quiet lunging for 15 minutes in the morning. Then give the horse a rest and a feed, and work again perhaps after lunch for another ten or 15 minutes. Don't sweat off the fat that he has put on during the rest, but just do slow, steady work on the lunge to build up the muscles gradually. Then resume work mounted, progressing quietly so you have no set-backs.

Whatever direction you are channelling your horse's career, remember that he needs building both bodily and mentally. If he is kept in the stable, whenever possible turn him out for an hour or two on good grass, so he can relax and enjoy himself as he grazes. Being his natural food, grass is good for him. Being fed in his stall all the time becomes boring for any horse. All this will help you with his training; a happy, contented horse is always going to work better for you than a bored one.

145

Breeding

Breeding a foal from your own mare is a thrilling experience indeed, but one that should be carefully thought about before any action is taken. The mare's age needs to be considered. Some people are unwise enough to breed from two-year-old mares, and indeed even yearlings are able to give birth. It seems to me to be unkind to put the demands of carrying and bearing a foal on a horse whose own body is still immature. And it will almost certainly lead to her getting "sprung ribs" and never quite regaining the juvenile elegance of her youth. Generally it is better not to breed from a mare before she is four or five, at which stage the bones are fully developed and she has had a chance to prove herself under saddle. A good mare can then go on breeding until she is 23 or 24. Some people follow a practice of breeding a mare when she is seven or eight, then using her for the next 12 to 15 years or so as a riding horse, before breeding from her again. Providing she has already had one foal, there should be no problem, but it would be less wise to breed a first foal from a mare in her 20s.

Some of the questions you should ask yourself before reaching a decision to breed are: have you sufficient pasture in good condition with adequate shelter to keep your mare and her offspring? Do you have the time, money and dedication to raise a foal to maturity? Does your mare have enough good points in her favor to justify reproducing her, remembering that you want to make sure there is a future for her foal, too?

Above: Mares and foals out at grass.

Below: A new arrival.

Mares and Stallions

If the answer to all these questions is yes, the next thing is to decide the type of foal you hope to breed, which will influence your choice of stallion. Study your mare objectively to decide which points can be improved. You might want to produce a foal with a better head or stronger hindquarters, for example.

Many people like to put their mare to an Arab stallion, in order to produce the attractive Arab characteristics in the foal. If you are breeding from a pony mare and want to produce a pony using an Arab stallion, study some pictures first so you know what points to look for. In my opinion, there are two types of Arab: those that show a strong likeness to a pony, and those that give you the impression you are looking at a small horse. Obviously, it will be the former type that you want in this case.

I was told in Jordan by Sheriff Masser that there are two main types of pure Arab, too – the mountain type and the desert type. The difference can be best spotted by looking at the head. The mountain type gives the impression of broadness between the eyes, which are set far apart and well to the sides of the head, so that the horse has better vision over a wide spectrum when he is standing on high ground. The desert type has a narrower head with the eyes generally positioned more towards the center of the forehead.

Still on the subject of a stallion to breed with a pony mare to produce a pony, a good cross if you wanted to breed a bigger pony would be with a Thoroughbred sire. The right Thoroughbred stallion will be more difficult to find, though, for there is no such thing as a Thoroughbred pony, and only very few Thoroughbreds have real pony characteristics. Once again, the head is the guide and you should look for a stallion which has a pony's head rather than that of a horse. Thoroughbreds with pony-type heads probably owe this characteristic to the original Arab blood from the three famous Arabian stallions that helped to found the English Thoroughbred breed.

If your mare is a registered pony, you will probably want to breed a pure-bred foal which can also be registered. In this case, you must choose a sire that is true to type and, preferably, the best possible one available.

Having decided in your own mind on the kind of foal you want to breed, it is helpful to look at stallions in the same objective way as you did your mare, to assess what they have to offer as sires. I look for a horse that appears masculine and dominant, as well as one that has the conformation and action I require. Even more essential is temperament, unless you are breeding racehorses, when temperament will often be sacrificed for performance. In all other cases a gentle nature and kind temperament are extremely important, because you undoubtedly want to breed a foal that can be enjoyed by its handler, breaker and owner!

Nowadays stallions are treated much more as "ordinary" horses than they used to be. They are ridden and exercised daily and generally lead more normal lives. Some even have their time divided between being at stud and competing in show-jumping events – to wit, the stallion Marius ridden in the show-jumping ring by Caroline Bradley.

Above and left: Two examples of Arab horses. The one pictured on the left displays pony characteristics as opposed to the horse qualities of the one above.

Ask to see the stallion led so you can check his movement and feet. Be slightly wary of those racehorses that broke down during racing and so were then retired to stud. It may be that there is an inherent weakness or a defect in the conformation. The fact that there are many more stallions kept now than at one time means, too, that there are many more imperfect ones. Look for a stallion that is as near perfect as possible, at least in terms of improving on the conformational defects of your mare.

When you have decided on a stallion, go and see the stud manager where the stallion is standing, to discuss the details – in particular the arrangements for visiting your mare while she is there. All stud owners and stallion men are helpful to inexperienced breeders. Besides the fact that it is their "bread and butter," they are genuinely interested in their work. They will advise you of the best time to send your mare, remembering that the foal should arrive 11

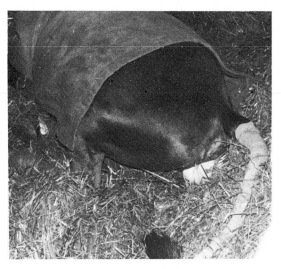

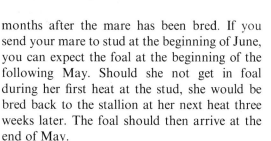

months after the mare has been bred. If you send your mare to stud at the beginning of June, you can expect the foal at the beginning of the following May. Should she not get in foal during her first heat at the stud, she would be bred back to the stallion at her next heat three weeks later. The foal should then arrive at the end of May.

The best time of year for a foal to be born is undoubtedly late spring, when the weather is getting warmer and the grass is at its best. This ensures that the mare has plenty of milk for its foal. Breeding has become very scientific, though, and racehorse foals are now bred earlier in the year, in February or March. This gives them the advantage of a few extra months in the year of their birth before they start to race as two year olds. On the other hand, it means that artificial conditions must be provided to protect the young foal from the cold winter weather. In big studs, where perhaps most racehorses are bred, these conditions are provided by the use of radiant-heat lamps in the stalls and covered exercise yards where mares and foals can stretch their legs without getting cold and wet.

Stud Procedure

If you arrange to send the mare to the stud when she comes into season, make sure you keep a check beforehand of when she comes into season, so you can make a note in your diary of when you expect to send her away.

You will need to arrange the stud fees and the price of the boarding of the mare. A cheap breeding farm can be a false economy, resulting in a mare returning to you very thin and worm-ridden, which will almost certainly affect the foal in some way. So look at the fields where the mare is going to run and make sure that you are happy she will be well cared for during her stay.

Different breeding farms have different conditions of payment regarding the stallion. "No foal, no fee" means what it says – if your mare is not in foal by the first of October, you do not pay a stud fee. If these are the terms the stallion owner offers, it indicates that he has every confidence in getting your mare to foal. "No foal, free return" means that if your mare does not get in foal she can come back to the same stallion the following year, without your having to pay another stud fee. In both these cases, you will have to pay for the board of your mare while she is at the farm. A "straight fee" means that if your mare does not get in foal, it's just bad luck – you have lost the stud fee!

On the whole, pony mares are easier to get into foal than bigger mares. Some mares do not breed when they have a foal at foot, although others will. Some mares will not breed to a certain stallion but are quite all right with another. The usual practice is to leave the mare at the farm for three to six weeks so that she can be tried to see if she has "turned," which means she is not in foal. Should she be in foal, however, and appear to be "holding," as it is called, she can be tested manually by a veterinary surgeon at six weeks. After that she can return home.

If you are sending a mare with a young foal at foot to stud, you should be even more particular about the facilities at the stud farm. It is essential that there are stalls available for use in wet, cold weather, especially as the foal will be very young when its mother returns to stud. Most breeding farms like to have the mare six or seven days after she has foaled.

The Mare in-Foal

When the mare returns home, you can use her for very light hacking – that is, if she does not have a foal at foot. In my opinion it is much better to leave her resting in a quiet, shady field away from other horses. The feeding of a brood mare is very important and some people will tell you that the period of a foal's life in the uterus is the most important time of its development. The unborn foal takes all its food from the mother's bloodstream, so the mare needs sufficient, good food all the time, to sustain her and her foal. Some mares put on a lot of weight when carrying a foal, while others, just like some people, retain a trimmer figure until late in pregnancy. Do not listen to people who tell you a mare does not need extra food; I think she should be given extra rations whenever she looks as if she needs it. If she is prone to laminitis, it is safer to rely on hay for her bulk feed rather than grass, which is richer in protein. There is actually a theory that no mare carrying a foal will get laminitis, but I have proved this to be wrong with a Welsh pony mare of mine. It is fair to say, though, that it is unusual for in-foal mares to contract this disease since the nursing foal is taking a great deal of nourishment from the mare.

Lippizana mares and foals.

149

As the mare gets heavier and the foal takes up more space, there is less room for bulky food. At this time increase her concentrated food, giving, say, 2–4 lb. (1–1.5 kg.) extra oats and some additive such as Equivite of Stud Malcodig. This is rich in minerals and helps both the unborn foal and the mare's milk. Seaweed meal is another good food additive. It is very rich in iron, which is good for the blood, and also salty, which makes the mare drink more water. A mare should be encouraged to drink lots of water at this stage as it is good for the system, keeping the kidneys working so that the legs do not fill out. Mares that are turned out the whole time rarely fill out in their legs, for walking around the field helps to keep the circulation going. Mares that are brought in at night will often have puffed-up legs by morning. To prevent this, put on bandages when she comes in at night, taking them off in the morning before turning her out in the field for the day. Puffed-up legs point to kidney trouble, which is not unknown in pregnant women as well. Carrying a baby is a strain on the system. Some people and some horses cope better than others.

Each mare must be treated as an individual, and since you know your own mare you should be able to recognize any unusual or unnatural signs that she may display.

Come the winter, I think mares in foal deserve to be kept warm and dry at night at least. Then they will need a short feed at night and in the morning with additional hay, but limit the hay ration if they are carrying a lot of extra weight over their quarters and their necks. It is a good idea to mix the morning feed in particular with plenty of chaff, which will make them eat it more slowly. This will help the digestion, and it will ensure that they get the maximum benefit from the feed. As a guideline, I like my mares to spend at least half an hour eating their morning feed, before going out into the paddock to graze.

In making preparations for the foal, try to arrange to have a small paddock near to the house cultivated and left clean and ready to put your mare into, a week or two before she is due to foal. As her time gets nearer, keep a careful watch to see she is well herself and that her bowels are kept open.

There is a question, too, of providing com-

A mare stands patiently while her foal suckles.

of pregnancy, because young foals are very susceptible to worm infestation from grazing.

Foaling

Watch to see how the milk vein enlarges and runs down the underneath of her stomach to the udder. Watch the size of the udder and the relaxing of muscles around the top of her tail. All these signs will give you a guide as to how soon a mare will foal. Like people, mares can foal early or late. Extremes are unusual and in general there seems to be a three-week cycle, so that mares tend to foal three weeks either side of the appointed date. More mares seem to foal late rather than early, but this three weeks either side of the foaling date should not cause you undue concern providing the mare is well herself. If she is not, call the vet.

If you have never delivered a foal before, then if possible, arrange for a knowledgeable friend to be present. Your vet should be warned beforehand when you are expecting the mare to foal, in case something goes wrong and he needs to be called. It is generally felt that the birth of a foal is most likely to go smoothly when unaided, or unimpeded, by human intervention. In my opinion, it is essential for someone to be there in case the mare needs help.

Signs that the birth is imminent are small globules of wax-like material appearing on the mare's teats, possibly even running milk and the relaxing of the muscles by the tail. But be warned, some mares show none of these signs and foal quite unexpectedly. Some mares foal lying down, others standing up. Some show signs of excitement or distress, others are calm

An attractive Arab foal.

panionship if you have just one in-foal mare. Try to find a suitable old horse or pony to be her companion up to the time she is about to foal. Separate them at foaling time, but preferably only by a railed fence so that they can see each other, but the companion cannot interfere in any way. Both the mare and her companion should be wormed regularly during the period

Youngsters can be extremely inquisitive!

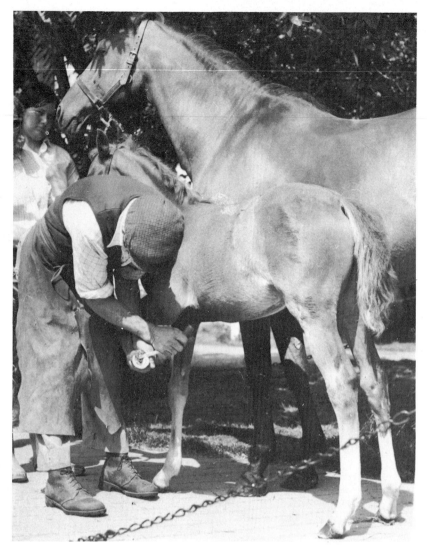

the other. After that the nose appears, lying between the legs, after which, with some pushing from the mare, the whole head will appear. The foal's nostrils should be cleared and his face slapped to make sure he is breathing. As soon as the shoulders are through the pelvic arch, the body and hind-quarters should slide through with no problem. At this stage the foal should be towelled to dry him off and stimulate his circulation. He will still be attached to the mare by the umbilical cord, which is good because, although he is breathing himself and thus getting oxygen on his own, he still has the benefits of the blood line from his dam through the cord. The cord will rupture when the mare gets up, if the foal struggles. There should be only a few drops of blood; should there be any more, tie the cord with previously prepared sterile tape.

It is essential that the person attending the birth make sure that all the afterbirth is removed from the mare. If any is left behind, it will turn gangrenous very quickly. The vet must be called within four hours of foaling if the afterbirth is incomplete when the mare drops it.

Of course, not all births go smoothly and on occasions things go wrong. The foal may be mispresented or awkwardly placed in the womb, so that it cannot be born without expert help. But these occasions are rare, and it is extremely unusual for a foal to be born dead. Generally, one can expect all to go well with a healthy, normal mare, although it would be particularly advisable to have an experienced person present for a first foaling of a mare that is rather highly strung.

I have now had more than 30 years' experience breeding foals, beginning with one small Welsh pony mare and leading up to having bred my

Above: The blacksmith's visit is less frightening if the dam is present.

Below: A stable rubber is used to lead a very young foal.

and peaceful. You will just have to cope with the situation as it is presented to you.

The birth begins with the appearance of the water bag, which will rupture as the mare strains. After the flow of water the two front feet should appear, one often just in advance of

A quiet dam will always reassure a young foal.

own stallion and running a small stud. Of course, I have had disappointments and worries during this time, with nights sitting up looking after sick foals or foaling mares. But I would say that breeding ponies and riding horses has brought me a lot of fun, as well as some success. My best day was at one horse show some years ago where I got six first prizes, three reserve championships and two championships! That sort of day certainly makes everything worthwhile, but even that is not the main point. Nothing gives me greater pleasure than to walk through the fields on a summer's evening to visit the mares and foals. The old ladies are glad to see me and the youngsters are inquisitive. The day is over, there is no rush and everything is serene and peaceful. What more can one ask?

Handling and Raising of Young Stock

A foal's training and education should start almost immediately in terms of getting used to people. The first and most important thing to do is to gain his confidence, for all future training should depend on his confidence in people. Foals are curious by nature, but they are also afraid, particularly of something that is taller than themselves and moves hurriedly or noisily. When you are beginning to make friends with him stoop down so that you are on his level or even smaller; he will feel more confident to come and investigate. It will help too if the dam has confidence in you. If she doesn't, she is likely to try to stop you from getting near her foal. Some mares are very possessive about their foals, particularly to begin with, in which case it is best to leave them alone for a day or two until they have calmed down and will accept your presence.

Training could be said to begin after a few days, when a foal slip can be put on the foal's head or a stable rubber around his neck and he is led out into the field. Someone will be leading

153

the mare in front and the foal will follow. He can be encouraged by putting one hand behind his quarters to help him along if necessary. In following his mother, the foal will also learn to be led at the same time, but it is very important that the person leading the mare does not get too far ahead. If his mother gets out of sight, the foal is likely to get frightened, which will manifest itself by his stopping with all four feet firmly planted on the ground. He is not likely to move until his mother is brought back.

When the foal gets between four and six months old, he will begin to be too much for his mother. You will notice this as the mare begins to lose condition. The youngster will be taking so much milk from her that she will not be getting enough nourishment from her food to keep herself going. In any event, it is time the foal was weaned and started growing up. This is especially the case if the mare is in foal again.

Prepare a stall for the foal, well bedded down with sawdust and deep litter and banked with straw so that he does not damage himself if he gets upset and falls. Put food in his feed box and tie a bucket of water to the wall. Take the foal away from his mother and put him in the stall, preferably next to another foal. If this is not possible, try to find an older companion for him when he is first separated from his dam. Some foals will eat the feed right away and immediately settle down to enjoy this new independent life. Others will fret and pine for their mother and you may have more of a job on your hands to get them used to it. If the foal frets, let him settle down with someone he knows making a fuss over him, grooming him and so on. If the foal is very upset, it may be necessary to have someone hold his head while the other person carefully grooms him.

This growing up stage is very important in regard to discipline and behavior. Your voice is better than hitting, although on occasion a good slap does no harm, just as it doesn't with a child. I would say be slow to hit; I have found my voice does more to help me handle youngsters than a stick. They are babies, though, and like children will often "try you out" to see how far they can go. Any tendency to kick must be stopped at once.

After a couple of days in the stall, turn the foal or foals out by day and bring them in at night. If you are dealing with several foals, try to separate the sexes, even if they have been gelded. Boys will play boys' games and can be very rough. This shows how you should plan ahead when breeding to make sure you have

The State breeding farm at Haras du Pin, France.

154

enough room for everybody. Get a foal used to wearing a New Zealand Blanket as soon as possible. This will mean they can stay out in the rain and there are none of those mad rushes to get the horses in when a storm blows up.

As summer comes, if you are not showing your youngsters, worm them, trim their feet, toughen them up by doing no more grooming than just brushing the muck off them and then turn them out. See that there is some shade to protect them from the hot mid-day sun, either in the form of trees or hedges or a shed. Make sure this is big enough to accommodate however many youngsters you have turned out in the field, so that there will be no crowding and kicking.

As the grass gets less nourishing, keep an eye on the foals' condition, perhaps giving a small feed each evening to keep the flesh on and help them to grow. See that you have one or two mineral blocks tied up in convenient places, and have the soil tested so you know which minerals your land is lacking. (The Department of Agriculture will test your soil as part of a free service, available on request.)

When youngsters are growing, it is all important that their bone structure develops well. No deficiency should ever be overlooked. Good oats with a mineral added, fed in chaff so that they are thoroughly digested, are the best feed of all. I tend to mistrust nuts, particularly for feeding to these young horses, as it has been proved that the additives lose their value quite quickly after manufacture. All horses have their likes and dislikes and they will be developed even at this early stage. One of my present foals likes to have his breakfast in bed – the bowl has to be placed for him to eat while he is lying down. Breakfast finished, he condescends to get up!

The question of whether to keep young stock out or bring them in each night is a personal decision, which will be made in the light of the type of foal you have. From a cost point of view, I think there is little difference. They will eat more if they live out all the time as half their intake goes to keeping them warm.

There are very few countries where the decisions and choices connected with breeding are left to the individual. In many countries,

Feeding time for the Lippizana mares and their foals at the Austrian National Stud at Piber, Styria. The black coats of the foals will turn gray as they mature.

breeding farms are under some kind of general State control or jurisdiction.

In Austria, for example, the government's control on the breeding of the Haflingers is so strict that all colt foals are inspected at weaning with a view to being used later for stud, and if they do not pass this scrutiny they are sold for meat. Apparently no more than 20 or so are selected each year from about 400. Nor does

Below top: A handsome yearling.

Bottom: A mare and foal being shown.

this mean that the chosen few will definitely be used as stallions in the future. They have to measure up to another set of high standards when they are three years old, and only if they pass this examination are they included in the Haflinger stud book.

This control has been generally enforced only for the last 20 years, during which time it is said to have made an enormous difference, and marked improvements may be noticed in the examples of this breed.

The breeding of horses in France has some measure of government control, mainly because few private owners keep their own stallions. Those stallions that are privately owned have to be examined by government stud inspectors before they are allowed to breed with any mares. Rather than go through this, most owners of brood mares breed their mares with the high standard stallions kept at the several government stud farms situated throughout the country. Stallions found at these stud farms are mainly Normandy half-breeds. Thoroughbreds, Anglo-Arabs and Trotters.

Showing Brood Mares and Foals

Many shows include classes for brood mares with foals at foot, but to compete in this way does make for some extra planning. It is unwise for a very young foal to travel as it is still so susceptible to infection. Also, if the mare is in foal again, the excitement and anxiety could cause her to lose the fertile egg before it becomes firmly attached to the wall of her womb. In my opinion, it is also unwise to show a mare which

A successful day! Note the smart show tack worn by mare and foal.

is very heavy in foal as it puts an undue strain on her just before foaling.

The shows generally begin in April and then continue throughout the summer. This means that a foal to be shown in the early shows should be born in March, when often the weather will necessitate mare and foal being kept inside. From January on, a mare will need extra attention in the form of careful feeding and grooming to get her into tip-top condition. This is when it is particularly important to supplement her feeding with the extra concentrates and minerals that make all the difference to her condition. Don't let the mare get too fat, though. Fat mares seem to take all the goodness for themselves and tend to produce skinny foals.

If you are keeping the mare in all day because of bad weather, she should be walked out in hand to get some exercise. A small, short feed at noon, with a few carrots and apples added to it, will help to break the monotony. Better still, turn the mare out during the day in a New Zealand Blanket, bringing her into the stable at mid-afternoon.

It is unusual to leave show mares at breeding farms for any length of time as most of these establishments do not have the time to give them the extra care they need. You can stress to the stud groom that you are willing to pay for extra food or, better still, send your own food along with the mare.

Get your entries in to the shows in which you want to compete well in advance and plan your schedule from then on. Practice showing in hand at home during the preceding weeks, finding out which is the best way to run the foal with the mare. It may be that they both do best if you hold the foal in front of the mare as she trots towards it. How you practice during those preceding weeks can make all the difference to your final placing.

If you need to stay overnight at the show, take all the food you will need for the mare and take some extra bedding for her and her foal, as there never seems to be enough provided. Have an attractively stitched show halter made for the foal either with leather reins or a white lead one. The mare can wear an ordinary double bridle.

More Advanced Riding

Riding – the Next Steps

As the training of a horse progresses and the ability of a rider increases, there are a number of different fields of equestrianism available to both. Hitherto, the rider has probably done little more than go for pleasant hacks and maybe enter in a few small, local shows. Should he want to take his riding career further, he will probably have to make a decision about which aspect interests him and his horse most.

The pictures on this and the opposite page illustrate some of the different advanced fields. Right, a horse is demonstrating the supreme art of classical equitation – that of *haute école* – and although it is seen here without a rider, all the movements recognized in *haute école* are also performed with a rider. Classical equitation at this very high level is a very specialized field, which comparatively few horsemen pursue. Below is the field of three-day eventing, which, in spite of the fact that it places great demands on horse and rider, has become increasingly popular over the last decade or so. Opposite, top is a picture of an international show-jumper – a very competitive field of horsemanship which has proved itself an extremely popular spectator sport. Beneath this, are riders demonstrating the skilled and exacting demands of a specific dressage movement performed in split-second unison.

Whatever field you may choose to enter, the beginning stages of advanced training are common to all, and are based once again on achieving obedience and cooperation.

Left: The supreme art of classical equitation demonstrated at the Spanish Riding School in Vienna.

Right: One of the most successful show-jumping personalities — Hans Winkler, seen here at the 1976 Olympics.

Below left: Eventing is one of the most demanding of all equestrian sports. Here Princess Anne and Goodwill demonstrate their obvious ability.

Below: Perhaps the most elegant field of horsemanship, dressage requires immense skill and concentration as well as split-second timing.

As a rider becomes more relaxed on a horse and more proficient in the saddle, he will often find that as much as he enjoys hacking around the countryside, he would like to learn more, to know how to demand greater things from a horse. At this stage he should attempt to go deeper into the whys and wherefores of riding. He should read widely and talk to knowledgeable people to learn more about horses and explore different fields of equestrianism. Then he should try out these new ideas, either to adopt or discard them. Horses and riding are never dull, and no one, however experienced – top riders and instructors included – ever knows it all. In all spheres of involvement with horses, be it breeding, training, learning to ride, or teaching of riding, there are always new ideas, new angles and new things to learn. Everyone should have an open and enquiring mind if they really want to proceed. My advice to everyone is to take regular lessons. Find out your weaknesses and what you are doing wrong. Have them corrected and learn the right way to work so as to overcome them. Go over all points in theory and practice. It is never pleasant to be found wrong, but you are aiming at being able to ride better, which in turn will lead to your riding life being ultimately more enjoyable and infinitely more satisfactory.

The rider by now will find himself applying the natural aids automatically, but he should begin to take a close look at each of them, studying the reasons for why and when he applies them the way he does.

He should ask for explanations in areas of uncertainty. His aim is still to attain a mixture of balance and suppleness which allows him to follow the movement of his horse, giving a picture of unison that is delightful to watch. Everyone makes mistakes and sometimes anticipates certain reactions from the horse which do not in fact occur. This is obvious from photographs of even the best riders being left behind or being out of balance with their horse. But this is all the more reason to work continually towards gaining a strong seat, which allows hands and legs to work independently. Then aids can be given clearly and without contradictions caused by tension resulting in involuntary movements of the rider's hands and legs. When the rider has more control over his legs and hands, he can begin to ride a more sensitive and better trained animal.

The importance of developing some rapport

Below: The ordinary walk.

Right: Loose rein walk.

160

between horse and rider has been stressed in various places throughout this book. If you are to progress together towards more advanced work, it becomes even more crucial. It will come about by quiet, sensitive, harmonious working with a definite aim in mind.

Dressage

As one begins to learn how to ask for more advanced movements from the horse, one could be said to be entering the field of horsemanship now known as "dressage." Dressage is a French word, with no real equivalent in English, but a definition in the French-English dictionary translates it as "erecting, setting up, raising, training."

Thus we can get a picture of a trained horse with elevation, which is just what it is all about: a balanced horse with good carriage. "Dresseur," the noun, means a trainer, a raiser. If we take the word "training" to be the equivalent of the old-fashioned "schooling" of a horse, we are as near to the meaning as we can be. But to clarify it still further, the international equestrian authority, known as the Federation Equestre Internationale (F.E.I.), gives the following definition of dressage – "harmonious development of the physique and ability of the horse. As a result it makes the horse calm, supple and keen, thus achieving perfect understanding with its rider."

The objects of dressage upheld by the F.E.I. are "to preserve the Equestrian Art from the abuses to which it can be exposed and to preserve it in the purity of its principles, so that it can be handed on intact to generations of riders to come." The Federation instituted an International Dressage Event in 1929 and since then there have been many international, national and local competitions in all countries. The latter competitions will be within the scope of many riders.

The Dressage Committee in charge in England presides over official dressage competitions and holds courses for those of its members who are interested. It has a selection committee which chooses teams to go abroad, but the main object is to improve the standard of dressage generally in this country.

The F.E.I. also gives the following definition of the qualities looked for in a horse:
– "freedom and regularity of gaits.
– harmony, lightness and ease of movements.
– lightening of the forehand and engagement of the hind quarters.

Below: The rider is asking the horse to walk more actively by the use of her leg. Note the horse's hind leg.

Left: The collected walk. Note the different styles of riding between this rider and the one above. The rider shown on the left was trained by a German dressage expert and the influence is clearly evident in the higher position of the hands, for example.

161

Right: The working trot. The horse is balanced and responsive.

Above: The medium trot.

maintain an even gait, and can alter gaits at given points. From here you can progress to a variety of work at the different gaits of the walk, the trot and the canter.

The Gaits

Until recently we talked of the three types of walk, trot and canter – that is, ordinary, extended or collected (or slow) walk. The F.E.I., in considering that no young or inexperienced horse could demonstrate real extension or collection, decided to change this slightly to the collected walk, medium walk, extended walk and free walk, and collected, working, medium and extended gaits of the trot and canter. Collected gaits are not asked for until a fairly advanced stage. The word "working" is meant to convey a gait between collected and medium, with no loss of rhythm or hock action – not real collection, but an attempt at more balanced movements with greater elevation than an ordinary gait.

"Medium" means a gait between the working and the extended gaits. It is more active than the working gait with greater energy from the quarters, which frees the forehand to move with a longer stride. The head is allowed to move a little "in front of the vertical."

The extended gait comes when the horse is really moving forward with long strides to cover as much ground as possible. The rider allows the horse to lower his head, lengthen his neck and yet remain on the bit. The horse should show great activity behind, which will

– an ability to remain absolutely straight in any movement along a straight line, and bend accordingly when moving on curved lines."

All this you have been seeking to attain in your regular school work so far. In fact, the first steps in dressage are those that most riders will already have been practicing for some time – that is, simple school figures ridden at the walk, trot and canter, aimed at making the horse obedient and showing that the rider can

162

allow his forelegs to really move forward. Extended gaits are very attractive to look at when the work is done in balance, but a common fault can be to lengthen the stride in front, while leaving the hind legs trailing behind.

The "free" walk is a relaxed pace during which the horse is allowed to stretch his head downwards. This movement used to be termed simply "letting the horse see the ground" and this describes aptly the action of complete freedom of the head and neck.

Collected gaits are the hardest of all to achieve properly and the F.E.I. in their series of dressage tests do not ask for collected gaits until the "Advanced Elementary" test, which is preceded by the Preliminary, the Novice, and the Elementary. One of the reasons for this is that collection imposes a great strain on the muscular system of a horse, and until the proper muscles have been developed, it cannot be

achieved. Thus it is not for the novice horse, nor the novice rider.

Bringing a horse to a halt becomes important now, and as defined in dressage terms, it should be "square." In other words the horse must be straight in the direction in which he has been travelling, with his forelegs and hind legs evenly placed under him so that they make a complete rectangle.

In its definitions and descriptions of dressage, the F.E.I. also states that "in all his work, even at the halt, the horse must be on the bit. A horse is "on the bit" when the hocks are correctly placed, the neck is more or less raised, according to the extension or collection of the gait, the head remains steadily in position, the contact with the mouth is light, and no resistance is offered to the rider."

Extension in paces should never be asked for unless you feel the horse is really "on the bit" as described above. If so, you can push him into an extended pace from the ordinary pace by increasing the pressure with your seat and your legs. Remember that it is a lengthening of stride that you are asking for, not a quickening of the gait, nor a loss of the regularity of the steps. In an extended walk the hind feet touch the ground clearly beyond the footprints of the forefeet. At an extended trot, when great impulsion is coming from the quarters, the horse uses his shoulders to cover more ground with each step, but his action should not become higher. At an extended canter, the tip of the horse's nose points more or less forward as the horse extends his neck. The pace should be as light and as calm as the ordinary canter.

Counter Canter and the Flying Change

The work you have done at the canter so far with your horse will have been mainly in

163

circles, when you asked him to lead with the inside leg. Now extend this to working in a figure eight, bringing him back in the center of the "8" to a trot or walk for a few paces before asking him to lead off on the other leg. When this is well mastered, you can ask him to "counter canter," which means cantering in a circle with the outside leg leading. This exercise helps to supple a horse. And as he will be used to cantering with the inside leg leading, it will also test his obedience to you as the rider, as well as demonstrate how clearly you are giving the aids! When counter cantering, the horse should remain slightly bent to the leading leg, which automatically means that his spine cannot be bent to the line of the circle. Try to make sure, however, that the quarters do not swing to the outside of the circle.

I think riding at the counter canter should be done with great discretion, for I feel it somewhat contradicts a horse's previous training. Having spent hours instilling natural balance into a horse as he canters with the inside leg leading, it seems a pity to muddle the horse's brain. It can also give a feeling of great dependence on the rider, and there are some fields of equestrianism – cross country riding, for example – where it is important for a horse to be able to get himself and his rider out of trouble on occasions. However, it does test the rider's aids and the horse's obedience.

A considerably more advanced move at the canter is the flying change of leg. It is not asked for until the "Advanced Medium" dressage test, which is the sixth test in the scale. This means that the horse changes leg at the canter in the air in a single stride while still cantering. It should be executed at the moment of suspension at the canter with the horse remaining straight, calm and light. A common fault is to change the leading leg only, so that the horse is cantering disunited. As an exercise it should certainly not be attempted until the horse obeys the command to counter canter and maintains this gait quite happily through circles and serpentines.

Before attempting a flying change, try this exercise. Ride in a straight line, and from a walk give the aids for the horse to canter, clearly indicating which leg you want to lead. After a few strides bring him back to a walk, and then ask him to canter again, leading with the other leg. You should sit very still. If you move your body too much it will make the horse swing from side to side, instead of changing legs evenly in a straight line.

Repeat this a few times and, if all goes smoothly, try the flying change. If all does not go smoothly, wait until it does! To ask for a flying change, begin by counter cantering on a left circle. Making sure the horse is well balanced and attentive, shift your position, giving the aids for cantering on the other leg. It is easiest to ask for the change as you reach a corner of the ring, so that the horse changes to lead with his inside leg after his head position has been altered. The ease, or not, with which he achieves the flying change will depend on his balance and the work you have done before in leading off with different legs. If you have trouble in perfecting a flying change, it will be these things that are at fault, and it may be necessary to go back to practicing leading off with different legs from a walk and a trot when you are riding in a straight line.

Above top: The working canter, off-fore leading.

Above: The counter canter to the right.

The Half Halt

A movement you will have been performing throughout your schooling work is that of the half halt. Now you should give it a little more thought. The half halt is used in downward transitions and the idea is to bring the hocks underneath the body or "to engage the hocks" and thus lighten the forehand. This is why it is necessary to drive a horse forward when you want to reduce pace. A horse cannot reduce pace or come to a halt smoothly unless he is driven forward into the bit, with his hocks under him and his forehand lightened. A pull on the reins, with no supporting body and leg aids, will result in the horse lurching forward into a halt on the forehand. A half halt commands the horse's attention and warns him that you are about to give him some further instruction – to ask him either to change pace, shorten his stride or turn a corner.

Backing up is a far more complicated maneuver than might be imagined. As we have seen already, it is a gait in two-time – the legs moving simultaneously in diagonal pairs. If it is not done correctly, the horse will walk back in four-time. Backing up provides an excellent opportunity for the rider to feel the horse dropping its head as it both accepts the bit and prepares to obey an order. The procedure for backing up is to ask the horse to halt correctly, then use gentle pressure with the legs, just behind the girth, and a slight feel on the reins to flex the head so the horse accepts the bit. As soon as you feel the head drop, ask for the horse to back up, relying on pressure from your seat and legs rather than the reins. As he moves backwards, keep him going in a straight line by using your legs.

You should allow him to move back only a few steps and then ask him to move forward immediately, otherwise he may develop a tendency to run back rather than step back and it

Above: Educating the horse towards achieving a collected canter. This is not a true collected canter.

Left: The collected canter.

165

may also encourage him to get behind the bit. Backing up is a very important part of dressage tests and any signs of hurrying, deviating from the straight line, or inactivity of the hindquarters are deemed serious faults. It is said that a horse that is not obedient to the aids of the rider in this maneuver is insufficiently suppled, badly schooled or badly ridden!

As soon as a rider begins on this more advanced schooling work, he must think more about the action of the bit in the horse's mouth. The bit can be moved in the mouth by the rider so that the pressure is transferred and the bit made to work on the tongue, on the bars of the mouth or on the lips. As the bit is so moved, the horse's head can be positioned from one side to the other – a factor that is very important in certain movements, such as the shoulder-in or shoulder yielding.

Lateral Aids and Movements

The shoulder-in is an example of "lateral movement." In lateral work, the horse is bent uniformly from the poll to the tail and moves with the forehand and the quarters on two distinct tracks. The distance between the tracks should not be more than one step. Lateral movements should be practiced for only short periods at any one time and should be followed by energetic straight forward movements. The rider should have studied the theory of lateral aids, although so far he will have been using only the diagonal aids (the opposite hand and leg used together). Lateral aids involve the use of the same hand and leg working in unison and to my mind they can be termed the "forcing" or corrective aids.

A useful exercise to demonstrate the use of lateral aids is the turn or pivot on the forehand. It will teach the rider how to gain control of the horse's quarters, which are moved around by his legs. It is a movement which is not very popular with some members of the dressage

Left: Positioning the novice horse for a turn on the forehand by bringing it alongside a fence.

Left: Starting the turn. Note that the horse's head is straight and the quarters are yielding to the rider's right leg.

Below: Half the turn has been completed. The use of the fence is well illustrated – it prevents the horse moving forward at this stage.

Far left: During a turn on the forehand the horse effects a semi-circle with its hind legs. It pivots on the inside foreleg.

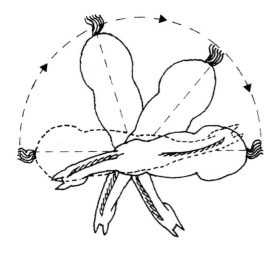

fraternity, although the Pony Club at one stage used to demand its execution in some of their tests. The inside leg is the active leg and is used behind the girth to push the quarters around, while the inside hand guides the horse's head around to follow them. The outside leg keeps an even pressure over the girth to keep up the impulsion and prevent the horse stepping backwards. It is supported by the outside hand which remains still, but resists any forward movement, since the horse should take only one step forward during the whole movement.

To translate this into terms of left and right to make it clearer, if doing a pivot on the forehand to the right, the horse's head should be bent slightly to the right. It helps to practice this move as you come into a halt from a walk so that the horse is still on the bit and there is still some impulsion in his body. Your aim is to pivot around so he is facing in the opposite direction, after which you should walk on. When you become expert at this, turning both to the left and right, try a complete pivot, after which you should walk on in the same direction.

The shoulder-in is an exercise used to supple the horse's back, but, more important still, it makes the rider position his horse exactly in the place he wants him, developing the horse's obedience. In effect, the horse is bent around the rider's inside leg and the outside shoulder is placed in front of the horse's inside hind leg.

In the turn on the haunches it is the forehand that effects a semi-circle. The horse pivots on the inside hind leg.

Left: The horse is brought into position for a right turn on the haunches.

Left: As the turn begins, the neck is bent too much. The bend of the neck should never exceed the bend the horse can give with his back.

Below: The turn is completed.

The horse is really moving unnaturally at the rider's commands, for his body is bent away from the direction in which he is to move. This is why it is a good exercise for developing obedience.

To do a shoulder-in to the right, keep the horse's quarters in a straight line going along the side of the ring and slightly incline his head and neck towards the center. His right foreleg is then brought inwards off the track. Then, with firm pressure from your right leg, push the horse forward so that he moves on three tracks – that is, his off fore is making a track of its own, the off hind follows the track of the near fore and the near hind has a track of its own. The quarters should remain perpendicular to the track of the school. Practice the shoulder-in movement to the left and right.

In the shoulder-out, the horse's head is positioned towards the wall with his quarters inwards. This movement is not as popular as it once was, since it is believed that there can be a loss of impetus when the horse's head is facing the wall. On the other hand, I feel it does force the rider to really use his legs to keep up the movement. Again the horse moves in three tracks.

Closely connected with the shoulder-in is shoulder yielding, wherein the horse is bent in the opposite direction to that in which he is travelling. Here the horse is asked to work on a circle and to move outwards, keeping his body bent around the rider's inside leg. The exercise teaches the rider to use the direct hand as he keeps the inside hand steady, i.e. the inside hand keeps the horse's head flexed on the circle, while the outside hand is used in an outward movement to lead the horse outwards. The outside hand should not have a backward tension as this will slow the horse down, for the outside hand controls the gait on the circle and can work as a brake. The sideways movement of the hand will pull the bit against the horse's inside cheek, which will encourage him to move away towards the larger circle. The rider's legs should be used to help to keep the bend, the outside leg operating behind the girth and the inside leg over the girth. The inside leg keeps the impulsion going as well as encouraging the horse to move outwards.

Although the position of the legs should not alter, the strength of pressure from either leg does in fact alter the position of the horse. This therefore excellently demonstrates the importance of developing independent use of the legs.

After shoulder yielding there is the controversial question of leg yielding. One school of thought is very much against this method of beginning to teach a horse lateral work. The critics claim that if you teach a horse to leg yield there is difficulty in getting him to move correctly afterwards. To other people, leg

Right: Practicing leg yielding on a novice horse at a walk. Note the rider's hand, clearly indicating the direction that she wants the horse to follow.

Right: The commencement of leg yielding at the trot. The rider's left leg is open (well away from the horse's side) thus allowing the horse to move to the left.

yielding is just a step towards more advanced lateral movement, and it is accepted that the position of the horse during it is not what is ultimately wanted.

In shoulder yielding, the horse was carried sideways while correctly bent on a circle. Now we are asking him to straighten his quarters, but still move sideways. In fact what we are really asking for is a half pass (see below) but with the wrong bend; the idea is to teach a horse to cross his legs. It is easier to do this by making him move sideways with his head bent in the direction from which he came. It means, too, that the neck is flexed and the quarters straight, and he is being asked to move away from a very active leg into a passive leg. This therefore allows him to move sideways, helped by an open hand. The main difficulty will be to keep the horse moving.

The half pass mentioned above is a beautiful and graceful movement when correctly executed. The horse is again moving on two tracks and bends slightly to look in the direction of the movement. His outside leg pass and cross in front of the inside legs (inside legs are those on the side toward which the horse is bent). The gait at which the horse is travelling before the half pass is executed should remain unchanged. It is better to work at the trot than at the walk, because it is easier to keep the horse moving. Do this exercise along the line of a wall or fence to begin with, in which case you want to put the horse at a 45° angle from the

Above: Leg yielding to the right at the trot.

Left: A typical fault in leg yielding — the rider's left hip collapses when moving to the right — and vice versa.

wall as you come alongside it from a corner. If half passing to the left, use the left hand slightly sideways, so the right rein supports on the right side of the neck. Apply very active pressure with the right leg just behind the girth, so the horse is pushed over to a more passive left leg. You will probably find it easiest to travel sideways from a line towards home at first, and as soon as the horse has responded with a few sideways steps, push him forwards into a posting trot.

When you can perform the half pass on the track against the wall, try the same movement diagonally across the center of the ring. Again it is the outside leg which is the most active and pushes the horse across, but the inside leg should be kept close to the horse's side as it will help keep him moving.

Half-pirouettes and pirouetting consist of the forehand moving in a half or full circle around the haunches. In advanced dressage tests, half-pirouettes are performed at a canter and the movement commences the moment the inside hind leg has ceased its forward movement. The half circle completed, the horse moves forward again without a pause. This is a very advanced movement, but turns or pivots on the haunches can be practiced by less advanced riders at a halt or walk. To execute a right turn on the haunches, lead the forehand around with the right rein, keeping the left rein still, and close the left leg behind the girth to prevent the haunches from flying out. The pivoting leg is the off hind.

All the movements and exercises so far described, besides being within the scope of most experienced riders and horses, have some practical purpose. They help in developing suppleness and obedience in the horse and help the rider to appreciate more about the finer arts of riding.

From this point on, the schooling movements become very advanced and specialized; indeed one could include the pirouette in such a category. Although the movements themselves can be described, it is not really sufficient to describe the aids for executing them. This is the time for practical lessons from an expert if you feel a real interest in dressage. I would also recommend that you read more specialized books than this one can hope to be on this fascinating subject.

The Passage and the Piaffer

Two very advanced dressage gaits, expected to be performed only in the Olympic Dressage Test known as the Grand Prix de Dressage, are the Passage and the Piaffer. The passage is described as being "a slow, shortened, very collected, very elevated and very cadenced trot."

As in an ordinary trot it is a movement of the diagonals, but each pair of legs is raised high and has a prolonged period of suspension. The exact action has to depend in part on the individual horse's conformation. Some give more rounded and longer action, while others have much livelier, shorter action. The ideal movement is stated in the directions for the execution of the Grand Prix de Dressage Test. According to the rules of the F.E.I., it is as follows: "The height of the toe of the raised

Opposite, above:
Commencing the half
pass to the right at a
walk.

Opposite center: Note
the near hind leg
crossing over the off
hind.

Opposite below: The
near foreleg crossing
over the off fore. The
horse is bent in the
direction in which he is
travelling.

foreleg should be level with the middle of the cannon bone of the other foreleg. The toe of the raised hind leg should be slightly above the fetlock joint of the other hind leg. The neck should be raised and gracefully arched with the poll as the highest point and the head close to the perpendicular. The horse should remain light on the bit and be able to go smoothly from the passage into the piaffer (see below) and vice-versa without apparent effort and without altering the cadence, the impulsion being always active and pronounced.''

The piaffer is the collected trot executed on the spot. Again a formal and ideal definition from the directions for the execution of the test is as follows:

"The horse's back is supple and vibrating. The haunches with active hocks are well engaged, giving great freedom and lightness to the action of the shoulders and forelegs. The neck is raised, the poll supple, the head perpendicular, the mouth maintaining light contact on a taut rein. The alternate diagonals are raised with even, supple, cadenced and graceful movement, the moment of suspension being prolonged. In principle, the height of the toe of the raised foreleg should be level with the middle of the cannon bone of the other foreleg. The toe of the raised hind leg should be slightly lower, reaching just above the fetlock joint

of the other hind leg. The body of the horse should move up and down with a supple and harmonious movement without any swinging of either the forehand or the quarters from one side to the other."

The piaffer, although being executed strictly on the spot and with perfect balance, must always be animated by an energetic impulse which is displayed in the horse's constant desire to move forward as soon as the aids calling for the piaffer are discontinued.

The Grand Prix de Dressage is performed in an arena that measures 60 m. × 20 m. (approx. 195 ft. × 65 ft.). The time allowed for it is 12 minutes 30 seconds, and it is extremely difficult. It includes movement at ordinary, collected and extended gaits of the walk, trot and canter, frequent changes of rein, gait and speed, halts and backing up, flying changes of leg at the canter (at one time 15 changes of leg are asked for – one at every stride as the horse moves diagonally across the ring), half pirouette, work on two tracks, and finally, the passage and the piaffer.

Haute Ecole

It has been said that if school work is logically developed, it leads to shorter and more complicated movements, which, though undoubtedly

Far left: Half pass at the trot to the right.

Left: Motion is maintained by the rider's right leg on the girth. The horse is bent in the direction in which he is travelling.

Far left: The rider's left leg is positioned approximately 4 in. (10 cm.) behind the girth.

Left: Note from the position of the barn how the horse has moved forward as well as sideways.

171

beautiful, have no practical value in leading the horse on to other things. In fact, this is a field of horsemanship that is an end in itself, known as "Haute Ecole." The aim is to achieve the highest levels of perfection in classical riding. Such is the work and aim of two of the most famous equestrian establishments in the world – the Spanish Riding School in Vienna and the Cavalry School, known as the Cadre Noir, at Saumur in France. These two places provide the supreme example of classical equitation and the movements performed on the magnificently trained horses can be compared to a classical ballet.

The Spanish Riding School of Vienna

The Spanish Riding School of Vienna was founded in 1560 at the Imperial Court. At this time the classical art of riding was at its peak, and there were similar establishments at the royal courts all over Europe. The name "Spanish" refers to the origin of the horses – the beautiful Lippizanas – who are descended from Spanish horses, and were bred specifically for the Imperial stables in Vienna. Except for a ten-year exile period after the Second World War, the Spanish Riding School has been training horses and practicing its great art in Vienna since the sixteenth century.

The training of the Lippizana stallions follows a long-established and carefully planned routine. Serious life and work begin for them when they are three years old, at which point they leave the pastures and are brought to the school. When they are accustomed to being handled, school work begins, just as it does for any young horse, on the lunge. If anything, such work is even more important for the Lippizana, for he must be perfectly balanced, a hundred per cent obedient to his rider and

The famous quadrille being performed by the Spanish Riding School of Vienna – a demonstration of *haute école* at its peak.

horse's natural reaction after a moment or two is to make a jump forward. When this is repeated two to eight times in a controlled manner, it forms the next air – the courbette. During the courbette, the forelegs never touch the ground. If a stallion is particularly exuberant he may initially lack the self-control necessary to execute a levade and instead leap into the air with all four legs off the ground. This is the basis of the *ballotade*. His body is horizontal to the ground and his hind legs are bent under and behind him. If he then stretches his hind legs so they extend behind him in a straight line, he has performed the *capriole*.

It is one of the factors of classical equitation that all the exercises or airs are based on ordinary movements which the horse will perform untrained in his native state. Thus, young colts, for example, may be seen performing "ballotades" in the field as they frolic and play. Haute Ecole works at bringing these graceful

Left: Perfectly matched – a pair of Lippizanas begins a demonstration of classical dressage.

Below: Horse and rider demonstrate the levade – one of the airs above the ground.

muscularly extremely well developed. As we have seen before, these are the things achieved by working on the lunge. So he is taught to walk, trot and canter, in perfect balance with supreme suppleness, to understand the rider's aids and to become completely obedient to the rider, concentrating entirely on what he is asked to do. He is said to have reached the stage of Haute Ecole when he has mastered these points and is able to perform half passes, pirouettes and flying changes with "graceful ease."

Haute Ecole is divided into exercises, more usually referred to as "airs," on the ground and above the ground. The piaffer and passage are among the airs on the ground which, as we have seen, are expected to be performed by horses in the Olympic dressage test. Lippizanas are taught the piaffer in hand and also "between the pillars." In the latter, the trainer is also on the ground, but does not hold the reins, these being attached instead to pillars on either side of the horse. It is apparently during this time that the trainer is able to judge whether the horse has the natural aptitude to be trained in the airs above the ground.

The main airs above the ground are the *levade*, the *courbette*, the *ballotade* and the *capriole*, and they may all be performed with or without a rider. The levade is when the hind legs are moved under the body to such an extent that the weight is taken off the forehand, which then lifts off the ground. The stallion in effect squats on his haunches – the hocks must be bent at an angle of 45° – and maintains this position. As it imposes a great strain and is also uncomfortable for any length of time, the

movements to perfection, so that they may be performed at a command with or without a rider.

The Cadre Noir

After a slightly checkered former history, the other notable center of advanced riding, the Cavalry School known as the Cadre Noir, was established at its present home in Saumur, France, after Louis XVIII had succeeded to the throne in 1814. Its original instructors and founder members came from two sources – from civilians from the School of Versailles and from military personnel of various regiments. A quarrel between the two led to the school being closed down in 1822 and it was reopened in 1825 as a cavalry school. Almost a century and a half later, in 1969, its exclusive ties with the military were broken and it is now primarily a civilian establishment.

In spite of the quarrel between the two factions, there remained the traditions of horsemanship and expertise each had brought with them: academic equitation from Versailles, and

The courbette being performed by a Lippizana stallion.

Opposite top: An officer at the Cadre Noir.

Opposite: The spectacular capriole, performed by a Lippizana.

word means to jump, leap and skip, which admirably describes the movement of these highly trained horses. Movements performed include airs above the ground – the courbette, ballotade and capriole. The horses are not shod, in order to avoid any danger of striking one another – for, with the exception of the capriole, the twelve riders in the display perform these extremely advanced movements in a very small school in breathtakingly precision-timed unison.

Each July the Cadre Noir holds a Tournament or Carousel which lasts four days. Besides the displays of Haute Ecole for which they are now world famous, events also include a lance display, hurdle races, and various equestrian games.

The Cadre Noir is still primarily a school of equitation, and it runs a variety of courses. Among the best known are those for people who wish to become instructors of riding. To gain one of the much sought-after places a candidate must already hold certificates of a certain standard in instructing. The pupils are provided with four horses, each of which is ridden with a specific objective, so the course in effect is divided into four sections. One is to improve the seat and balance, and the work includes much riding without stirrups, cavaletti work, etc. The next works on the aids and their delivery, and concentrates more on dressage exercises such as the shoulder-in, half-pirouette, rein-back, counter-canter and changes of leg. The third is jumping instruction, and particular emphasis is placed on the approach and take-off, strides between fences and jumping at various

equitation based on gaits and exercises leading to cross-country riding from the military. These form the basis of the curriculum and courses offered by the School today, although the whole operation has widened to embrace such fields of equitation as racing, polo, three-day eventing and show jumping.

The traditional indoor ring work which leads to Haute Ecole still forms a very important part of the Cadre Noir's routine, and regular performances are given. There are two main performances or exhibitions, both of which are shrouded in tradition. The first has come to be known as the "Black Mass" and is performed by the instructors, who are known as the *ecuyers* or equerries. It is led by the Equerry-in-Chief, and all the riders wear the superb traditional uniform and ride on magnificent, ceremonial saddles. The display consists of work on two tracks, walk, trot and canter, changes of leg and the passage. Finally the Equerry-in-Chief demonstrates both the school walk and the sustained trot.

The other display is the colorful performance of the "sauteurs." Literally translated this

angles. Finally, there is training for participation in competition work, such as eventing and show jumping.

Besides training civilians in the various fields of equitation, the instructors receive training themselves in Haute Ecole. They each ride two horses – one that is experienced and helps to teach them the movements, and a novice which they train to the required levels of perfection.

Side-Saddle Riding

Side-saddle riding is included in this chapter not so much because it is an advanced form of riding, but rather because nowadays it is probably practiced by people who can already ride astride. In the early part of this century, and for centuries before, all ladies rode side-saddle, as many famous paintings of aristocracy and royalty bear witness. But immediately after the Second World War it was a rare sight indeed to see anyone mounted this way. As with so many older techniques in all sorts of fields, side-saddle is enjoying a current revival, and a Ladies Side-Saddle Association and also classes for children riding side-saddle are held at many shows.

To ride side-saddle is undoubtedly a good idea for many women. After all, we're not all built in the same way and those of us with round thighs and somewhat bulky bodies can often find it difficult to balance cross-saddle. Hooked around the pommel of a side-saddle,

An elegant side-saddle rider at the Seville Fair in Spain.

The rider is shown without a skirt and is demonstrating the correct position of the legs for side-saddle riding. The right toe points down towards the left toe which points upwards.

The rider has the reins in her left hand and is holding onto the balance strap with her right hand.

The rider is sitting correctly – with the skirt now in position.

one not only looks more feminine, but is also infinitely more secure! Once the technique is mastered, it is also safer to ride side-saddle on a strong horse if he is prone to bucking, especially if you are a light-weight. I find if I ride a really strong horse cross-saddle, when he pulls my seat raises out of the saddle, and I cannot control him as well as I can side-saddle, when I can sit myself down into the saddle, really secure my knees in the pommel and defy him to unseat me! In addition to these points, no woman riding cross-saddle ever looks as smart as a well-turned out woman riding side-saddle proficiently. It is elegant, chic and correct and it is something that everyone rightly admires.

The secret of riding side-saddle is to sit right on top of the saddle, and not, as I heard someone described at a horse show recently, "sitting beside her horse, not on it at all"! It is easy to make such a mistake, particularly if you do not have a saddle that fits you. Besides fitting you, however, it must fit your horse. When buying a new side-saddle, I would stress the importance of having someone with you who knows what they are talking about. Fitting side-saddles is a tricky business, as there is a tendency for them to slip on the horse's back, and yet if they don't fit, they will result in a sore back very quickly. You will need a saddler who is prepared to take endless trouble in packing the side up so as to keep it correctly positioned and straight in the middle of the horse's back. The saddle needs to fit well behind the shoulder of a horse, so that the rider is able to sit into the movement. If the saddle is perched on top of the shoulder, the rider cannot sit properly and will be most uncomfortable. Most side-saddles today are suede-seated, which are certainly easier to sit on than the old-fashioned leather-topped ones on which I learned to ride.

Most modern side-saddles have their own patent safety stirrups. Old-fashioned side-saddles generally do not and therefore must be used with stirrup irons that have a safety catch. This is so that if the rider falls, the stirrup automatically opens and releases her foot. If this does not happen, there is a very real danger of being dragged, which can result in an accident. It is fair to say that one has half the number of falls when riding side-saddle as one does when riding cross-saddle, but once your right leg has dislodged itself and come over the pommel, you are almost bound to fall. It is much better at this stage to let yourself go, rather than try to hang on.

To mount for the first time, stand beside the horse and put your hands on the pommel, taking the reins in your left hand as usual. Get a leg up and sit down cross-saddle. Keep your right hand on the balance strap and put your right leg over, hooking it around the pommel. Keep the same position of your shoulders – that is, square with your horse's shoulders, so that you remain looking between his ears. This obviously makes you twist at the waist a little, but this straightness must be maintained because it makes the difference between an elegant and inelegant rider – and nothing looks worse than an inelegant one! The position in the saddle is therefore very important. The whole of the weight of your body is taken on the right seat bone and thigh and the closer the right thigh is pressed onto the outside of the saddle, the better. It should actually be possible to pass a hand under the left seat bone of a well balanced side-saddle rider.

For the first week of riding side-saddle, ride without putting your left foot in the stirrup iron. You will then get into the habit of not relying on it, and it should only be used as a foot-rest. Keep your left knee about a hand's width away from the lower pommel but pressed comfortably against the side of the saddle. There is a divergence of opinion on how your right foot should be held. The leg is crooked over the front pommel, and the foot will hang down naturally. Some people say it should be level and square, with the heel slightly down, and toe slightly up, but this does not give the skirt of the side-saddle riding habit a good line, nor does it help to keep your muscles well down over the pommel and into the saddle. I feel, therefore, that the old adage of the closer the two toes are together – i.e. your right toe pointing down and your left toe pointing up – is probably right.

However, there are two quite valid schools of thought so you must adopt whichever is best for you. Walk around for a little while with your hand still on the balance strap. This will

Below: The rider is sitting incorrectly – her body is not straight and her right shoulder is lowered.

Bottom: The side-saddle rider usually sits to the trot.

help to settle you into the saddle. If you begin to ache, take a rest by putting your leg over to sit cross-saddle for a while. Then try trotting. The trot is never very comfortable unless you ride a horse which has a really slow, controlled trotting pace. You will find you will bump around in the saddle quite considerably at the trot. Keep your right hand on the balance strap still and just urge the horse forward into a canter. This is a very comfortable gait, and you will find the rocking motion is very easy and it is enjoyable to sit to. It is also the best movement for getting yourself right down into the saddle.

In the old days, the horse was meant to canter only with the off-fore leading; today this would doubtless be considered badly schooled and one-sided. But in those days, when riding horses was done more to get from one point to another, or for a day's hunting, comfort was the important factor.

As with all forms of riding, the best way to begin riding side-saddle is on the lunge. This should ideally be for ten minutes to start with, followed by a quarter of an hour's rest and then another ten minutes. Rest again; then work for another ten minutes. Don't ever try to ride for two hours or so in the early stages of learning to ride side-saddle. You will merely rub your legs, strain your muscles, and get into the wrong position. By overworking yourself and taxing your muscles to this extent, you are more likely to develop a bad position and this will be very hard to correct.

To jump side-saddle, the same forward posi-

tion is adopted as in cross-saddle riding. Try to keep forward with your left heel well down. The grip of your knees around the pommel helps you enormously in making you sufficiently secure to allow the horse to have a free head. This is particularly important, because on landing the horse needs to be able to recover without being too much upset by the imbalance of your weight. If a horse does go down, he will be inclined to fall on his nearside because of your weight, so be careful when you go into a fence that your weight is central or, if anything, a little to the right.

Never try to learn to ride side-saddle on a horse that has not been well tried out in this way before. Most horses will take a side-saddle without any fuss, although the more high-spirited ones might try a little bucking at first. If the side-saddle is being introduced for the first time, do not do up the balance strap too tightly to begin with. Lunge the horse with the saddle but no rider and let him get used to the feel of it. Then get on him, sitting cross-saddle, while someone else lunges you. Finally try putting your leg over. He's not likely to buck unless you tighten the balance strap too much. In fact, most horses seem to go better side-saddle, maybe because we have a more independent seat, which makes for steadier hands and therefore allows for greater free forward movement. Admittedly, you lose the use of the right leg, but you should always carry a stick in your right hand which must act as a leg. In time, you will find you can rely on sympathetic hands and the left leg to balance the horse when you are riding side-saddle.

If you are going to do a lot of side-saddle riding, you need a proper "habit." In the old days, these had to be gray or black to be correct, but now blue has become an acceptable and fashionable color. If you are going to do a lot

Above top: Again, the rider sits well into the saddle as the horse trots downhill.

Above center: The rider is maintaining a good position as she canters on the left rein.

Right: Dismounting side-saddle.

of hacking side-saddle, it is a good idea to have a "covered coating habit" which is a dust-colored habit that does not show the dirt! Habits used to be made of two fabrics – a light-weight one for the coat and a double-weight one for the skirt. It is often claimed that it is hard to get the double-weight one, but it is, in fact, possible to have a skirt made of double material. It is essential if it is to hang correctly, and to look elegant that a skirt also cover the right boot. If you ride continuously, you will find you are inclined to wear out the top of the knee of the skirt, so quite often a leather patch is stitched here.

For country shows or "morning" shows, the correct dress is a blue habit, a polka dot tie, a white or white-and-blue striped shirt, a veil and a bowler hat. For afternoon or evening shows, you should change the tie for a stock and the bowler for a top hat, still with a veil.

Competitive Riding

I have often been asked how one begins competitive riding, and each time I find it a difficult question to answer. I think it is really a natural progression. One learns to ride, maybe enters for fun in a few small shows and gymkhanas, and thus finds that competition work is enjoyable. This will give any rider incentive to work at his or her riding, for all competitive work, of whatever nature, demands a high standard of horsemanship.

Top-class competitive work needs aptitude, dedication and tremendous hard work. Your body and mind must be kept fit and trim for whatever events you wish to enter. If there are big competitions ahead, energy must be conserved rather than expended on other pleasure activities. A competitor lacking concentration and forethought is not likely to reach the heights. You must want to learn and improve all the time. You must ask yourself, "Where did I go wrong? How can I do better?" But particularly in the early stages, competitive work should be approached in a slightly light-hearted manner, with good humor and, above all, good sportsmanship. Too much store should not be placed on winning and losing – tomorrow is another day and another opportunity to do better. I decided very early in our competitive life that we would try to avoid the pitfall of boasting of success, by never making note of what we had won. Then we could never give an answer to a question about the number of prizes we had collected, because we honestly did not know!

It is also worth noting that it is not always the most expensive horses and ponies that do well in competitions. More depends on the rider, and I have seen the most unlikely animals become winners because they had riders who were willing to take trouble and time for patient training and hard work.

There are so many forms of competition work connected with horses nowadays that I think it is best to look at them individually.

Showing

Having always looked after my own horses, and finding that I preferred to look at those that were good-looking rather than plain, the showing side of competitive work has long interested me. Shows and gymkhanas as such are a comparatively recent innovation. There were very few when I was young and they began to increase in number and popularity towards the end of the Second World War. My daughter and I began on our show career by riding at small gymkhanas, run for charities, and it was from these humble beginnings that we later attained marked success showing ponies.

Below, A beautiful Arab is shown in-hand.

Left: A considerable amount of equipment is necessary when competing at horse shows!

There are many categories in which horses and ponies can be shown. There are classes for ponies of different heights, based mainly on the pony's conformation and way of moving. There are classes for "working" ponies where their performance, including an ability to jump various fences, is more important. There are classes for different breeds – native ponies and Arabs in particular – which may be shown under saddle or in hand. There are classes for working hunters and show hunters (many of which have never been hunted in their lives!), and these are further sub-divided according to the country.

Finding top-class show ponies and horses is extremely difficult, and they are generally very expensive to buy. Those shown in specific breed classes are obviously meant to portray the finest characteristics in terms of conformation of their breed. Hunters are loosely described as those "that are suitable to ride to hounds." But, as I have said, valuable, top-class show hunters are unlikely ever to have been hunted, as their owners would be unwilling to subject them to possible damage or injury which they might incur on the hunting field. Instead, therefore, they are a model type, expected to be workmanlike and to look as if they have sufficient stamina to hunt. They should be sensible, with a good mouth and a comfortable ride.

The hack as a type has its origins in the days when members of fashionable society went riding in the streets and parks of towns and cities. Because the horse was constantly on view, in fact almost on display before the general public, it was particularly important that it presented a pleasing appearance. To do this it had to be well mannered, and look beautiful and elegant as it moved. Thus its conformation

and "presence" were very important. All of these things are looked for in the hack today. The hack, more than any other show horse, needs that indefinable "presence," so that it

Below: Bandaging a show pony's tail keeps it clean and neat.

Above: A prize-winning hack. Note the fine head and legs and neat compact body.

Below: A well proportioned hunter.

will be truly eye-catching. It is not a specific breed; in fact, hacks are usually cross-breeds which have inherited all the good qualities from either parent. Many hacks have a considerable amount of Thoroughbred blood in them giving a refined appearance.

Show ponies at one stage could almost be termed "freaks" of breeding, in that every now and then one pony of outstanding conformation and beauty would be born among a host of mediocre ones, for no apparent reason. Nowadays, however, there are several horse farms which concentrate on the breeding of "show ponies" and it has become big-money business. Most show ponies are crosses of native breeds and Thoroughbreds and many tend to be less hardy than their native ancestors. They are bred, trained and kept only to compete at shows. Not so beautiful, perhaps, but really more useful are the ponies shown in the "working" classes, where the judging is based more on their overall performance and ability than their conformation and movement. They will be required to jump, which pure show ponies are not expected to do.

Horses and ponies that are shown in-hand, as opposed to under saddle, include every type and breed, and it is an excellent way to introduce young horses to the demands and disciplines of the show ring. Classes range from those for heavy horses to small native breeds, and special classes for brood mares and foals. In addition, classes for young stock may be sub-divided into those for one, two and three year olds. Judging is based on conformation and type, and placings are bound to depend on the individual preferences of various judges.

In the US, hunter classes are divided into pony hunter, junior hunter, first and second-year green or novice/working hunter, open working hunter, conformation hunter and handy hunter. In England hunter classes are normally sub-divided into lightweight, middleweight and heavyweight as well as small hunters and working hunters. Then there are hack classes, for particularly elegant, eye-catching horses, usually of a Thoroughbred type measuring between 14.2 and 15.3 hands high. In addition, there are a number of show classes for horses registered with the various different societies – such as the Hackney Horse Society and the Palomino Horse Societies. The US has a popular class known as the Pleasure Horse Class, which is open to all types of horses and is judged on performance, manners, suitability to rider, and conformation, generally in that order.

Different types of horses are shown in various styles of riding (both in the Pleasure class and in others), known as the hunt seat, the saddle seat and the stock seat, which is used with the Western saddle. Generally, the

Above: The judges
make their decision.

style suits the horse, although some horses can be shown in more than one of the styles. Thoroughbreds are shown under hunt seat and are required to demonstrate smooth gaits and good manners. Their turn-out and tack is conventional – similar to that seen in showing classes in European shows. Three- and five-gaited horses, such as the Saddlebred and Tennessee Walker and Arabs, are generally shown under the saddle seat. Arabs are also shown under the stock seat. In the Pleasure class for Saddlebreds the correct turn-out and tack is a loose mane and tail (though part of the mane may be braided with colored ribbon), a double bridle and a straight-panelled saddle with big skirts. Horses shown under Western saddle are generally such breeds as the Quarter Horse, Pintos, Palominos and Appaloosas – and they are shown on a loose rein, the emphasis being on comfortable and easy gaits.

The saddle and hunt seat classes, other than the Pleasure class, are comparable to show classes in other countries and will be judged on similar criteria – performance, presence, quality and conformation. The horses are essentially for equitation or show riding and are judged as such. Gaits are particularly important in the showing of three- and five-gaited horses, and they are expected to perform the walk, trot and canter (three-gaited), or the walk, trot, canter, slow gait and rack (five-gaited).

The stock seat (or the Western style of riding) competitions have the greatest variety, for besides the pleasure and equitation classes there is a variety of events open to the Western-style riders. Many of these are more to test the

aptitude and skill of rider and horse in performing tasks they have to do in their daily work, rather than to "show" the horse.

The basic training for any show horse or pony is the same as for any other horse – that

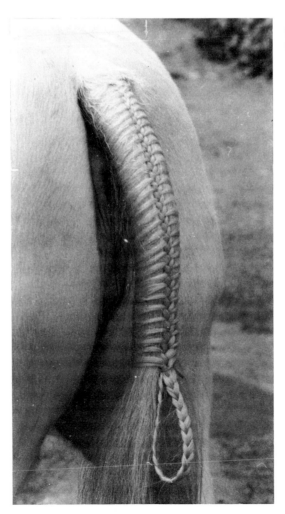

Left: An immaculately
braided tail showing the
looped end.

183

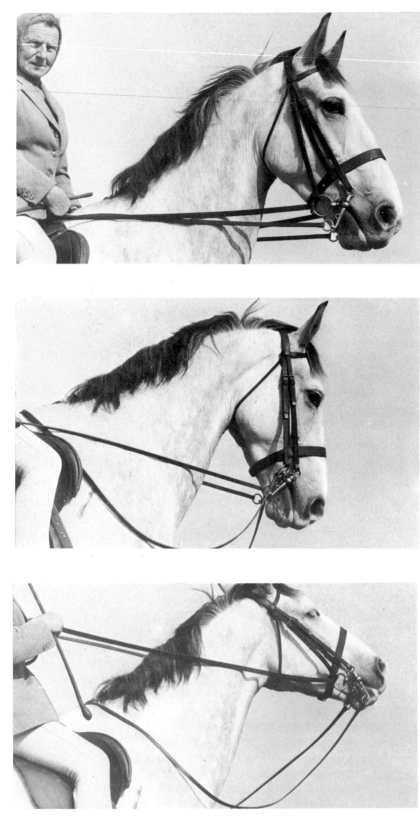

is, patient training and exercises on the lunge to make him supple and get him to move forward freely. This will be interspersed with gentle hacks, and it is a good idea to go out with others to get the horse used to being ridden in close proximity with other horses.

Carriage and Poise

Perhaps the main thing to try to develop is impressive carriage and poise, for these are the things that a judge will instantly notice. The head carriage is therefore particularly important and needs to be both elegant and fine, with the head held high and flexed naturally from the poll. This position must be maintained.

Horses and ponies are sometimes shown in a double bridle as it helps a rider to position the head. However, good head carriage is achieved by schooling in a snaffle bridle, and a well-schooled horse will accept a double bridle with little trouble. As explained on page 96, a double bridle comprises two bits – a bridoon or snaffle, which raises the head, and a curb which flexes it.

Anyone entering the show ring will have practiced using a double bridle and will be used to handling four reins, but I will explain the basic principles here. Keep the curb rein looser than

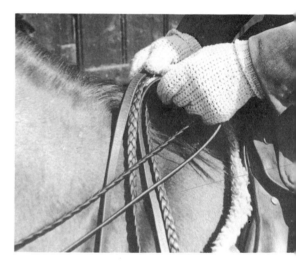

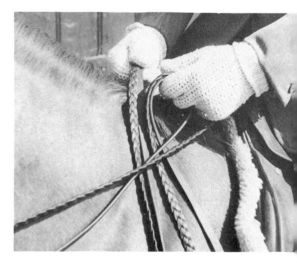

Above top: Horses are sometimes shown in a double bridle, although this horse and rider are not dressed for the show ring!

Above center: The curb flexes the head from the poll.

Above: The bridoon raises the head.

Right: Although the plaited rein can be used with either bit, it is more usually attached to the bridoon. Here the two ways of holding the reins are shown. Above right, the curb rein is on the outside. Right, the bridoon rein is on the outside.

the bridoon. Try holding the curb reins in one hand – and the bridoon reins in the other so you can see the different effect each set of reins has on the horse's head. Raise the head with the bridoon rein (using your legs) as you move forward and then use the curb rein to make him flex.

There are different, recognized ways of holding the reins of a double bridle, so try each of them in turn to find which you prefer. One way is to hold them with the curb rein running through one hand up and over the palm, with the bridoon rein running down and under the palm, your fingers closed on the reins. You can then operate either rein by just turning your wrist. Another way is to hold the reins with the curb rein coming around the little finger, with the bridoon below the third finger, or between the second and third fingers. In this method the curb rein is on the outside of the hand and, by use of the hand, has great pressure exerted on it. Holding the reins this way therefore tends to lead to lower head carriage of the horse.

The third, and perhaps most generally accepted, method is to hold the reins in a similar way to the above, but so that the snaffle rein comes on the outside of the hand and the curb on the inside. Greater influence can then be exerted on the bridoon rein, so that the head is raised. Most horses do tend to carry their head naturally too low rather than too high. Either of these last two ways of holding the reins may be adopted – the choice should depend entirely on your horse's own head carriage.

It is particularly important that show horses and ponies have a good, impressive walk, for this is the first gait a judge will see as the horse enters the ring. It helps to develop a good walk if the horse is led in-hand from both sides, so his muscles develop evenly. Walk out yourself as the leader, encouraging him to do the same by pushing him with an occasional flick of a long whip. Then practice walking – really striding out – mounted. Urge him on with pressure from your legs applied alternately with each stride, working first on a long rein and then with his head held in the correct position.

Lunging is still an important part of the training – maybe ride out one day and lunge the next. A good trot can be developed only if the horse really has his hocks under him so the forehand is lightened. This can best be achieved on the lunge when you can really check the horse's movement. In the same way, the easy-striding, calm canter so admired in the show ring is best attained through patient work on the lunge. Work at smooth transitions of gait both on the lunge and when mounted.

When training a hunter for the show ring in England, make sure many people ride him during the course of his training, because how he acts for any particular judge will make a considerable difference to his placing. A working hunter will have to be able to jump a few small jumps, so include this as part of the training, using both show-jump type fences and natural-looking ones. The aim with a hack is to produce a balanced and collected horse that moves forward with grace and ease and is comfortable to ride. The story is the same – lots of work on the lunge to create calm, collected gaits interspersed with trail riding with other people, so he does not become bored or stale.

Presentation of show ponies and horses is important, of course, for it can make so much difference to their appearance and thus their appeal. Besides trimming the horse at the heels and around the muzzle, and cleaning him to gleaming perfection, make sure all white markings – socks and stockings – are spotless. Manes look best braided but the tail will look equally attractive braided or not, providing it is well shaped and really clean and well brushed. Tails and legs can be kept clean in shipping by bandaging, and a summer sheet should keep the coat shiny and free from dust. It goes with-

out saying that all tack should be clean and immaculate. In fact, many people will have special show tack – a fine, neatly stitched double bridle and so on – that is kept in immaculate condition for nothing else.

Always allow yourself plenty of time when travelling to shows, getting there long before your class, both to guard against any time-consuming mishaps and to get the horse settled and used to the new surroundings. Horse shows can be upsetting affairs, with all their bustle and activity and so many people and horses milling around.

Above: A well turned out show pony and rider. Presentation is a very important aspect of showing horses and ponies competitively.

185

Show Jumping

In a period of 30 years, show jumping has grown from a little-practiced, seldom viewed sport into one that has major international appeal. People who have little intrinsic interest in horses nevertheless flock to the big horse shows or watch the exciting international competition on the television. For those that compete, it has become a professional and big-money sport, in which large companies and commercial organizations sponsor many of the individual professional riders.

The first records of organized show jumping competitions appear around the 1860s but it was a century later, after the Second World War, that the sport began to really catch on in a big way. Italy, France and Germany were ahead in holding show-jumping competitions, which doubtless explains in part the success of riders from these countries in major events.

Show jumping undoubtedly owes its increased popularity to the vast efforts of those involved in its organization. Competitions used to be held over dull and boring courses with unimaginative and unappealing fences that all looked much the same. There was no time limit imposed, so a rider could circle endlessly in front of a fence if he felt his horse was not going correctly. Each round could thus be, and usually was, a highly protracted affair, boring to watch and probably neither very interesting nor rewarding to ride. From a competitor's point of view, too, the "rules" were far from satisfactory. Penalties were given for touching a fence as well as actually knocking it down. As most fences had slats resting on top of them which were easily dislodged, it was necessary to jump very high to make sure of clearing each obstacle. In addition, competitors were penalized for landing on or within the demarcation lines of spread fences, and more penalties were given if mistakes were made by forelegs than if they were made by the hind ones. As may be imagined, there were endless margins for human error in judgement with such a system, with much resulting dissatisfaction! The shows were also very lengthy.

Nowadays the system of judging is extremely simple, which has made it a much more attractive prospect for both spectator and competitor. The rules decree four faults for a fence knocked down, whether it be just one pole dis-

J.G. Maathurs of Holland takes a jump in the ring.

Competitive show-jumping calls for much hard work in training to achieve accurate timing and precision. In these pictures of the approach (left), take-off (right), suspension (bottom left) and landing (bottom right), the horse and rider are demonstrating great harmony and balance.

lodged or the whole fence demolished, and whether it be hit by forelegs, hind legs or anything else. Three penalty faults are given for the first refusal at a fence, six for the second and elimination for the third. Circling in front of a fence constitutes a refusal. Faults are also given for the fall of a horse or rider. There is generally a time limit set for a course, and if the competitor runs over the time allowed, he collects time faults. This system is now internationally instituted by the F.E.I., so everyone knows what to expect.

As with eventers there is no recognized breed that makes a show jumper, and many different types of horses will be seen in the show-jumping ring. Characteristics to look for are boldness and a natural love of jumping. In addition, show jumpers have to be trained to be very obedient to their rider's commands, but, at the same time, they need sufficient intelligence to get themselves out of difficulty if problems occur, such as they might at awkwardly spaced combination jumps.

They also need to be very supple to cope with the twists and turns that comprise most jumping courses. Most successful show jumpers

will have powerful quarters and strong hocks.

Training a show jumper is every bit as long and exacting a task as training a horse for any competition work. We discussed on page 143 the very beginning stages of teaching a horse to jump, although this is really only to give a trainer an idea of whether the horse has natural jumping aptitude, while helping to instill more natural balance in his general movements.

The early training for a show jumper is much the same as for a rider learning to jump – in other words, to get the horse moving freely over heavy poles on the ground, first at a walk and then at a trot. Start with three evenly spaced poles and then add a fourth and a fifth, placed close together, but a little way apart from the others, so that the horse has actually to hop over these two. Then start using four to six cavaletti placed in a line, the correct distance apart for the horse to step over one at each stride. Trot over them in both directions, both on the lunge and mounted. Finally make the last two into a hurdle, which actually has to be jumped rather than trotted over. The four cavaletti to be trotted over will be about 4 ft. 6 in.

(1.4 m.) apart; then leave a double space of 9 ft. (2.8 m.) before the two cavaletti placed together as a jump. Remember the advice about not piling cavaletti up too high on top of each other, which is very dangerous. Never put more than two together on top of each other.

When the horse is really at ease with his basic cavaletti exercise, you can begin popping over a variety of small jumps which, for a time, you should make no higher than 2 ft. (60 cm.). It is very important throughout teaching a young horse to jump that his personal confidence in himself and in you is never shaken. Never overwhelm a youngster. He will be learning all the time if you constantly introduce new and different-looking obstacles, so that he is perpetually jumping things he has not seen or come across before.

As with training an eventer, build lots of strange and unusual multi-colored jumps, using anything you can find, providing it does not have sharp protuberances such as nails or jagged edges. Put the jumps in different places so that the horse does not get used to jumping the same thing in the same position all the time.

When first teaching a horse to jump, you can make use of his natural homing instinct and jump him in the direction of home. If he appears happy and at ease, try jumping him away from home – or in some completely different place, such as a friend's field. Even the low jumps you build should be solid, for if they knock down easily, it could instill carelessness into the horse and he will think all fences will knock down when he hits them. Make sure these fences have a good ground line, which will encourage a horse to lower his head and really look at the fence. If he does not lower his head enough when jumping, concentrate on jumping him on the lunge, putting bright-colored poles on the ground to attract his attention. Watch to see that he is lowering his head correctly and attaining the correct bend of his back. Try jumping low double oxers – that is, jumps comprising two lower poles with a small brush fence or something that looks solid in between them. This type of construction helps in getting a horse to bend his back correctly as he goes over the jump.

Top right: The horse is standing off at the jump and the rider has lost some contact.

Center right: At the same fence the rider has been left behind. This is making the horse hollow his back and therefore jump flat.

Right: A good position from the rider, although she is looking down at the jump.

Again, in these early stages, I think it is a good idea to intersperse jumping lessons with long rides and some schooling on the flat. Some people advocate jumping every day for the potential jumper, but I don't think it is a good idea. He needs to think of other things as well, and a ride in the country can be relaxing and therapeutic. You can always pop over small fallen logs and the like during the natural course of the ride.

As you progress to higher jumps, say of about 3 ft. 3 in. (1 m.), build fewer of them and space them further apart. This is probably best done outside the ring, using the fence of a field as a natural starting place. It is much easier to ride or lunge a horse over a jump positioned close to a fence or hedge than one stuck out in the middle of a field. To some extent, it is a substitute for the walls of a covered school, but it is essential to introduce jumping in an open space into the horse's training, so that he gets a feeling of freedom too.

It will help both you and your horse if you seek the advice of some experienced person whose opinion and judgement you respect, asking him to watch as you ride over fences. Sensible criticism from someone who knows what they are talking about, from an observation point on the ground, can help you considerably, for it is not always easy to assess the overall picture from on top of a horse. And do practice school work as well – particularly all those exercises on the lunge. They help so much in giving a horse natural balance, suppleness and calmness – all essential attributes in a show jumper, who is going to be asked to jump a number of varied, and often tricky, fences in a confined space.

If you start your training well in advance of the show season and all goes well, with your horse jumping small and varied fences with ease and confidence, it will be a good idea to take him along to a small show. The idea initially is not to compete, but just to get him used to the sights and atmosphere and to meeting lots of other horses. Lunge him in a quiet corner of the field, so that he calms down, maybe even gets slightly bored. Then ride him about, stopping to chat with people, or to watch the horses in the ring. At the next show, enter him into a novice event, providing the fences are no higher than those you have been jumping at home. But never force him around the course. He has to get, and maintain, "ring confidence," which is an extremely important factor for any horse entering competition work. He must never dread the ring, for if he does he can never make a successful show jumper. Instead he should enjoy it, feeling all the time that it is something of a party. Many years ago, I took a seven year old mare to a show. She was white with sweat and bucked and jumped around from 9:30 in the morning

until 4:30 when I got off her. Yet within two months she was winning at shows. Patience will be rewarded when you are training a show jumper – as is the case with all other horses, too, of course.

From here on, the training of show jumpers becomes more complicated and specialized and you would be well advised to read as much as you can about the subject. Watch the top-class riders in the ring, and listen to their comments before and afterwards. You can learn a great deal from the experts, not least that they never neglect basic exercises – work over cavaletti and

Above top: The rider is teaching the horse to land on a given leg (a useful attribute for speed competitions). The horse's head is bent slightly to the right so he will strike off on the off-fore.

Above: It is said that if you feel the horse's tail on your hat, he is bound to be a good jumper!

189

on the lunge – even with their top-class, experienced horses.

The show jumper will need to be trained how to jump water jumps and tricky combinations. Water jumps used to present an enormous amount of trouble, but now, as they appear in more and more competitions, they have become less of a problem. This is doubtless because they are generally better built than they were at one stage, but also because any show jumping rider will include the technique of jumping them in his horse's basic training. They call for great extension on approach so that the horse is really able to stretch himself. The important thing to remember, however, is that a horse cannot attain great length in a jump unless he also attains height. That is, his body must follow the same natural curved arch that it does as he goes over any jump.

Horses are very often frightened of water jumps or ditches when they first come across them, as they are not quite sure what horrors may lurk within. Hence it is a good idea to dig a ditch in your training field, and practice over this. Don't make it too wide, perhaps not more than 3 ft. 3 in. (1 m.) or so initially, and construct wings on either side that slope slightly forward, so the horse is drawn into it. It will help to begin with to put a pole or hedge in the center – again so that he is encouraged to jump upwards as well as to spread himself. Later you can abandon this.

Combinations can often present problems, and the only way to try to avoid these occurring

Above: The essence of competition show-jumping is to *stay* at the top. Here Lucinda Prior-Palmer, in the top league of today, is competing at Hickstead, England, in 1969.

Below: Teaching a horse to jump over ditches and water jumps is an essential part of training.

is by constructing a number of different combinations. Fences are classified as being part of a combination if they are within 39 ft. 4 in. (12 m.) of each other, and it is the distance between them, rather than the fences themselves, that makes them hard to jump. Try building different types of combinations – leading off perhaps with an upright type of fence placed before a spread fence with just one stride in between, again keeping the fences small to begin with. Then reverse the order. Add another fence two strides farther on. Vary the distance, so that you have to ask for two long or three short strides. Just practice a number of different things, so you both are able to cope with whatever you meet in the ring, even if it is something quite new.

As you enter more show jumping competitions, you will constantly find new obstacles or combinations of obstacles that differ slightly from those you have come across before. Course building is now an art in itself, and a highly sophisticated one at that. Course builders are at pains to build new and interesting courses, sufficiently demanding to ensure that not every horse in the competition gets by them all. Basically there is only a limited number of types of fence – the upright, the pyramid, the parallel, the staircase and the water jump. An imaginative course builder interprets each of these in different ways to provide variations of each type. His aim is always to build a demanding course that ensures a challenge, but he is also working towards making a course that encourages a horse to jump his best, not one that is really difficult and dangerous to ride. Often you will find there is one fence on a course that consistently causes trouble, but this, in fact, is often more psychological than anything else. Riders see those before them knock a hurdle down and

immediately they think that they are almost bound to do the same thing, thus riding accordingly.

In show jumping competitions you are always allowed to walk the course before the jumping starts, and this is a very valuable time for the rider. Study each jump with care, and assess it from your own horse's point of view. Measure the distances between each fence, particularly in combinations, and decide before you enter the ring whether you are going to push on to ask for two strides between fences or whether you think it would be better to hold back slightly and ask for three. Decide from which angle you want to approach any particular jump, and also where you can cut corners and where you should give yourself the maximum amount of room.

A special kind of show jumping event, held at only some of the major international shows, is the puissance, or high jump. This is the only event in which the result depends solely on jumping ability and not on speed; the horse that wins is, quite simply, the one that jumps the highest. The first rounds usually comprise a shorter course than usual, perhaps only six or eight fences, and in successive rounds this number is reduced still further. Finally, there are a couple of deciding fences, most often a high wall and a triple bar, perhaps with a smaller "warming-up" fence. In jumping great upright heights, such as the high wall of a puissance event, the jumping technique changes again. At such a height a horse quite literally has to "buck" himself over the top. Many spectators dislike puissance events, feeling they are not altogether fair on the horse, who must be pushed to the limits of his capacity. However, most top-class riders would disagree, feeling that it is asking no more from a horse to jump great heights than it is to ask him to race around a course of large jumps at speed. A rider of the caliber to enter such events should in any case know his horse's capabilities. Thus, if he feels it has already reached its limit, he can withdraw, and certainly no one would think less of him for doing so. In fact, quite the reverse.

A competitor in a Puissance or high jump event. Different techniques of jumping have to be employed by horse and rider to clear the great heights reached in these competitions.

Racing

For those people that love speed, racing is their sport, and a highly competitive one it is, too. Racing in some form is probably as old as the practice of riding horses, and there are records of mounted races being held by the Greeks in 600 B.C. The ancient Egyptians certainly counted horse racing as one of their sports, and the Romans ran mounted races as well as their almost legendary chariot races. Today racing is probably one of the commonest sports connected with horses in every country. It is particularly enjoyable in that it involves so many people – the jockeys or drivers; the stable lads, the race organizers and ground staff; trainers and owners and their friends and the many members of the general public who love the excitement and exhilaration of a "day at the races."

Nowadays the most highly organized forms of racing are those run on the flat, and those over fences, known as steeplechasing. In addition, there are the very fast and highly competitive trotting and pacing races – so popular in the US, Russia and parts of Europe – and the point-to-points run in England which are affiliated with specific Hunts.

The first record of flat racing in Great Britain appears to be around 1377 when the Prince of Wales, later to be Richard II, raced his horses against the Earl of Arundel. Racing then prospered, except under Cromwell, who added it to his list of "forbidden sports." It was restarted by Charles II from whence it became known as the "Sport of Kings." The British Royal Family since this time has taken a keen interest in racing and has done much to further its popularity. It was Queen Anne who was responsible for Ascot Race Course, and the race meeting held on this course is still one of the most fashionable occasions in any horse lover's calendar.

Flat racing and steeplechasing are instantly connected with the Thoroughbred, which for years was bred most successfully by the British – so much so that the English Thoroughbred Race Horse became a breed in its own right. English Thoroughbreds have been exported all over the world at various times, but now other countries – the US, France, Italy, Ireland, Australia and New Zealand, to name just a few – are equally successful in producing these quality race horses. American race horses in particular are a force to be reckoned with on race tracks the world over.

South Africa's premier National Hunt race is the S.A. National Hurdle which is run over a course of 18 hurdles.

192

There are five classic races held every year in England– the Derby, the Oaks, the St. Leger, the 1000 Guineas and the 2000 Guineas. These races began over 200 years ago. In France there are many famous races that carry considerably higher prize money than in England. Among them are the Grand Prix du Paris and the Prix Royal Oak held at Longchamps and the Prix du Jockey Club held at Chantilly. In the US, races are held at different "tracks" and several racing meets continue for some time – in fact for up to 100 days, although it is more usual for them to last 50 or 60 days. The most famous flat races are the Kentucky Derby and the Preakness Stakes. The racing fraternity in the US was the first to use the mechanical starting gates which are now a familiar sight to all racegoers.

Steeplechasing and point-to-points have the same origin, for they both undoubtedly sprang out of the hunting field in the eighteenth century. The races themselves almost certainly began as rather friendly, if keenly contested, affairs between a few people, each claiming his hunter to be the best. An early story of such a race tells of the gentlemen and horses assembling at the gates of one churchyard and racing to where the spire of another church could be seen, hence the name "steeplechasing." From these beginnings, slightly more organized affairs began to emerge such as the St. Albans' steeplechase in 1832. But even in 1839, when the world-famous Grand National became the

highlight of a steeplechaser's career, an old rule still existed which stated that "no rider was to open a gate or ride through a gateway or more than 100 yards down the road."

The Grand National, held each year at Aintree, near Liverpool, is probably the most famous steeplechase in the world. When it began in 1839 most of the 29 fences consisted of little more than low banks with gorse on top of them. However, among them were two fences which concealed brooks, and these have ever since presented riders with a certain amount of concern. The most famous, now known as Becher's Brook, was named after a certain Captain Becher, who was apparently the first person to find himself deposited in its unfriendly waters.

Steeplechasing is most popular in France and in the US, where there are rich rewards for the winners of races. France has an equivalent of the Grand National in its Grand Steeplechase de Paris, run annually in June. Of equal fame is the Grand Course de Haies d'Auteuil – a hurdle race also staged in June.

In the US racing over fences has been further divided into steeplechasing or hurdle races, where the fences are made of soft brush or light branches, and the "hunt" meetings where the fences are made of timber and constructed very solidly, such as in the world famous Maryland Hunt Cup. Jump racing seems to have begun in the late eighteenth century in the US and the races were known as

A point-to-point meeting.

"pounding" races – the aim being to "pound" the other competitors.

There is a race held every year in Czechoslovakia which compares with the English Grand National. Called the Grand Perdulice, it was once won by an Englishman, Chris Collins, well known as an event rider as well as an amateur race rider. It is interesting to note that in 1976, out of 37 starters, only seven finished and the first and second horses came from the same farm in Czechoslovakia. Very satisfactory for the manager!

Point-to-point races, as mentioned earlier, have common ancestry with steeplechasing. The name "point-to-point" was coined for that is just what the early races were – a race run from a specified point to another specified point. As these races increased in popularity, the Hunt gradually began to make them more organized and festive affairs, with huge lunches given for the farmers as a "thank you" for allowing the hunt on their land. Up until this stage, there had probably been only one race – just for the members of the Hunt – and often the course was kept a secret until they were all ready and assembled. But, as the races changed and became an important way for a Hunt to raise much needed funds, "fair" courses were built. The lay-out and jumps varied according to the part of the country. More than one race was

The Hialeah Park Race Course in Florida.

held at each meeting – an Adjacent Hunt Race (for members from five nearby packs), a Members' Race, a Farmers' Race, and an open Race in which anyone could compete providing their horses complied with the regulation of being hunted through the season and providing they could produce a certificate from the Master of their pack of Foxhounds in order to prove it.

Ladies began to compete in point-to-points after the First World War and at first races were held to include both sexes. In around 1930, races exclusively for ladies were held and ladies became barred from the other races. Nowadays they can also compete in the Members' Races. Up until comparatively recently, however, point-to-points were really held as fun affairs. as a way to mark the end of the hunting season. Hunting dress was worn – the pink and black coats and top hats, which were a common sight in the hunting field. Gradually these gave way to the traditional racing colors and the jumps took on a "steeplechase" construction. Although the horses still have to have hunted during the previous season and must not have been in a licensed trainer's yard since the previous November, they are no longer hunters, but race horses probably trying out their prowess before moving on to greater things.

Very exciting from a spectator's point of view are the trotting and pacing races that comprise the two forms of modern harness racing. These obviously date back in some ways to the Roman and Egyptian chariot racing. Over the ensuing centuries, lighter carts have been developed and horses specially bred to participate in the sport.

In both trotting and pacing races, the horses pull a light sulky, which holds the driver. The difference between the trotters and pacers is that a trotter's movement is a trot of the diagonals like that of ordinary riding horses, but much faster, while a pacer's legs move laterally – that is, the two nearside legs move together as do the two offside legs.

France, the US and Russia are probably the countries most famed for their trotting and pacing horses, although the sport is popular in many other countries, too. In the US the races were started by the early settlers who staged trotting, pacing and timber-pulling races among themselves. Doubtless the races themselves were for relaxation, but they had to do with everyday life – getting from place to place in a horse-drawn vehicle and pulling timber from the virgin land the settlers were attempting to clear and cultivate.

For many years the Russian Orlov Trotter was considered the best breed of trotting horse, but now the horses bred in the US have proved their worth by holding all the world records. The most famous harness racing breed is the American Trotter, which may be a trotter or pacer. It descended from an English Thoroughbred imported to the US, but the conformation of the Trotter today is markedly different from the Thoroughbred, mainly because they are not bred to carry a rider.

Nearly all countries of the world hold races of some sort. The Arab countries are great supporters of racing and Arab horses are bred specifically for racing in the same way as the Thoroughbred is produced for this sport. Whatever its form, all racing has one thing in common – it is man's wish to prove his horse is the best, and that hasn't changed since those first races in 600 B.C.

An Arab fine-Harness horse.

Eventing

Eventing is fast becoming one of the most popular of all equitation sports, and yet it is perhaps the most demanding of them all. Although a sport that appeals primarily to the young, in England there have been two notable older gentlemen connected with the sport who have done much for it. One is Brigadier Bolton, who consistently produced good eventers, all of which he had schooled himself. The other is Major Alhusen, who could also be relied upon to produce good horse after good horse. Even more to his credit, he had bred them all himself, using a German mare as foundation stock, which he had brought home with him after being stationed in Germany.

Eventing demands high standards in three different types of competitive riding, namely dressage, cross-country riding and show jumping. The cross-country aspect usually includes a section across roads and tracks and a steeplechase course to test the horse's stamina and endurance, before it is asked to do a gruelling ride across a course of cross-country jumps. Clearly, eventing is extremely exacting on both horse and rider, and its aim is to test the all-around ability and versatility of a horse. It reduces the tendency, often inherent in competi-

The event rider and horse have to be skilled in competition dressage (above), as well as able to maintain fast speeds over prolonged distances and a steeplechase course (left).

tive work, to over-specialize but instead encourages the breeding of good horses and subsequent thorough training of both horse and rider. A horse has to be obedient, supple and balanced to execute a good dressage test; bold enough to face big, awkward and sometimes real problem fences; with sufficient stamina to take them at speed, after it has completed the roads and tracks section. And then, after all this, it still has to be supple and calm to face a fairly exacting course of show jumps, which will include upright and spread fences different from those encountered during the cross-country course.

A tall order for any horse, and, as one can imagine, horses that can compete in this kind of competition are not trained in a short time. Perhaps more than for any other equestrian event, a horse needs to have complete confidence in his rider, so that he will be obedient to the many different demands placed on him in a short space of time. In addition he has to maintain a very high standard of fitness. It can take years of hard, patient work to produce a top-

class eventer. Understandably, such horses are worth a great deal of money.

Eventing began as part of army training, to encourage members of mounted regiments to train their horses well in these separate fields of horsemanship. It is what the French call "the complete test" and work at the famous Cadre Noir (see page 176) has always placed justified emphasis on this type of training. Belgium, Sweden and Switzerland all held military three-day events in the first decades of the twentieth century and in 1912 they were included in the Olympic Games, all the competitors being military personnel. Eventually, after the Second World War, eventing spread from the military to civilian life, and one-day, two-day and three-day events began to be held. The most famous three-day event held in England is the Badminton Horse Trials, first promoted by the Duke of Beaufort after he had been present at the 1948 Olympic Games. He gave Badminton Park in Gloucestershire for the event, and the first one was held in 1949. Eventing was less popular in England than other places at this time, army officers still being suspicious of "dressage" and preferring instead to play polo! Happily, it became popular among civilians, particularly among lady riders who now consistently do well in national and international competitions.

To describe the ideal horse for eventing is not difficult. To find it is quite another matter!

Yet if you look at advertisements for horses today, every other one claims to be a "potential eventer." This may be taken as an indication of the sport's increasing popularity, rather than all these horses' aptitudes! An eventer must have a certain amount of substance, combined with a quality that shows he will be fast across country. He should have a proudly carried head with bold eyes. He needs intelligence and kindness, courage and obedience, stamina and suppleness. The great Eddie Goldman once said that the first thing he would look for in a

Above and below: In addition to the aspects mentioned opposite, an eventer has to tackle a demanding cross-country course, incorporating many formidable obstacles. A formal show-jumping course completes the event.

potential eventer was an even temperament. A horse that is going to be asked to perform many different but equally demanding exercises and tasks, in a comparatively short space of time, must have an even and easygoing temperament if he is to remain calm at all times.

Training and caring for an eventer is extremely time-consuming, for they need lots of work and lots of exercise to keep them fit and to keep their minds occupied and sharp. The first thing is to instill suppleness and natural balance in them, which calls for training on the lunge with side reins attached (see page 134), first without a rider, and then with a rider on top. Intersperse this work with hacking in the country unless he has not been hacked, in which case drive him out on long reins attached to a Cavesson with an assistant at his head. But progress to riding him as soon as possible so that he can be lunged with a rider. Next you can begin cavaletti work, which will follow the same procedure as when you are teaching a potential show jumper to jump.

After this, read every book you can find on jumping methods advocated by other people so that you find what suits your horse. I feel the best principle is to keep to small fences – no more than about 2 ft. 6 in. (70 cm.) high, but as varied as possible. Paint them all the colors of the rainbow. Use straw bales, oil drums – anything that looks peculiar. Throw a horse blanket over a small jump, or some colored coats over poles. Makers of cross-country courses dream up some amazing jumps these days to test a horse's boldness, so at this stage

you are saying to your horse, "go on, it isn't going to hurt you." This is why it is so important that he has complete confidence and trust in you – he must know that when you tell him it won't hurt him, it won't! As long as you keep the obstacles small with a good ground line, there is no reason why the horse should not work for some time just at a trot, hopping over the jumps as you put him to them, and coming back to a trot, even a walk, after and between jumps. As you raise the height of the jumps, place them farther apart to give more of a feeling of space to the horse as he jumps.

Don't neglect your dressage training through

Above: A successful event rider – S. Strachen.

Below: A. Argenton competing at Badminton.

goal take heart at the examples set by two great event riders, Lorna Sutherland and Lucinda Prior-Palmer. I was rude enough to tell Lorna her horse "Poppadum" was an overgrown cob and would never make a top-class eventer. She persevered – and proved me very wrong! Her other horse at that time was called "Nicholas Nickelby." He had a cleft palate and she had bought him out of pity. He went on to do very well for her. "Be Fair," Lucinda's brilliant horse, first came to my stable when Lucinda was still in school – never an easy time for anyone to work and train an eventer. He was not an easy horse, but she worked hard and overcame the troubles.

To conclude, I quote an old saying: "The bigger the eye, the better. The deeper the heart the stronger. The prouder the lift of the head, the more courageous. The swifter the action, the more fearless." This surely describes an eventer. Look at all the great eventers – not the one-time winners but those who consistently do well – and you will find big eyes, deep chests with plenty of heart room, and the proudness and courage that will not be beaten, however tough the competition.

all this, for the horse has to progress evenly and equally in all the aspects of eventing. Divide your time between the school work and jumping work, never doing either so much that the horse becomes bored and disinterested. Always let him know when you are pleased with what he has done and achieved.

Progress quietly and methodically; it is going to take at least 18 months to two years before you can compete in even a Novice Event. Build a small cross-country course at home. Have a table that can be taken both ways. Build narrow fences – some with drops on landing. Try to find a small, steep bank you can slide down. As you go out for rides, look for steeper banks to ride up and down. Pop over fallen trees and logs.

Try taking your horse to a small show in the same way you would a potential show jumper (see page 189). Then enter a Novice Hunter Trial to discover the fences he fears or does not like. Build similar ones at home and practice him over them until his fear has gone. If you go to an event where you feel the cross country is going to be too much for your horse, do the dressage and retire gracefully. Better this than to spoil your horse at this stage. This happened to us with what would have been a brilliant horse. Three stupid fences were included in the course, at which any novice horse was almost bound to hurt himself. It may be argued that no horse with brains is going to hurt himself for the fun of it, but then eventers have been trained to have confidence in their riders. Our horse jumped these jumps, hurt himself and then jumped two more fences before he lost his nerve. He stopped at the next awkward fence, and ever since then this horse's jumping has shown marked lack of confidence.

If the rigors of eventing seem an impossible

Above: Britain's Richard Meade on Tommy Buck.

Below: America's Bruce Davidson on Irish Cap.

International Events and the Olympic Games

For many people, success in local equestrian events will encourage them to enter bigger horse shows, where the competition is tougher and the rewards correspondingly more satisfying. This in turn can lead to participating in national competitions and then to international competitions – possibly as a member of a team chosen to represent one's country. Many factors are needed to compete internationally, and to be able to do so one needs considerable experience as well as calmness and wisdom to rise above the additional stresses and strains imposed by such events. Nowadays many young riders take their horses abroad each year to compete in various countries, in order to gain this experience and to see if their horses have the drive and ability to compete under strange circumstances. Competing internationally will

Above: Holland's J. Heinz on Trohnforger competing at Hickstead, England.

Below: Cachica from Argentina jumping off the Hickstead bank.

also test how both horse and rider stand up to the strain of travelling, and to the attacks of "nerves" brought about by the tense atmosphere of such events.

The equestrian event most instantly associated with international horse shows is probably show jumping, although there are also many international dressage and eventing competitions. The US, Canada and most European countries hold horse shows which are open to international competitors. Individual riders may compete in a variety of events, and in addition there is often a team event known as the Nations' Cup, for which four riders will have been selected from each of the competing countries.

In all national and international show jumping events, the rules are laid down by the Fédération Equestre Internationale, and those that apply to the Nations' Cup events are clearly itemized and must be adhered to wherever the competition is held. The reason for the rules being stricter in this event is to try to ensure the building of a course that presents the same problems to all riders, whatever their nationality. There could otherwise be a tendency for the course built in any particular country to favor the host riders. The course has to be about 867 yards (788 meters) long, except at indoor shows, and has to contain 13 or 14 fences. There must be at least one double or one triple, but not more than either one of both or three doubles. Fences have to be between 4 ft. 3 in. (1.34 meters) and 5 ft. 3 in. (1.6 meters) high and must include a water jump of not less than 13 ft. (3.9 meters) in overall width.

The four riders chosen by each country to take part must jump two rounds over the course. Penalties are given under the same system as any other F.E.I. show jumping event – that is, four penalty points for a fence knocked down, three faults for a refusal, six for the second refusal and elimination for the third, eight faults for the fall of the horse or rider and a quarter fault for each second taken over the alloted time. The final score is achieved by combining the penalties for the three best riders of each team, the winner being the team with the lowest score.

Every show jumping rider undoubtedly has an ambition to represent his country in a Nations' Cup event, but it takes a special sort of person to achieve it. Besides the obvious ability needed, such qualities as team spirit, sportsmanship and a calm but good-humored temperament are essential. It is the reputation of one's country that is at stake, not just an individual's personal reputation. The national selectors will nearly always choose one older, more experienced rider as a member of the team – one who has represented his country many times before and knows what to expect. Even if he is no longer at the very peak of his career, his wisdom and experience gained over many years will be an invaluable and vital asset to the team, particularly if his co-members are younger riders.

Another highlight and aim of any show jumping rider's career is to become the recognized World Champion. This event is held in various countries – the host nation at any one time usually being the home of the current holder of the title. It is an extremely tough event, made even more so for the four finalists who have to jump the course riding each other's horses. Thus, they have to prove their ability as horsemen, riding a strange horse over a

David Broome on Black Water.

201

course of jumps that would cause concern to most riders when riding a horse they know well! No wonder the World Champion is a much-coveted title.

If it is the ambition of every show jumping rider to represent his country in a Nations' Cup event, or to become the World Champion, it must be the zenith of every rider's career to be chosen to go to the Olympics – be it in the show jumping team, the eventing team or in the dressage event. The Olympic Games, held in a different country every four years, are looked forward to and followed by everybody. They originally started in 776 B.C., but events involving horses did not take place until the 25th Olympiad in 690 B.C. Even then the competition was not for mounted riders, but consisted of chariot races. A thousand years later, in 393 A.D., the Olympic games were abolished and were not reinstated as an event until Baron Coubertin did so in 1896.

It came as a great surprise to me to learn that the Olympic flame had been extinguished for so many centuries, for I had always imagined such spectacles as the grand tournaments of

Above: A consistently successful show-jumping personality, Nelson Pessoa of Brazil, mounted here on Bord de Loine.

Left: P. Weier of Switzerland on Wulf.

Opposite top: Alwin Schockemohle from Germany competing at Hickstead.

Opposite right: Ireland's popular Eddie Machen.

the middle ages were part of the Games. Even when the Games were resurrected at the end of the last century, there were no events for horses. One of the reasons for this could well have been the expense of transporting horses to some far-off place to compete. Transportation for animals, horses in particular, was a great problem anyway and I have heard many "horror stories" told to me by my father's groom about the rough boat journeys across the English Channel. This would have made taking horses any great distance extremely impractical and they certainly would have been in no state to compete in a gruelling and challenging event at the end of it. Nowadays, the transportation arrangements for horses are highly organized and sophisticated, with specially equipped airplanes and an exclusive trans-European "horse train."

In spite of the difficulties and expense of transportation at the beginning of the century, there were people who felt strongly that equestrian events should be included in the Olympic Games, which were, after all, supposed to represent all sporting activities. The guiding light in the move to have them incorporated was Count von Rosen, who was Master of the Horse to the King of Sweden. He felt that to include equestrian events in the games could only have a beneficial effect upon international standards of horsemanship. His enthusiasm was such that the Olympic Committee of 1906 asked for details of proposals to be drawn up for consideration at the meeting to be held at the Hague in 1907. The Swedes formed a committee which drew up a program of events with suggested rules, and the Olympic Committee agreed that they should be included in the Games that were due to be held in London in 1908. Eight nations put in a total of 88 entries, which proved too many both for the newly built Stadium in London, and, as was subsequently proposed, for inclusion in the International Horse Show held in London the same year. Equestrian events thus made their debut in the Olympic Games held in Stockholm in 1912, and they proved tremendously popular.

In the interim period between Count von Rosen's proposals in 1906 and the Olympic Games in 1912, various riding events were included in the Berlin Congress of 1909, on an international competitive basis. These included "prize riding," which later became the Grand Dressage event, and the "military competition," which was the forerunner of our three-day event competition. On the whole only the Army teams from affluent countries competed, and the jumping competitions were filled with military uniforms. However, my father did win the International Jumping Competition in London in 1909 riding in hunting dress. In addition there was the famous "Festival of Riding" which was

held at Spa in Belgium each year under royal patronage.

This, too, was an "international" event of sorts, and cross-country racing, ordinary racing, show jumping and *haute école* events were all held. The latter included movements that were more akin to circus riding than true *haute école*, which involves only the natural airs on and above the ground.

The first show jumping team event held at the Stockholm Olympics in 1912 was won by the host nation, with France and Germany coming in second and third. The First World War obviously made it impossible to hold another Olympic event until 1920, when again it was the Swedes who were victorious in both the three-day event and the show jumping. In Paris in 1924, the Swedish team took the gold medal in the show jumping event, but the Dutch team claimed the gold in the three-day event, as they did again in the 1928 Olympics.

The Amsterdam Olympics marked the beginning of the three-day event in the form that it is known today – that is, a dressage event, followed by the cross-country events, and finally the show jumping competition. Still no real competition for the Continental riders, Britain nevertheless showed they might be a force to be reckoned with in the future by placing sixth in this event. In the ensuing Games in 1932 held in Los Angeles and those in 1936 held in Berlin, it was the host nations in both cases who

achieved most notable success, although in Los Angeles none of the competing teams completed the show jumping event.

The Second World War then broke the four-year continuity of the Games, and the next time they were staged was in Great Britain in 1948. The show jumping gold medal was claimed

Above: Edgar Gupper on Le Champion riding for Belgium in the team show-jumping event at the 1976 Olympic Games.

Left: Canada's Michael Vailloncourt on Branch County – winners of the individual silver medal for show-jumping at the 1976 Olympic Games.

Opposite top: Lucinda Prior-Palmer and Be-Fair in the dressage section of the three-day event at the 1976 Olympic Games.

Opposite right: Luis Alvarez-Cervera from Spain competing in the team show-jumping event at the 1976 Olympic Games.

by the Mexican team, and a British Army team took the bronze. The Americans took the gold in the three-day event and the Swiss won the

Up until this time, it was often army officers who were successful in competitive riding. With their military training on horsemanship, this was hardly surprising. As the Olympic Games progressed into the 1950s, civilian riders came into their own. It was at the 1952 Olympics that Britain got her first gold medal in the show jumping event. Her three-day event team followed this in 1956 by claiming the gold at the Stockholm games.

In the Olympic Games held over the last two decades, medals have been claimed by a variety of nations, showing that international standards are much the same in many countries. Germany has done consistently well, claiming gold medals for show jumping in 1956 at Stockholm, 1960 in Rome, 1964 in Tokyo and 1972 in Munich. Canada took the gold for the show jumping team event in 1968 in Mexico. The United States has done well too, collecting a silver in the show jumping event in 1960, silvers for the three-day event in 1964 and 1968, and silver for both these events in 1972. After consistently collecting silver medals in the equestrian events in previous Olympics, France carried off the gold for the show jumping event in the 1976 Games at Montreal, with Canada taking the gold for the three-day event.

Driving

Horses have been used to pull carts for the transportation of goods, possessions and people from place to place for thousands of years. Even before the invention of the wheel, which clearly made it possible to build more efficient carts, a contraption on "skids" was widely used. At first, man probably only moved around to find fresh pastures for his stock, in much the same way as the nomadic tribes of today still do. The "carts" used by such tribes consist of a primitive arrangement of poles to which they strap their entire belongings as they wander from place to place.

Harnessing horses to a cart may have begun for practical purposes, but the indications are that it very soon, if not simultaneously, developed into a sporting activity too. The chariot races of the early Greeks, Romans and Egyptians are not just legendary; we know that the sport was included in the Olympic Games held in 680 B.C. It is undoubtedly the sporting aspect of driving, as much as practical necessity, that has led man to develop and improve the vehicles he has harnessed to his horses over the centuries. In addition, horses were bred specifically for driving purposes, the types produced varying according to the type of coach or cart they were required to draw. Thus heavy horses were used to draw loaded farm carts while a lighter breed of horse would be used

to pull the lighter carriages. Horses would be harnessed in teams to pull stage coaches or to pull the great covered wagons over rough tracks.

By the seventeenth and eighteenth centuries, driving as a sport had become a possible means of earning huge sums of money – by the placing of large bets between owners on races. A general interest in driving horses competitively began

Above: Driving through the snow in Mount Royal Park, Montreal.

Below: A four-in-hand competing in the Grand Prix Driving competition.

A smart turn-out at a horse-show.

to be shown by the wealthy in all countries. In Russia, the "dare-devil" Count Orlov produced his famous "Orlov Trotter." He established a stud farm which bred horses specially to trot very fast and to have great powers of endurance. They undoubtedly made a great contribution to the popularity and perpetuation of trotting races. A name integrally linked with making the sport exciting and spectacular in England at this time was that of the Marquess of Queensberry, known as "Old Q." He was the instigator, and winner, of many one-horse chaise matches.

By the late eighteenth century, driving in England had become a fashionable pastime. This was considerably helped by the royal patronage given by the then Prince of Wales, later to be King George IV. In just the same way the interest shown by the British monarchy in recent years has done much to effect a revival in driving. HRH Prince Philip is a regular competitor in Driving Club events.

As the interest in driving increased, so the breeding of suitable horses became even more selective and specialized. In England the Norfolk Roadster, originally bred for utility and farm work, was developed and used for trotting races that became popular in East Anglia. From this the Hackney Horse was developed. It is a showy type of high-stepping animal, which looks most elegant and attractive harnessed to a light carriage. Although it has

some drawbacks for competition driving as laid down by F.E.I. rules, it became popular for elegant driving at the end of the last century and the beginning of this. It still has a very active following all over the world.

In the north of England heavier types of horse were bred for drawing coaches – namely the Yorkshire Coach Horse and the Cleveland Bay. The latter is the breed generally used to pull the royal carriages on State occasions. In Holland the Fresian and Gelderland were widely used for driving purposes, and in Germany, the Oldenburg and Holstein were found to be admirably suited to pulling heavy vehicles such as road coaches. In Austria the Lippizanas and Haflingers are used. Hungary and Poland are two countries which have a great interest in driving horses, and representatives from both places have consistently proved themselves in international competitions.

One of the most widely supported driving competitions is that of "combined driving," for which the F.E.I. produced a set of rules in 1969. The competition is divided into three sections: Turnout and Dressage, a Cross-country Marathon, and Obstacle Driving. The Obstacle Driving entails precision driving at speed between pairs of markers, which provides great excitement for spectators. Extremely fit, sound, obedient and versatile horses, with great stamina, are needed for this event, and their training is rigorous.

A smart turn-out at a horse-show.

Endurance Riding

Endurance riding as a competitive sport is comparatively new, although as a practice it has been in existence since the horse was first used to convey man from place to place. The cavalry horses of a few centuries ago, and those used to carry mail when the first postal systems went into operation, would certainly have covered the distances which are now usually undertaken only in endurance-riding competitions, as a matter of course.

The sport of endurance riding was begun by the US Cavalry in North America in the 1920s. Now it is practiced fairly extensively in the US, Canada, Australia and, more recently, England. The idea is to ride horses over a measured and carefully marked-out route, most frequently of 100 miles (160 kilometers) at an average gait. (However, Britain's most famous endurance competition, the Golden Horseshoe ride, is only 75 miles, or 120 kilometers, long). How many days the ride takes varies according to the competition. The Tevis Cup, for example, the 100-mile (160-kilometer) route which follows that taken by the gold miners over the Sierra Nevada, is done in one day. Britain's Golden Horseshoe ride is staged over two days, and those run in Florida and North Carolina require that the 100 miles (160 kilometers) be ridden over three days. In Australia, the best known endurance ride is the 100-mile (160-kilometer) Quilty ride, which takes place over very rugged terrain in the Blue Mountains of New South Wales and is ridden in one day.

One of the attractions of endurance riding is that it is open to any kind of horse, from a pure-bred animal to a variety of crosses. In any one endurance ride, you are likely to find a motley collection of Arabs, Thoroughbreds, Quarterhorses, Standardbreds, German Trakehners, and various native ponies as well as a variety of crosses of all these breeds. Although there is no reason why almost any horse, providing it is sound and fit, could not compete in endurance competitions, it is those with

Endurance riding puts great demands on both horses and riders.

considerable Arabian blood that consistently do well. The stamina and staying ability for which the breed is renowned comes out in this kind of competition.

To enter most of the really long-distance endurance rides, horses and riders must first have qualified at one of the shorter rides, previously held over distances of between 40 and 60 miles (60–95 kilometers). In Britain, rulings require that horses are at least 14 hands high and must be five years old. In most endurance rides, the judging is done in two ways. There are awards for the horses that complete the distance in the shortest time and awards for the horses which finish in the best physical condition. The best horse is that which manages to take both awards!

Rigorous veterinary checks are compulsory before, during and after endurance rides, to make sure such things as the horse's pulse and respiration are in order. In addition the vets will look out for signs of fatigue, lameness or tender legs, heavy sweating, fever swellings, clear eyes and so on. Any horse which does not pass the veterinary examinations at any stage must withdraw – this is an essential ruling which is designed to safeguard the horses in these gruelling events.

That horses have to be in prime physical condition and really fit to compete in endurance riding is obvious, and they need to be conditioned and trained for the task accordingly. If a horse is to be entered for a ride – particularly one of the 100-mile (160-kilometer) ones, training should begin four or five months previously. It would take the form of going for at least four short rides a week, at which strong walking is interspersed with shorter periods of steady trotting to get the horse really fit.

After a few weeks this could be reduced to three days a week, which after two months should be at least 20 miles (30 kilometers) long. On other days the horse should have no more than half an hour of gentle exercise on the lunge.

The month before the ride takes place, you should be going out for five rides a week, alternating rides of 15 miles (24 kilometers) with longer ones of about 25 miles (40 kilometers). During this time too, you should try a couple of 50-mile (80-kilometer) long rides, and use these to really assess the fitness and physical condition of your horse when he has finished the distance.

To make sure the horse is in good physical condition, worm him at the outset of training. Pay particular attention to correct feeding, giving only top quality grain and hay, with mineral and vitamin additives. If the horse is prone to sweating, make sure he has additional salt. Blood tests during this time give an indication of whether the food is adequate and of whether it is being used properly by the horse.

Legs and feet will obviously need constant care and attention too. Shoes with leather pads are a good idea as they protect the soles of the feet from bruising by stones or rugged terrain. Make sure too that saddlery fits properly and is consistently comfortable. Keep a watch throughout the training period to make sure that there is no piece of saddlery rubbing anywhere.

If you are training a young horse specifically for endurance riding, pay particular attention to his gait and stride at the trot, working to make it as smooth and even as possible. This is the most used, and therefore the most important, gait in endurance riding, and a comfortable trot can do much to make an endurance rider's long periods in the saddle easier and generally more pleasant.

Competitors in the Arab Horse Society's Golden Horseshoe Ride.

Glossary

Aids

Artificial

Items of equipment such as whips, sticks, spurs and martingales which assist the rider and his natural aids in controlling the horse.

Natural

The rider's hands, legs, voice and body weight used in conjunction to control the horse.

Airs

Above the Ground

Movements performed by the horse in classical equitation in which the horse's legs leave the ground on command.

Artificial paces

Certain movements used in circus work, such as the Spanish Trot and the Spanish Walk, which are not executed naturally by a horse. Also refers to some gaits, other than the walk, trot and canter, executed by certain breeds.

Backing

Term used in breaking, for when a horse has a rider on its back for the first time. Also used to mean backing up.

Backing up

When a rider asks his horse to step backwards.

Ballotade

One of the classical airs above the ground. In this movement, the horse leaps into the air with his body horizontal to the ground. His legs are bent beneath him.

Behind the bit

A horse is behind the bit when he drops the bit in his mouth and thus avoids the direct pressure.

Breaking roller

A wide strap that buckles around the horse's body in the same place as the girth, with rings or dees attached, to take side reins or a crupper.

Bridoon

A small snaffle bit used in conjunction with a curb bit to form a double bridle.

Capriole

One of the classical airs above the ground. The basis is the same as the Ballotade (see above), but in the Capriole, the hind legs are stretched out straight behind the horse's body.

Cantering united or disunited

Cantering with hind and forelegs following the correct sequence is cantering united, and in the incorrect sequence is cantering disunited.

Cavesson, breaking

Item of tack, similar in construction to a head-collar, although much stronger, used in breaking and early training. A breaking cavesson is heavier than a lunging cavesson.

Cold-blooded horse

A horse of strong working type as opposed to the lighter, more refined types, such as a Thoroughbred or Arab.

Conformation

The bone structure and shape of a horse (see chart on page 110).

Counter canter

To canter in a circle with the outside leg, as opposed to the inside leg, leading.

Courbette

The courbette is one of the classical airs above the ground. The horse stands on his hind legs, which are bent at the hocks, and then performs a series of leaps without his front legs touching the ground.

Covering

Term used in breeding, to describe the serving of a mare by a stallion.

Creamola

Cream-colored horse or pony which lacks strong pigmentation in the coat. It is usually the resulting offspring of a palomino sire and dam.

Curb bit

A bit used in conjunction with a chain or strap that passes under the lower jaw. Forms the second element of a double bridle. There are two kinds of curb bit, the fixed mouthpiece and the sliding mouthpiece.

Diagonal

Opposite fore and hind legs – i.e. off-fore and near-hind or near-fore and off-hind. Also refers to the aids when a rider uses his right hand and left leg (or vice versa) in conjunction.

Direct rein

This is the "natural" rein used for turning a horse's head, i.e. the right rein to turn right or vice versa.

Double oxer

A fence of three elements, the highest part being in the middle.

Dressage

Dressage is a term of French derivation which is used to describe the schooling or controlled physical exercise of a horse. The German "prize riding."

Equerry
An officer in charge of horses. A French word used in particular at the Cadre Noir School in Saumur, France, for the instructors.

Eventing
A competition staged over one, two or three days, which includes a dressage test, riding over roads and tracks, a steeplechase course, a cross-country course over natural obstacles, and a show-jumping course.

Faults
Penalty points for mistakes in show-jumping competitions, or incorrect actions developed in training.

F.E.I.
The initials of the Federation Equestre Internationale – an international body which draws up and controls the rules for international equestrian events or competitions.

Forward seat
When the rider adopts a forward position, as in jumping.

Free forward movement
Displayed by a horse that is working well and going forward freely at all gaits without restriction.

Feathering
The narrowing of a horseshoe's edge, so that the horse is less likely to injure itself by brushing – i.e. the action of hitting the inside of the opposite leg with the shoe. Also the long hair on the lower leg of heavy horses in particular.

Flexion
The bending of the horse's head to the left or right, or flexing it from the poll, thereby dropping the nose.

Free walk
A walk during which the horse is allowed free movement of its head by the rider.

Frog
The "V"-shaped, soft part of the sole of the foot, which acts as a natural shock absorber.

Half halt
A slowing down from a faster pace – i.e., a rising trot to a sitting trot, or a sitting trot to a walk.

Half pass
Movement by the horse sideways and forwards crossing the front and hind legs.

Half pirouette
Turning through 180° using one hind or foreleg as a pivot.

Hands
Official term of measurement to describe the horse's height, a hand being 4 in. (10 cm.). It can also refer to the hold on the reins and thus the means of control over the horse by the reins.

Haute Ecole
The French term for classical equitation, Haute Ecole means "high school" or, in other words, advanced riding.

Hogged mane
When a horse's mane is cut short or it is clipped off.

Holding
A term which is used in breeding; a mare is holding to a stallion's service or covering when she is in-foal.

Horse sick pasture
When a field has been over-grazed by horses, so that the pasture has turned sour through an excess of droppings or manure that has been left on it.

Hot-blooded horse
Horses of fine breeding, i.e., Thoroughbreds or Arabs, as opposed to horses which are cold-blooded.

Hunting seat
A position in the saddle that is not necessarily a correct seat as practiced by classical schools, but is comfortable for the rider who is in the saddle for many hours.

Italian forward seat
Position in the saddle first developed in Italy by Federico Caprilli, the Italian forward seat is now universally adopted as the recognized, correct jumping position.

Lunging
Exercising and schooling a horse on a long lunge rein, attached to a cavesson and held at the other end by the trainer.

Mouthing
The first time a bit is introduced into a horse's mouth during breaking.

Neck reining
Guiding a horse by the use of the reins against his neck.

On the bit
A horse is on the bit when it is fully accepting the pressure of the bit in its mouth, is moving forward freely and is ready to respond instantly to the rider's commands.

Palomino
A specific creamy-colored horse.

Passage
A French word to describe an elevated trot.

Pelham
A bit which combines the action of a curb and snaffle in one bit.

Piaffer
A pace at the trot. The action is performed on the spot and in effect is marking time in two-time.

Piebald
A horse of black and white coloring. The patches of each color are irregular.

Pirouette
This is a short turn of the horse in a small circle which is not more than the length of the horse itself.

Pivot on the forehand
A turn through 180° or 360° in which one foreleg remains in the same spot and the horse pivots on it.

Pivot on the haunches
A similar turn to the above except that one hind leg remains in the same spot and acts as a pivot.

Points of the horse
The names given to the different parts of the horse's body.

Pony
Any horse that measures 14.2 hands high or less is a pony.

Posting trot
This is the action of a rider rising, or posting, from the saddle in rhythm with a horse's trot.

Puissance
A show-jumping competition in which the winner is the horse that jumps the greatest height.

Rack
A pace used by American bred horses for pleasure riding.

Running walk
A hurried walk in which the horse's legs do not move in true four-time.

Saddle seat
This is a term for a type of riding position in the US.

Sauteurs
The French word for jumpers.

Selective breeding
The selection by man of mares and stallions to be mated, as opposed to natural breeding in the wild.

Shoulder in
A school movement, worked on three tracks, used in training the horse and in schooling exercises. The horse is bent around the rider's inside leg, so the forehand is brought off the straight track and the head and neck are bent towards the center of the ring.

Shoulder out
As above, except the horse is bent around the rider's outside leg, and its head and neck are bent towards the outside of the school.

Showing-in-hand
When horses are led, as opposed to being ridden, in showing competitions.

Sitting trot
The action of a rider as he sits in the saddle at the trot, instead of posting.

Skewbald
A horse whose coat comprises irregular patches of different colors, in particular brown and white.

Spavin
A bony or soft enlargement of the hock.

Square halt
When a horse halts with his legs correctly placed, thus making a rectangle beneath the body.

Stock seat
The rider's position in the saddle when working in a Western saddle or an Australian cattle saddle.

Stud
The name given to an establishment where horses are bred.

Warm-blooded horse
The resulting offspring of the mating of a cold-blooded and hot-blooded horse.

Western riding
The type of riding practiced by American (and also Australian) cattle men using a stock or Western-type saddle.

Wisping
Massaging a horse's muscles with a wisp, made from straw or hay.

Index

Figures in italics indicate illustrations.

Abscesses, *91*, 93
Aids
    artificial, *60*, 61
    lateral, 166–170
    natural, 60–61, 62–65, 160–161
Ailments, common, 86
Airs
    above the ground,
        ballotade, 173, 175
        capriole, 173, 175
        courbette, 173, *174*, 175
        levade, *173*
    on the ground,
        passage, 170–171, 173, *175*
        piaffer, 170, 171, 173
Alhusen, Major, 196
Alvarez-Cervera, Luis, *205*
American Quarter Horse, 12, *13*
American Saddle Horse, *14*
American Trotter, 195
Anatomy of a horse,
    foreleg, *86*
    internal organs, *78*
    lower leg and foot, *92*
    muscles, *53*
    points, *52*
    skeleton, *53*
Andalusian, *34*, 45
Anne, Princess, *158*
Appaloosa, *15*, 45
Arab, *39–40*, 45, 146–*147*, 151, *180*, 181, 183, 195, 209
Ardennes, *20*
Argentina, horses of, 16–*17*
    Argentine Polo Pony, 16–*17*, 126
    Criollo, 16
Argenton, A., *198*
Army horses, 41, 45, 49
Art, horses in, *8, 9, 11*, 34, 38, 39, *46, 47, 48, 49*
Artificial paces, 14
Asia, horses of, *39–41*
    Arab, *39–40*, 45, 146–*147*, 151, *180*, 181, 183, 195, 209
    Barb, 41
    Timor Pony, 41
    Waler, *41*
Australia, horses of, *41*
    Australian Waler, *41*
Austria, horses of, *18*, 207
    Haflinger, *18*, 156, 207
    Lippizana, *18*, 45, *47*, 149, *155*, 172–*173*, *174, 175*, 207

Backing or mounting for the first time, *136*–137
Backing up, *144*, 165–166, 171, 175
Badminton Horse Trials, 197, *198*
Ballotade, 173, 175
Bandaging
    a knee, *90*
    for protection, 106
    a tail, *181*, 185
Barb, 41
El Bedavi XXII, 18
Belgium, horses of, *19*
    Brabant, *19*
Bits, *94–97*, 132–*134*, *184*
Bitting, 132–134

Black Mass, 175
Blankets, *77, 107*
Blaze, 25
Blistering, 87, 88
Bolton, Brigadier, 196
Bone spavins, 87, *88*
Brabant, *19*
Bradley, Caroline, 147
Braiding a mane or tail, *85, 183*
Bran, 80
Breaking a horse, 128–145
    western style, 128
Breeding, 146–157
    best time for, 147, 148
    birth of a foal, *149*, 151–152
    feeding while in foal, 149–150
    selecting a stallion, 147
Breton, 21
Brewery cart horses, 31, *42*, 43
Bridles, *94–98*, *184*–185
Bridling, *96*
British Isles, horses and ponies of, *24–31*
    children's ponies, *29*
    Cleveland Bay, *29*, 207
    Clydesdale, *31*, 43
    Connemara Pony, 28–*29*
    Dales Ponies, 26–*27*
    Dartmoor Pony, *26*, *109*
    English Thoroughbred, 11, *24–25*, 192
    Exmoor Pony, *9*, *26*
    Fell Pony, 27
    Hackney, *24*, 25, 207
    heavy horses, 10, 19, *21*, 30–*31*, 182
    Highland Ponies, *29*
    Irish Draft Horse, *25*
    Irish Hunter, 25
    New Forest Pony, 27–*28*
    Shetland Pony, *27*, 45
    Shire Horse, *31*, 43
    Suffolk Punch, 31
    Welsh Ponies, *30*
British style of riding, 51
Brood Mares
    age of, 146
    care of, 150–151
    feeding, 149–150
    getting into foal, 149
    showing, *156–157*, 182
Broome, David, *201*
Buying a horse, 108–111
Byerly Turk, 24

Cachica, *200*
Cadre Noir, 49, 172, 174–176, 197
Calgary Stampede, *125*
Camargue Pony, *20–21*
Canter
    counter, 164, 175
    description of, 64
    position and aids for, 64–65
    show-ring, 185
    united and disunited, 65
Capped hocks and elbows, 87, *88*
Caprilli, Federico, 50, 51
Capriole, 173, *175*
Care of a horse, 74–111
    ailments, 86
    care of the feet, 90–93
    feeding, 76, 78–81
    first aid, 86, 89
    grassland management, 74–75
    grooming, 82–85, *112*
    injuries, 87–88

    skin complaints, 88–89
    stable management, 76–77
Cavaletti, *71–72, 73*, 143, 187–188
Cavalry School
    of France; *see* Cadre Noir
    of Italy, 32
Cavendish, William, 49
Ceremonial horses, 15, *40, 43*, 44
Changes of leg, 164, 171, 175
Children's show ponies, 29
Circus horses, 15, *42*, 45
Cleveland Bay, *29*, 207
Clip, types of, 85
Clydesdale, *31*, 43
Coach horses, 23
Colds, 86
Colic, 86
Competitive riding, 180–209
    driving, *206–207*
    endurance riding, *208–209*
    eventing, *158*, *196–199*, 205
    international events, *200–205*
    racing, *192–195*
    showing, *180*–185
    show jumping, *186–191*, 196, *197*, 200–*202*, 205
Confidence, instilling in the horse, 189, 198, 199
Conformation, 109, *110*, 111
Connemara Pony, 28–29
Corn (grain), 78, 80–81
Corns (foot disorder), 93
Coughs, 86
Counter canter, 164, 175
Country code for riders, 113
Courbette, 173, *174*, 175
Cow horses and ponies, 43, *44*, 45
Cracks
    heel, *88*–89
    sand, 93
Creamola, 38
Cribbing strap, *77*
Criollo, 16
Cross-country riding, *35–36*, 49, 196, *197*, 204
Curb bit, 94, 96–97
Cuts, 89

Dales Ponies, 26–27
Darley Arabian, 24
Dartmoor Pony, *26*, *109*
Davidson, Bruce, 199
Denmark, horses of, 35, 36–37, *38*, 45
    Fredericksborg Horse, 36
    Jutland Horse, 36–37
    Knabstrup, *38*, 45
Derby, *46*
Direct reining, *61*
Dølahest, Norwegian, 36
Draft horse, 21, *31*
    Dutch, 19
    Irish, *25*
Dressage, 48, 50–51, 100, *159*, 161–171, 196, 203–204, *205*
    clothing for, *55*
    events for, 18, 22, *35–36*
    horses for, *35–36*
Driving, *206–207*
    horses and ponies for, 19, 27, *29*, *206–207*
Dutch draft horse, 19

Eclipse, 24
Endurance riding, 208–209
England, horses of; *see* British Isles

213

English Thoroughbred, 11, *24—25*, 192
Equipment, *94—107*
Equitation
    history of, 47—50
    modern, 50—51
    styles of, 47—51, 183
Europe, horses of, 11; *see also* Austria, British
        Isles, France, Germany, Hungary, Italy,
        Netherlands, Poland, Scandinavia, Spain
Eventing, 49, *158*, *196—199*, 204, *205*
    horses for, *35—36*
Evolution of the horse, 8—10
Exercises for the rider, *66—69*
Exercising the horse, 69, 76, *77*, 112
Exmoor Pony, 9, *26*

Falls, 65
False quarter, 93
Federation Equestre Internationale (FEI), 161
    driving events, 19
    show jumping events, 200
Feeding a horse,
    amount and types of food, 78, 79—81
    rules for, 78—79
    times for, 76, 78, 81
Feet, 109
    care of, 90—92
    disorders and diseases, 92—93
    shoeing, 92, 93
Fell Pony, 27
Fencing, 74
Festival of Riding, 204
Finland, horses of, 36—*37*
    Finnish Horse, 36—*37*
First aid
    equipment, *86*
    rules, 89
Five-gaited horses, showing, 183
Fjord Pony, Norwegian, 9, *36*
Flat-racing, 192—193
Flying change of leg, 164, 171
Foals
    birth of, *149*, 151—152
    early handling of, 153, 154
    feeding, 155
    showing, 156—157, 182
    weaning, 154
Forward seat, *50*, *70*, 71, *73*, 99
"4H," 120
France, horses of, 20—21
    Ardennes, *20*
    Breton, 21
    Camargue Pony, 20—21
    French Trotter, *20*, 21
    Percheron, *21*
Fredericksborg Horse, 37
French style of riding, 50
French Trotter, *20*, 21
Fresian, 19, 207

Gaits, *63—65*
    artificial, 14
    collected, working, medium, extended or
        free, *162—163*, *164*, 165
    see also Walk, Trot, Canter, Gallop
Gallop
    description of, 64
    position and aids for, 65
Galls, girth, 87, 88
Games, mounted, *124*, 125—*127*
Garron, 29
Gates, opening and closing, *144—145*

Gelderland, *19*, 207
German style of riding, *50*
Germany, horses of, *22—23*, 207
    German Trotter, 22
    Hanoverian Horse, *22*, 50, *51*
    Holstein, 22—23, 207
    Oldenburg, *23*, 207
    Trakehner, *23*, 50
Gidran, 32
Girths, *58*, *101*
    galls from, 87, 88
Godolphin Arabian, 24
Golden Horseshoe Ride, 208, *209*
Goldman, Eddie, 197—198
Gotland Pony, 35
Grand National, 193
Grand Prix de Dressage, 170—171
Grand Prix Driving competition, *206*
Grasses, *75*
Grassland management, 74—75
Grazing, 74—75
"Great Horse," 10
Grisone, Federico, 48
Grooming, 82, 85, *112*
Gupper, Edgar, *204*
Gymkhanas, 121—125, 180
    training for, 122—124

Hack, 181, *182*, 185
Hackamore bitless bridle, *96*
Hackney Horse, *24*, 25, 207
Haflinger, *18*, 156, 207
Half halt, 165
Half pass, *51*, 169—*170*, 171
Half pirouettes, 170, 171, 175
Halters and head collars, *94*
Halts, 165, 171
Hambletonian, 13
Handler, Colonel, 51
Hanoverian, 22, 50, *51*
Harness horses, 25
Harness racing, *195*
Haute Ecole, 18, 45, 48, 49, 171—176
Hay, 78, 79—80
Heavy horse, 10, 19, *21*, 30—*31*, 182
Heels, cracked, *88*—89
Heinz, J., *200*
Hickstead, *200*
Highland Ponies, 29
Holidays, riding, 114—118
Holland, horses of; *see* Netherlands
Holstein, 22—23, 207
Hoof; *see* Feet
Hoof oil
    making your own, 90
    using, 90
Horse of the Year Show, 124—125
Horse
    evolution of, 8—10
    national and native breeds of, 10—41
    gaits of, *62—65*; *see also* Gaits
    points of, *52—53*
    role of in society, 9—11, 42
    working, 42—45; *see also* Working horses
Horseshoe
    fitting of, 93
    invention of, 48
    problems with, 93
    types of, *92*, 93
Hungary, horses of, *32*, 207
    Gidran, 32
    Shagya, 32
Hunter classes, 181

Hunters, 181, *182*, 185
    Irish, 25
Hunting, 193, 194—195
Hunt seat, 182—183

Iceland, horses of, 9, *37*
    Icelandic Pony, 9, *37*, *118*
Injuries, leg, *87—88*
International events, 200—205
Ireland, horses of, 25, 28
    Connemara Pony, 28—29
    Irish Draft Horse, 25
    Irish Hunter, 25
Italian forward seat, *50*, *70*, 71, *73*, 99
Italy, horses of, *32*
    Neapolitan, 32
    Salerno, 32

Jonsson, J., *51*
Jumping
    cavaletti, *71—72*, *73*, *143*, 187—188
    forward-cut saddle, *99*
    forward seat, *50*, *70*, 71, *73*
    horse's movements during, *70—71*
    learning, 70—73
    show, 186—191, 196, *197*, 200—202, 204,
        205
    side-saddle, 178—179
    training for, *143*
Jumps
    constructing, 72, 188—189, 190, 198, 199
    practice, *72*
    types of, 190, 191
Justin Morgan (stallion), 12
Jutland Horse, 37

Kentucky Derby, 193
Knabstrup, *38*, 45
Knees
    broken, 87
    swollen, *90*
Kranich, 23

Lameness, 87, 88, 89, 111
Laminitis, 92, 149
Lateral aids, 166—170
Lateral movements, *166—170*
Legs
    injuries to, *87—88*
    protection of, *106*
Leg-yielding, *168—169*
Lessons, riding, 54, 160
Levade, *173*
Lippizana, *18*, 45, *47*, *149*, 155, 172—*173*, *174*,
    175, 207
Literature, horses in, 8, 34
Long-reining, *137—138*, *139*
Lunging, *67—69*, 71, *130*—136, 138, 139, 142,
    143, 145, 185

Maathurs, J. G., *186*
Machen, Eddie, *203*
Man O' War, 24
Martingales, *103—104*
Meade, Richard, *199*
Mongolian Pony, *33*
Morgan Horse, *12—13*
Mounting and dismounting, *56—57*
Mouthing, 132—134
Mucking out, 76
Mustang, 14
Muzzle, *77*

Nail binding, 93
Nations' Cup, 200, 201, 202
Native breeds of the world, 10—41
        classes for, 181, 182
Neapolitan, 32
Neck reining, 61
Netherlands, horses of, 19, 207
        Dutch Draft Horse, 19
        Fresian, 19, 207
        Gelderland, 19, 207
New Forest Pony, 27—28
New Zealand, horses of, 41
Norfolk Roadster, 207
North Swedish Horse, 35
Norway, horses of, 9, 36
        Norwegian Dølahest, 36
        Norwegian Fjord Pony, 9, 36
Nosebands, 45, 97

Oats, 80
Oldenburg, 23, 207
Olympic Dressage Test (Grand Prix de Dressage), 170—171
Olympic Games, 22, 159, 197, 200, 202—205, 206
Orlov Trotter, 11, 32, 195, 207

Pacing horses, 13, 195
Pacing races, 192, 195
"Palfrey," 10
Palomino, 38
Passage, 170—171, 173, 175
Pastures, 74—75
Pelham bridle, 94, 97
Percheron, 21
Peru, horses of, 17
        Peruvian Stepping Horse, 17
Pessoa, Nelson, 202
Piaffer, 170, 171, 173
Piebald coloring, 14
Pinto, 14—15
Pirouettes, 170
        half—, 170, 171, 175
Pivot
        on the forehand, 166—167
        on the haunches, 167, 170
Pleasure Horse Class, 182—183
Pluvine, Antoine de, 49
Points of the horse, 52
Point-to-point races, 192, 193—194
Poland, horses of, 207
Police horses, 43—44, 45
Polo, 48, 125—127
Polo ponies
        Argentine, 16—17, 126
        Australian, 41
Ponies
        Camargue, 20—21
        children's, 29
        Connemara, 28—29
        cow, 43
        Dales, 26—27
        Dartmoor, 26, 109
        Exmoor, 9, 26
        Fell, 27
        Gotland, 35
        Highland, 29
        Icelandic, 9, 37
        Mongolian, 33
        New Forest, 27—28
        Norwegian Fjord, 9, 36
        polo, 16—17, 41, 126
        Shetland, 27, 45

Timor, 41
        Welsh, 30
        Western Isle, 29, 118
Ponies of Britain Club, 29
Pony Club, 119—121, 124, 125, 167
Poulticing, 90, 91, 92
Preakness Stakes, 193
Primeval horses, 8—9
Prince Philip Cup, 123, 124
Prior-Palmer, Lucinda, 190, 199, 205
Przewalski's Wild Horse, 9, 10, 33
Puissance, 191
Pulling matches, horses for, 12

Quarter Horse, American, 12, 13
Quilty ride, 208
Quitter, 91, 92

Racehorses, 11, 22, 192—195
Races, famous, 193
Racing, 192—195
        clothing for, 55
        position for, 65
Rack
        fast, 14
        slow, 14
Rakush, 38
Reining
        direct, 61
        long—, 137—138, 139
        neck, 61
Reins, 98
        side, 134—135
        using, 59, 60—61, 184—185
Riding
        advanced, 158—179
        clothing for, 55
        competitive, 180—209
        exercises for, 66—68, 69
        Haute Ecole, 172—175
        learning, 52—73, 160
        mounting and dismounting, 58—59
        for pleasure, 112—127
        position for, 58, 62—65, 67
        preparation for, 112
        side-saddle, 176—179
        styles of, 47—51, 182—183
        use of aids in, 60—65
Riding Clubs, 120, 121
Riding masters, famous
        Cavendish, William, 49
        Caprilli, Federico, 50, 51
        Grisone, Federico, 48
        Pluvine, Antoine de, 49
        Robichon de la Guerinère, François, 49
        Xenophon, 47—48
Riding schools, choosing a, 54
Riding schools, famous
        Cadre Noir at Saumur, 49, 172, 174—176, 197
        School of Naples, 48—49
        Spanish Riding School of Vienna, 18, 47, 48, 55, 158, 172—173
Ringworm, 88
Roads, riding along, 113—114
Robichon de la Guerinère, François, 49
Rodeos, 125, 126, 127
Royal Canadian Mounted Police horses, 44, 45
Royal Tournament, 122
Running walk, 13, 14
Russia, horses of, 11, 32—33, 206—207
        Mongolian Pony, 33
        Orlov Trotter, 11, 32, 195, 207

Przewalski's Wild Horse, 9, 10, 33
        Russian Saddle Horse, 33
        Russian Trotter, 32—33
Russian style of riding, 50—51

Saddlebred, 183
Saddle Horse, American, 14
Saddle Horse, Russian, 33
Saddles, 98—101
        position in, 58, 62—65, 67, 70, 71, 73
        positioning of, 53
        side, 99, 177
Saddle seat, 182—183
Saddle sores, 87, 88
Salerno, 32
Salt, 81
Sand cracks, 93
Scandinavia, horses of, 35—37
        Finnish Horse, 36—37
        Fredericksborg Horse, 37
        Gotland Pony, 35
        Icelandic Pony, 9, 37, 118
        Jutland Horse, 37
        North Swedish Horse, 35
        Norwegian Dølahest, 36
        Norwegian Fjord Pony, 9, 36
        Swedish Ardenne Horse, 35
        Swedish Riding Horse, 35—36
Schockemohle, Alwin, 203
Schooling a horse, 128—145
        advanced, 158—175
        for jumping, 142—143
School of Naples, 48—49
Scotland, horses of; see British Isles
Seedy toe, 92
Selective breeding, 9, 10
Shagya, 32
Shales, 25
Shetland Pony, 27, 45
Shire Horse, 31, 43
Shoeing, 92, 93
Shoulder-in, 166, 167, 168, 175
Shoulder-out, 168
Shoulder-yielding, 168—169
Show horses, 12, 181—183
Showing, 180—185
        brood mares and foals, 156—157, 182
        in hand, 180, 182, 185
Show jumping, 186—191, 196, 197, 200—202, 204, 205
Show-jumping horses, 12, 22, 35—36
Side reins, 134—135
Side-saddle riding, 176—179
        habit for, 179
        holidays to learn, 118
        jumping, 178—179
        mounting and dismounting, 177—178, 179
        technique, 176—178
Side saddles, fitting, 99, 177
Skewbald coloring, 14
Skin complaints, 88—89
Snaffle bit, 94—96, 97
Sores, 87, 88
South America, horses of, 16—17
        Argentine Polo Ponies, 16—17, 126
        Criollo, 16
        Peruvian Stepping Horse, 17
Spain, horses of, 34
        Andalusian, 34, 45
        Spanish Horse (Spanish Jennet), 34
Spanish Riding School of Vienna, 18, 47, 48, 55, 158, 172—173
Splints, 87

Spotted horses, *38; see also*
    Appaloosa *and* Knabstrup
Sprains, 87
Spurs, *60*, 61
Stable, construction of, 76
Stable management, 76–77
Stable vices, 77
Stallions, famous
    El Bedavi XXII, 18
    Blaze, 25
    Byerley Turk, 24
    Darley Arabian, 24
    Eclipse, 24
    Godolphin Arabian, 24
    Hambletonian, 13
    Justin Morgan, 12
    Kranich, 23
    Man O' War, 24
    Rakush, 38
    Shales, 25
    St. Simon, 24
Standard Bred, 13
Steeplechasing, *192*, 193–194
Stirrup leathers and irons, *102*
Stock seat, 182–183
Strachen, S., 198
Strangles, 86, *88*
St. Simon, 24
Stuckelberger, Christine, 51
Stud farms
    governmental control of, 156
    procedure at, 148–149
    selecting, 148, 149
Suffolk Punch, 31
Sutherland, Lorna, 199
Sweden, Horses of, *35–36*
    Gotland Pony, 35
    North Swedish Horse, 35
    Swedish Ardenne Horse, 35
    Swedish Riding Horse, *35–36*
Swedish style of riding, 50, *51*
Sweet itch, 88
Swiss style of riding, 51

Tack, *94–107*
    bits and bridles, *94–98*, *132–134*, *184–185*
    care of, 104–*105*
    clothing for protection or warmth, *106–107*
    halters and head collars, 94
    history of, 46–47
    saddles, *98–101*
    show, *157*,*185*
    stirrup leathers and irons, *102*
Teeth, judging age from, *108*, *109*
Tennessee Walking Horse, *13*, 49, 183
Tetanus, *89*
Tevis Cup, 208
Thoroughbred horses, 22, 183, 192
    English, 11, *24–25*, 192
Three-gaited horses, showing, 183
Thrush, 90
Timor Pony, 41
Training a horse, 128–145
    for endurance riding, 209
    for eventing, 198
    for jumping, *142–143*
    for showing, 183–185
    for show jumping, 187–190
Trakehner, *23*, 50
Trekking, 115
Trot
    description of, 62
    position and aids for, 63

posting, *63*
show-ring, 185
sitting, *62–63*
Trotters, 11, 13, *20*, 21, 22, *32–33*, 195
    American, 195
    French, *20*, 21
    German, 22
    Russian, *32–33*
Trotting races, 192, *195*
Turn
    on the forehand, *166*–167
    on the haunches, *167*, 170

United Kingdom, horses of; *see* British Isles
U.S., horses of, 11, *12–15*
    American Quarter Horse, 12, *13*
    American Saddle Horse, *14*
    American Trotter, 195
    Appaloosa, *15*, 45
    Morgan Horse, *12–13*
    Mustang, 14
    Pinto, *14–15*
    Standard Bred, 13
    Tennessee Walking Horse, *13*, 49, 183
U.S.S.R., horses of; *see* Russia, horses of

Vacations, hacking and trail-riding, 112–118
Vailloncourt, Michael, *204*
Vices, stable, 77

Waler, Australian, *41*
Wales, horses of; *see* British Isles
Walk
    description of, 62–63
    position and aids for, 63
    show-ring, 185
Water jumps, *190*
Water, when to give, 78
Weier, P., *202*
Welsh Cob, *30*
Welsh Mountain type pony, *30*
Welsh ponies, *30*
Welsh Riding pony, *30*
Western Isle pony, 29
Western riding
    clothing for, 55
    holding the reins, 59
    holidays to learn, 118
    horses for, 12, *38*
    horse show events, 183
    mounting and dismounting, *56, 57*
    neck reining, 61
    position in saddle, 47, *58*
Whips, 61
"Wild" horses and ponies, 14
    early handling of, 129–130
    primeval, 8–9
Winkler, Hans, *159*
Working horses, *42–45*
    army, 41, 45, 49
    brewery, 31, *42, 43*
    carriage or coach, 49
    ceremonial, 15, *40, 43*–44
    circus, 15, *42*, 45
    cow, 43, *44*, 45
    eventing, 49
    farming, *42, 43*
    jousting, 48
    plantation, 49
    police, 43–44, 45
    polo, *16–17*, 41, *48*, 126
Worms, 74–75, 86, 151
Wounds, 89

Xenophon, 47–48

Yorkshire Coach Horse, 207

Photographic Acknowledgements

Austrian Tourist office 116, 149, 173. Belgian Tourist office 117. Paul Brichieri Colombi 50. Hugo M. Czerny 55. Light Horse 193. Leslie Lane 51, 182, 191, 209. C. J. Marsden 23, 29, 32, 206. Maurice Michael 48. © Bibliotheque Nationale), 32, 33, 48, 49 © British Museum). Peter Roberts 6, 10, 17, 24, 26, 27, 28, 29, 30, 34, 42, 43, 44, 45, 54, 55, 56, 57, 58, 59, 68, 69, 71, 73, 82, 83, 113, 118, 119, 120, 122, 123, 124, 125, 126, 127, 128, 142, 144, 145, 147, 158, 159, 161, 162, 163, 167, 170, 172, 174, 175, 176, 178, 179, 184, 186, 187, 192, 195, 196, 197, 198, 200, 201, 202, 203, 207. Betty Skelton 24, 40, 51, 58, 111, 148, 185, 190. Sòlarfilma, Reykjavik, Iceland 118. Swiss Tourist office 113, 115, 117. Syndication International 159, 204, 205. Sally Anne Thompson (Animal Photography Ltd) 12, 13, 14, 15, 19, 21, 22, 23, 25, 30, 31, 32, 35, 38, 39, 154. John Topham Picture Library 2, 8, 11, 13, 16, 18, 19, 20, 31, 33, 34, 36, 37, 39, 40, 41, 42, 45, 46, 47, 48, 79, 101, 108, 112, 113, 114, 124, 127, 151, 153, 155, 156, 157, 158, 180, 181, 183, 185, 194, 206. Transworld Feature Syndicate (England) 147. The other photographs were taken especially for this book by Ian Gibson Smith, Mike Coomber, Stella Robinson and Paul Turner of D.P. Press Ltd.

Design, picture research and illustrations by D.P. Press Ltd, Sevenoaks, Kent, England.